THE JUNIORS

THE BEST FOR THE BEST

PLAYRIGHT PUBLISHING

A photo symbolic of the proud South Sydney Juniors ...
a day when winning didn't mean everything.

THE
JUNIORS
THE BEST FOR THE BEST

IAN HEADS

PLAYRIGHT PUBLISHING PTY LTD

WITH THANKS

The thanks of the author and publisher are extended to the many people who shared their time, their memories and in some cases their personal material relating to the club to make this book possible. Special thanks to:

Jenny Bolton, George Wintle, Maxine Driscoll, Margaret Child, Tom Adams, Clem Kennedy, Bob McCarthy, Robbie Wallace, Jessica Brown, Claire James, Norm Nilson, Barry Dunn, Berkeley Burns, Phil Tresidder, Geoff Prenter, Bill Mordey, Paul Cross, The Hon Lionel Bowen, Brad Ryder, Frank Cookson, Ron Harder, Joan Child, Brad Stanford, Geoff Knight, Errol Pinkerton, John Riordan, The Meyer Family, Lionel Huntington, Alan Gilbert — and to Henry Morris (chairman) and the Board of the South Sydney Junior Rugby League Club for their enthusiastic commitment to the project.

Published in 2000 by Playright Publishing Pty Ltd.,
PO Box 548, Caringbah, NSW Australia. 2229.
Telephone: 02 9525 5943. Facsimile: 02 9524 7485.

National Library of Australia
Cataloguing-in-Publication data

Heads, Ian
  The Juniors: The Best for the Best

  Includes index
  ISBN 0 949853 72 0

1. South Sydney Junior Rugby League Club. 2. Rugby
League football – New South Wales – South Sydney –
History. I South Sydney Junior Rugby League Club. II Title.

796.33362099441

Publisher: Gary Lester
Designed by Kerry Klinner, Mega City Publication Design
Printed by Tien Wah Press, Singapore

CONTENTS

FOREWORD

It was the sheer ability and leadership qualities of the team leading South Juniors some 40 years ago that convinced my great friend and neighbour, Jack Brown, to sell the building then known as Bell's Ballroom and formerly the Kensington Club at Kingsford on an 8 000 pounds ($16 000) deposit.

George Wintle had previously visited me and said that he knew I acted for Jack Brown and that he would like to buy the old Kensington Club but that all he had was eight thousand pounds and did I think that 'Mr Brown' would sell the building on terms. I arranged for George to visit Browns' home to discuss the matter. I had a feeling that these two personalities would get on very well and while subsequent events made this forecast come true, nevertheless the most persuasive thing that George did was to arrive at their home with the greatest bunch of flowers that Mrs Brown had ever seen. Jack Brown was most impressed to think that George Wintle and his team had raised 8 000 pounds by 'selling chocolates and ice cream on Redfern Oval'. Sadly Jack Brown passed away but his wife, Jessica, still talks with great affection of the visit and George's enthusiastic personality.

The story of Souths Juniors' great success as a licensed club goes back to the political history, which brought about the change to the *Licensing Act*. Joe Cahill was the Premier of New South Wales and Bob Menzies was the Prime Minister. Menzies' govern-ment decided to discontinue giving to the States sums of money for the housing of the aged and infirm. This money was used by the State Housing Commission to build appropriate accommodation. With the termination of this policy Joe Cahill, as Premier, stated that New South Wales would contin-ue to provide housing for the many elderly and invalid in need and that he would amend legislation to allow clubs to have poker machines. The result is well known and the results have been most beneficial for the people of New South Wales.

The story of Souths Juniors, the acquisition of its building and its subsequent outstanding success as a club is a practical example of allowing people in a social context to provide entertainment for them-selves as well as assisting the needy.

Ian Heads' story of Souths Juniors clearly shows what can be done when Australians can organise themselves into groups that not only provide friend-ship and entertainment but also engender the mobil-isation of capital and labour for the benefit of society and in particular the less privileged in the society.

The Australian qualities of 'fair go and mate-ship' have made our country a good democracy and this history of a sporting club and what it has been able to achieve for society makes great reading.

Well done Souths Juniors.

The Hon, Lionel Bowen AC
Former Deputy Prime Minister of Australia

INTRODUCTION
THE BEST FOR THE BEST

The story of South Sydney Juniors Leagues Club is one of the great community sagas in the life of Australia's biggest city. For 40 years now the 'club on the corner' at Kingsford has added value to the everyday affairs of the district it serves. With the club itself (558A Anzac Parade) as the permanent focal point — ever-changing in the years since its modest beginning — there has been an unflagging reaching-out to the wider community within the boundaries of the Juniors' bailiwick. On one level the club has been a source of entertainment and enjoyment for countless thousands of members and visitors over the years. On another, the club has never stopped 'doing its bit' in the support of community services, hospitals, charities and a huge range of sporting organisations and clubs within what it has always accepted as its area of responsibility. For many people the club has been, and is — a home away from home.

Right from the beginning (1959) there was a determination to build a club that provided magnificent facilities for its members. That determination went hand in hand with the Juniors' reason for existence — to nurture, build and support the best Junior Rugby League organisation in Australia. The cost of that ongoing labour of love, manifest in the countless matches played within the district every weekend of the season, stood at around $1.5 million per year in 1999.

In club facilities provided over the span of 40 years, the Juniors has never been anything less than the pacesetter in the highly competitive world of Sydney clubland — via such attractions as its holiday hotel on the Hawkesbury, holiday units, luxury cruiser and constantly updating of in-club facilities. As this book went to press, plans were afoot for an ambitious $12 million redevelopment program. This sort of restless progress … the desire to make things ever-better for members has been very much the way of things at Souths Juniors throughout its life …

The story tackled via the project that produced this book is a remarkable and colourful one. The year by year progress of the Juniors since 1959 has in no way been smooth-sailing. There has been much drama and controversy down the years and more than enough black days when the club's good name was dragged through the mud, or could have been. At least once, the club's licence was at threat.

Commissioning the book, the Juniors' long-serving chairman Henry Morris did so with the words: 'We believe the story must be told warts and all. There is no point publishing a history of the club if it paints over the rough bits. It is then not a genuine history. We've had our troubles, sure and we don't back away from that — but we are secure in the knowledge that the story of the Juniors over 40 years is an overwhelmingly positive one. We are proud of the role we have played in our community — and proud of the place we hold in it today.'

There have been difficult times at the club and some highly questionable events — and it is for history to judge the contributions of some of the main players of those times — men such as Darcy Lawler and Wally Dean. This telling of the story of the 40 years may aid that process. Whatever the judgment may be of the legacy left to the Juniors by such men, it can be said without hesitation that they too possessed a great affection and feeling for the club.

Inevitably, one man — George William Wintle — looms larger than all others in the telling of the story of the beginning and the early years. Again and again, in interviews conducted and primary sources of material investigated, Wintle's energy and drive shine through — and so too does his unwavering dream to build a great club at Kingsford. That George, not so well these days, could play a part in the book via the memories and stories he volun-

teered, was a wonderfully positive aspect of the project. Most see him as the Founding Father — although without in any way stealing credit from the other fine men who made a decision in 1957 that the South Sydney Junior League deserved a club — and they would help build that need into something real.

This then is the story of a unique club — or a determined crack at telling it, anyway. The story of the Juniors is a large and restless and picaresque one — unmatched in the entertainment industry in Australia. To pin it down is not easy. But some things emerge, as certain as the rising sun — that the club on Anzac Parade has played a valuable role in the life of its district, and its city. And that in trying to live up to the target it set itself in early years — The Best for the Best — the Juniors has done itself proud.

IAN HEADS, May 1999

FOUNDATION MEMBERS

ABERLINE Peter
ADAMS Thomas Clarke
ALCOCK Eric
ANDERSON Brian Roy
ANDERSON Francis Anzac
ANDERSON John Thomas
APPEL Conrad Ernest
BADGER John Gordon
BAKER George Stanley
BAKER Stanley Francis
BEAZLEY Clarence Williams
BELL Leslie
BELL Norman
BENNETT William Keith
BENSON Neil Colin
BESANT Donald William
BINGLE William Charles
BLANDY Harry Richard
BLUNDELL George Howard
BONOMINI Frank
BRENNAN Victor Leonard
BROCK Robert James
BRODIE Thomas
BRODIE Raymond
BROGAN Kenneth Francis
BROGAN Thomas Francis
BROWN Alfred James
BROWN John
BROWN Robert William
BUCHANAN Douglas
BUCKLEY Raymond Lawrence
BURCH Ernest
BURGESS Walter Alfred
BURGESS Walter James
BURNS Berkley Moffitt
BURNS Lawrence
BYRNES Harold
CAMPBELL Malcolm Atkinson
CARROLL Robert
CHAPMAN John Henry
CHEERS Percy
CLEARY Frederick Thomas
COATES Walter Albert
COCKING Thomas Henry
COGHLAN Joseph William
COGHLAN William Vincent
CONLEY Keith Walter
COUGHLAN Thomas Arthur

CUSH Kenneth Richard
DALE Allan Bruce
DALE Roy
DAVIS Edward
DENNEY Thomas John
DEVINE Phillip George
DEVINE Samuel Morgan
DOWNES Roy Thomas
DOYLE Barry
DRUMMOND Arthur Allen
DUGGAN John Thomas
DUNBAR Arthur Hedley
DWYER John Henry
DYKES Robert
GALVIN Mark Frederick
GARTON John Arthur
GIDDINS Leslie John
GLANVILLE John Frederick
GLOVER Walter James
GOLDING Leslie John
GRAHAM Leonard Gordon
GRANT George Henry
GURNEY Laurie Clive
HACKETT William
HAGARTY Harold James
HALL Roger Bannister
HANSEN Raymond
HARRIS Charles Ashley
HARRIS John Anthony
HART Frederick Ernest
HEARNE Revilo
HENDERSON Edward Charles
HENDERSON Percy Edward
HOGG Norman Frank
HOLLAND John Frederick
HOLMES Aubrey Keith
HOLMES Cyril Roy
HOLMES James
HORDER Charles Henry
HUNT Charles Arthur
LOFTS Arthur Edward
LAMEY Frederick James
LAMPRELL William Joseph
LANE George Albert
LANGRISH John Arthur
LAWLER Darcy
LEAL Raymond Leslie Bruce
LEE Charles David

LEE George John William
LEE Lionel
LEFTLEY Stanley Herbert
LLOYD Warwick Thomas
MACKEY Raymond Edward
MAGEE Edward Francis
MAHON Phillip Alexander
MATHER John
MATHERS Kenneth
MAY George Clarence
McCARTHY Donald Kenneth
McCORMACK Allan Keith
McCORMACK Archibald
    Emmett
McCROSSIN Noel
McCULLOCH Keith
McGAURR Arthur
McGLINN Kenneth Patrick
McGUIRE Samuel
McKEE Maurice
McPHERSON Francis Leslie
McWILLIAM William John
MEADER Leslie Albert
METCALFE William
MEYER Norman Henry
MEYER Ross Lang
MILLER Frederick
MILLS John Edward
MILLS Kenneth Raymond
MIRKIN Michael Leon
MOFFATT William Joseph
MOLAN Kevin
MOONEY George Edward
MORGAN Richard Dennis
MORSCHEL David
MOSS Noel Aubrey
MURPHY Clifford Francis
MURPHY William James
MURPHY Edward Lawrence
PARKER Frank
PARROTT Albert John
PARSONS Stanley Robert
PAYNE Peter
PHILLIPS John
PORTER Arthur Edward
PORTER Raymond Charles
POWER Joseph
PALMER Frederick Eric

SAIT Noel Thomas
SCULLION Robert
SHARLAND Lloyd Arthur
SHAW Alfred Henry
SIMMONS Victor James
SLOWGROVE Donald Richard
SMITH Alfred Alexander
SMITH Linton Hamden
SMITH Thomas Richmond
STANFORD John Albert
STAUNTON Allan Willoughby
STEVENSON Jack
STIG Wallace
SULLINGS Tom
SWEET Peter Norman
SWIFT Edmund Walter
TATTERSALL William
    Alexander
THOM Jack
THOMPSON Darcy Edward
TOCCHINI Frank
TOMBS Jack
TONKIES Peter Brian
TRUMAN William Ernest snr
TRUMAN William Henry
    James
WALKER Eric Maxwell
WALLACE Alfred George
WALSH Thomas
WAY Bruce Edward
WAY Neville Raymond
WATSON Charles Harland
WATSON Kenneth Leonard
WATSON Kevin Elliot
WATSON Lance Allen
WEAVER Reginald
WEBBER Clarence James
WEYMAN Charles George
WHITE John Reginald
WILSON WalterWINTER
    Raymond John
WINTLE Donald Joseph
WINTLE George Lyttleton
WINTLE George William
WITTINGSLOW Norman
WUNSCH Augustus Patrick

BIRDS GULLY

Down the hill behind the spot where South Sydney Junior Leagues grew into the finest club in the land from its modest beginnings in the late 1950s, there once ran a fast-flowing stream. Birds Gully was (and is) its name — a creek which flowed down from marshes that existed on the Struggletown side of where the Prince of Wales Hospital and the Royal Hospital for Women stand on the high ground at Randwick today. Birds Gully is still there somewhere today, gurgling underground as it makes its way beneath Rainbow Street, traverses Anzac Parade and bends back towards the Nine Ways, close to the club. The creek, a significant feature of the Aboriginal and early European landscape, is hard to picture in the mind's eye now — and so too the rough track that once passed out front of where the club now stands so imposingly on the wide, divided boulevard of Anzac Parade (named in 1917).

From the early years of the century trams passed that way — steam first, then electric — carrying excursioners to La Perouse or visitors to the hospital at Little Bay. From 1909 a specially constructed bogie car, No 948, featuring six cells off a side corridor, travelled from Darlinghurst siding, carrying prisoners bound for Long Bay Gaol. Gradually the track alongside the tram rails widened over the years — and became a road. As the La Perouse line in its early years passed through a relatively isolated area a post box was carried by some trams for the benefit of local residents. And due to the lack of good road access to the Little Bay area in those earlier days, trams provided a limited parcel service too. It was not unusual for a consignment of fish or a can of milk to be bundled aboard at Circular Quay for the La Perouse run. The total journey time was 56 minutes.

Until 1936 the area in which Souths Juniors now stands was just 'South Kensington'. Then, in August that year the Postal department announced that from October 1, 1936 South Kensington's new name would be 'Kingsford' in the Municipality of Randwick (proclaimed February 22, 1859). The name was selected by the members of the South Kensington Chamber of Commerce to honour the late aviator and national hero, Sir Charles Kingsford-Smith. The *South Kensington News*, which promptly changed its name to the *Kingsford News* commented: 'We who live in Kingsford have a shopping centre with a future. We are as a large family. Cut off from the city we make our own destiny, our own suburban progress is in our own hands. Let us eliminate bias and prejudices and move forward with a new resolution that is born of the new name of Kingsford.'

The district has always had its sense of local pride. There was great excitement in the 1930s when South Kensington's 'white way' opened along Anzac Parade. It was a time when the Sydney County Council encouraged shopping areas to set up 'white ways' — roads with street lights installed. Along the length of the shopping area large white pendant lamps were hung. In hard, Depression times residents were urged to 'shop locally'. A local paper wrote disapprovingly of 'the unhappy spectacle of tram loads of shoppers going to Oxford Street'.

The Daceyville Junction was christened the Nine Ways in 1932 — and the complicated crossroads long proved a problem for all — 'a menace of forest and poles' — until the construction of the relieving (and present) roundabout in the 1980s. Over the years Kingsford has seen a large migration of Italian and Greek communities — the most high profile being the Castellorizians, who migrated from the 1940s. In the late 1980s the President of the Randwick and District Historical Society, Frank Doyle, observed of Kingsford: 'The suburb is not old enough to have developed an identifiable character, as much of it was built from the 1920s on. The boundaries of Kingsford are a little blurry. The rule of thumb is that if you have a shop you say Kingsford, but if you have a home you say you are in Kensington.'

The focus now switches just south of the 'Nine Ways' to the wedge of a building once known as 'Bell's Ballroom'. The plaque set into the wall down near the 'sharp end' of the club today, gives more than a hint of its beginnings. It is the foundation stone of the 'Kensington Club', opened on the spot in 1927. A later newspaper reference when the ballroom had been established in the building, suggests it was, for a time, a centre of the fistic arts too. An excerpt from a local paper reads: 'on the other side of South Kensington 'Bulldog' Bill Bray taught boxing at Bell's gymnasium.'

Significantly, all of the uses of the old building in its original, then growing forms, have had to do with the gathering of people for relaxation, health and fitness … or just enjoyment. And so it is today, 70 years on. Just as Birds Gully gurgles away deep down, so the spirit of the building at 556A Anzac Parade, lives on.

ABOVE: *A busy Sunday afternoon, with the trams in full swing. The old tram tracks which used to run in front of where Souths Juniors now stands.*

BELOW: *Sydney trams ran past Bell's Ballroom when George Wintle and his team moved in to begin the extraordinary saga of the Juniors, in 1959.*

CHAPTER 1

A BLOOMIN' GOOD START

A bunch of fresh-cut flowers played their part in the foundation of the club which was to become an institution in Sydney life — and the most famous in all Australia. The exact date is uncertain — but on a morning in 1957 George William Wintle had the blooms firmly in his grasp when he trekked across town to visit, at his Waverley home, colourful businessman JJ Brown, an Eastern Suburbs boy who had had some success with investments in Broken Hill. At the door Wintle, a man with an old-fashioned sense of chivalry (a 'charmer' in the words of one female interviewee for this book), presented the flowers to Brown's wife Jessica. The pugnacious Wintle had something different to offer John Brown — 8000 pounds ($16,000) as a downpayment on securing the splinter of a building just past the intersection at Kingsford, heading south.

For many years — the exact number indeterminate — the bottom floor of the wedge-shaped two-storey building had operated as 'Bell's Ballroom'. On Saturday nights for 30 years or so, with the seats arranged in traditional Aussie style around the perimeter, Bell's had hosted local lads and lasses at a regular dance. Romances had no doubt begun there … ended there. George Wintle had been one of the regulars. 'I went to every dance,' he declared, reckoning he was 'pretty fair' at the Foxtrot and the Quickstep. A renowned local, Lionel Bowen, later to become Deputy Prime Minister of Australia, remembers Bell's in use as a Child Care Centre in the

OPPOSITE: *The Founding Father — George William Wintle, pictured in 1999.* Photo courtesy of Ern McQuillan.

JJ 'Jack' Brown, who owned Bell's Ballroom on Anzac Parade. He liked George Wintle's style and agreed to accept the offered downpayment on the building. It was the beginning.

middle '50s, run by the Sydney Day Nursery Association. 'The Day Care Centre was a separate part of the building in the sense that it had its own entrance which was close to the apex of the triangular block,' he recalls. Bowen, at that time a solicitor based in Macquarie Street, acted for JJ Brown when Brown eyed the building, then decided to make a bid at an auction in the mid '50s.

'Brown said go along … and pay 9 000 pounds,' Lionel Bowen remembers. 'So I went to the auction and the top bid was 8 000 pounds. The auctioneer said to me — 'you can have it for 8 750' — and I said okay.' Bowen believes that the building's days as a dance hall were over by the time of JJ Brown's ownership.

It was sometime later that George Wintle's eyes turned to the old building on Anzac Parade which, as long-serving deputy chairman, Barry Dunn, recalls in conversation, carried a sign designating it as the Kensington Club ('KC Club'). A metal plaque on the wall at the 'pointy end' gives the clearest clue to beginnings. It reads:

The Kensington Club Ltd
This stone was set August 6, 1927
TD Mutch Esq., MLA
JH O'Dea, Esq.,
Patrons

By the late 1950s Souths Junior League, with Wintle a fierce driving force as secretary, had accumulated more than 8 000 pounds in funds — a small fortune in those days — much of it through the unrelenting hard work of Wintle and his fellow club officials and Junior League administrators in flogging pies and ice creams at Redfern Oval and the other junior

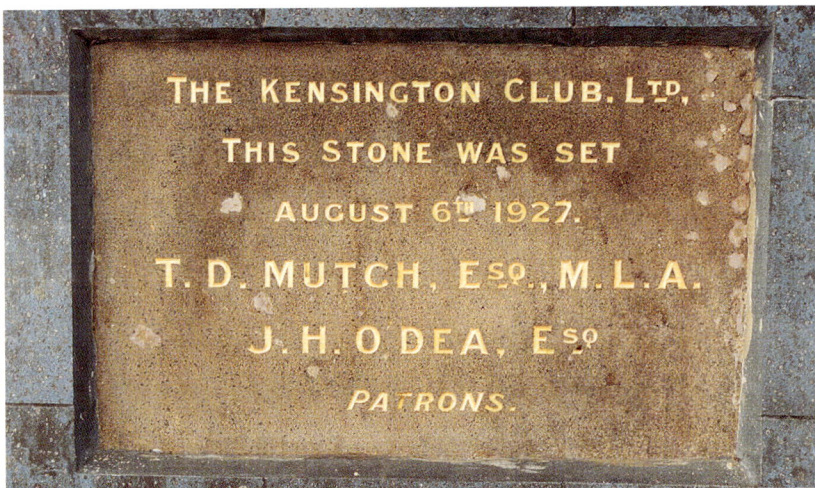

grounds. That money provided the foundation for conditional purchase of the building that became the club, although it was only part of the story. Tom Adams, one of the club's original 246 members, makes the point with considerable emphasis that the club wasn't just built on money from pies and ice creams. 'The 'A' grade clubs pitched in whatever they could,' he says. 'There were donations as high as 500 pounds from individual clubs to help get it going.' Over the years the straight-talking Adams — who runs the library at the Juniors these days — had a number of clashes with Wintle, a man driven by his dream … and one who was never easygoing. Old-timers recall Monday night meetings with George as secretary during which he would gather up his papers and storm out if the vote went against him. Tom Adams remembers too that war bonds held by the Junior League, or an individual club member, contributed to the early 'pool' needed to make the licensed club a reality.

Mrs Jessica Brown, widow of the late JJ 'Jack' Brown, remembers well the old building in Anzac Parade, and remembers too George Wintle's visit to the Brown home in Langlee Avenue, Waverley that fateful night in 1957. 'He came bearing the biggest bunch of gladioli I've ever seen,' she said. 'They reached to the top of the door. Jack knew George — or at least had seen him around. He always had time for anyone who was a worker … and there's no doubt George Wintle was a worker.' Jack Brown had bought the old building when it was largely unwanted. Talk was that the Eastern Suburbs railway was to go right through the spot. Jack thought otherwise … he doubted it would ever happen. 'I don't know that he had anything specifically in mind for the building — he just thought it was a good buy. George Wintle shared his views about the railway.'

Tom Adams — a foundation member in 1959, and still going strong in '99. Photo courtesy of Ern McQuillan.

At the end of that convivial night at the Brown household, George Wintle effectively went home with the building on a virtual lease arrangement, with potential to buy — although Jessica Brown's memory, at 85, was that there wasn't too much money changed hands at the start, and that her husband waited uncomplainingly until the club was up and thriving before he was fully recompensed for the total sale. The eventual price paid is somewhat clouded by the passing years. In one of the club's weekly newsletters of the early 1960s, George Wintle wrote: 'After two frustrating years and many thousands of pounds of debt, we opened the doors 19 December, 1959. The building was optioned at 32 500 pounds, not a bad little sum for a building originally costing about 13 000 pounds.' There are other solid references to that figure 32 500 pounds.

Among private papers generously made available by Jessica Brown for this book were documents which throw light on the ongoing financial arrangement:

Nov 4, 1957 — Letter from George Wintle, Oscar Nilson and Darcy Thompson to JJ Brown:

'By resolution of the Finance Committee of the above Association we, the undersigned, are authorised to seek a loan of 2 500 pounds, repayable in five years at 5.5 per cent. The South Sydney Junior League to lodge as part security, receipts for Bonds and Water Board loan — same to be held by you and the Rural Bank, Kingsford. Be advised that such Bonds and Loan Certificates are not to be lodged for payment without Mr. Brown's express approval.'

March 22, 1960 — Letter from George Wintle to JJ Brown:

'Enclosed please find cheque for 1 500 pounds in part payment of indebtedness of the SSDRLFC. A further cheque will be forwarded shortly. On Saturday April 2, Isador Goodman will be featured in the Club as a guest artist and you and Mrs Brown would be very welcome.'

June 20, 1961 — Payment made to JJ Brown:

'Balance of principal and interest owing in respect of premises at Anzac Parade and Wallace Street, Kingsford 1 645 pounds; interest at 6% to June 9, 1961, 24 pounds 15 shillings. Total 1 669 pounds 15 shillings.'

October 20, 1961 — Letter from George Wintle to JJ Brown:

'Enclosed please find cheque for 1694 pounds, 10 shillings — being balance due on money owing for above property. I might take this opportunity of stating that the success of the Club is entirely due to the efforts of the people who created it and the sociability of the Club members who enjoy its amenities.'

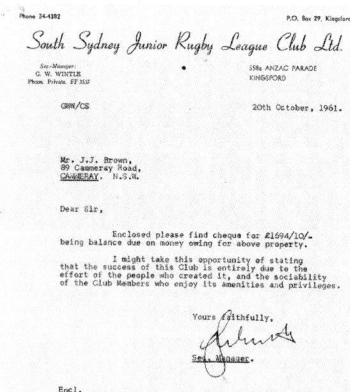

The South Sydney Junior Rugby League presentation night, 1955.

In the early 1960s George Wintle gave his clear view of the way it had all happened: 'We formed a club by securing 246 members, formed a company and with money derived from selling lollies, chocolates, pies, Coca-Cola, chips etc and from raffles and doubles, we took a lease of the original building on the basis of no licence within a certain time, option to be cancelled.'

In eventually selling the building that grew into the giant of South Sydney Junior Rugby League Club and in kicking of Eastern Suburbs Leagues Club (JJ Brown obtained the first licence for Easts through his connections with Miller's Brewery, and backed the club with his own money) Jack Brown stands as a towering — if largely forgotten — figure in the Sydney club industry.

Anyone who ever had even the slightest connection with the Juniors over the years, recalls George Wintle. Lawyer John Riordan, a notable contributor to the Souths (and rugby league) cause over the years remembers him 'up and down the grandstand' at Redfern one afternoon, selling his ice creams. Said a bloke near Riordan: 'Got any pies George? … it's too bloody cold for ice cream.' Riordan: 'George disappeared immediately … and

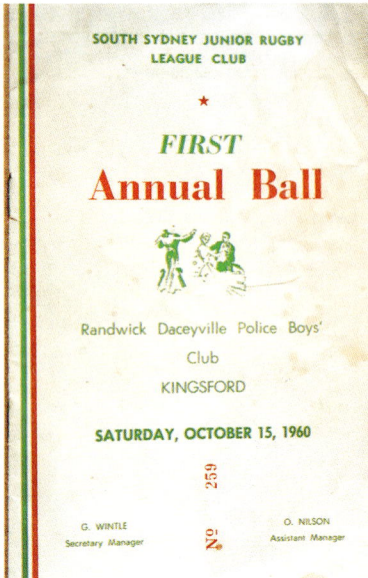

SOUTH SYDNEY JUNIOR RUGBY LEAGUE CLUB

★

FIRST

Annual Ball

Randwick Daceyville Police Boys'
Club
KINGSFORD

SATURDAY, OCTOBER 15, 1960

G. WINTLE
Secretary Manager

No. 259

O. NILSON
Assistant Manager

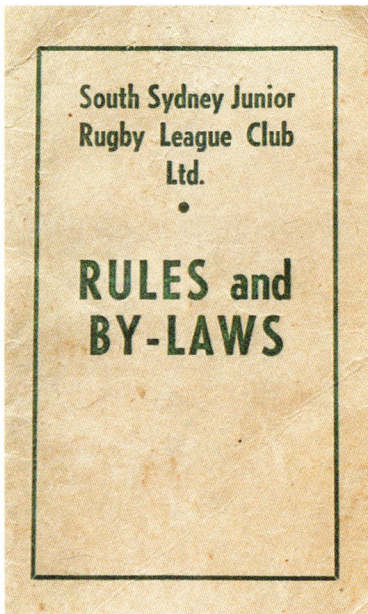

South Sydney Junior
Rugby League Club
Ltd.
•
RULES and
BY-LAWS

TOP: *A souvenir programme of the club's first Annual Ball, held at the Randwick Daceyville Police Boys' Club in October 1960.*

ABOVE: *A slice of club history: Ern McQuillan's photo of the Club's first booklet of rules and by-laws.*

returned with a box of hot pies.' John Ireland, long-serving President of the Sydney Catholic Club, and a man with a long association with the Juniors, remembers Wintle as 'the best worker I've ever seen', relentlessly pushing his pies on the colder days, ice creams when the weather was a little kinder.

The Juniors had never had a permanent home base. In the '50s the regular Monday night meetings in season were held, variously, at Mascot Town Hall, and the Mascot School of Arts. On Monday mornings Oscar 'Occa' Nilson, treasurer of the Junior League and a wonderful worker for the cause for many years, would take the weekend proceeds up to the bank — on a pushbike.

Like all such organisations the success achieved was built around a core of wonderfully committed workers. The Juniors' Grand Final program of 1950 gave a glimpse of those who 'dug the well':

'President: Mr J Stanford — Honorary Treasurer of the Junior League from 1938–40, and the President through most of the '40s.

Honorary Secretary: Joe Healey. In 1950 Joe had been secretary of Souths Juniors for 25 years — and had the distinction of having held office longer than any junior league official in any district. From Lauriston Park Club he had become secretary in 1925 after two years as assistant secretary. 'The program commented: 'He has given a lifetime of service to the Juniors and by a dint of hard work has brought the league through its trials and tribulations to a point where it is, without doubt, the strongest junior league in NSW.' In 1955 the beautiful 'Joe Healey Memorial Club Championship Trophy' was struck in his memory.

Honorary Treasurer: Clem Kennedy snr — he had held the financial reins since 1941.'

Many others were mentioned too: Tom Craigie, Gus Hahn, Sam Devine, Bill Fletcher, Fred West, Ern Coupland, Joe Power, Jim Harris, Reg Weaver, Harry Bilton, Arthur Langrish and Jack Kelly — all of them contributors to what the Souths Junior League had been over the years … and would be in the future.

It was at the office at the School of Arts, in Coward Street next to the Fire Station, that the big decision was taken. What the Junior League needed was a club of its own …

After all, the Juniors had been in existence for half a century, building a wonderful tradition of enjoyment and opportunity for the young men of the South Sydney district. The playing numbers had progressively grown over the years. When George Wintle took over as honorary secretary of the South Sydney Junior League in late 1953 (succeeding Joe Healey), there were 48 teams and 1 200 players.

The legacy of what Souths Juniors had become lay back in the mists of time. When rugby league began in Australia in 1908, only two (district) clubs had junior leagues in place — Balmain ... and South Sydney. In the Tom Brock collection at the University of NSW is a copy of the program published for the Australia v New Zealand match in early June 1908. The curtain-raiser features a team from South Sydney Juniors — against Balmain.

In his 88th year, Percy Horne, a great and enduring South Sydney man, recalled the beginning of the Juniors, in 1908. Perc remembers Johnny McGrath, a foundation committeeman at Souths District Club (and who was to become the first secretary of the Juniors) attending a meeting of the Waterloo Oaks (rugby union) Club in 1908, and convincing the players to switch to the new game. 'If we won the competition in rugby union we'd get a silver medal,' said Horne, an Oaks player at that time. 'Rugby league promised us a gold medal, plus free doctor's treatment if we got injured, and pay for time off work if we got hurt. The honorarium for an injured player would be one pound [$2] per week.' The players were also promised, and given, country trips for switching to league. In 1908 a team was sent to Newcastle, in 1909 another to Queensland.

It was the work of men such as Percy Horne in the early days that gave South Sydney football its chance. Perc was a wonderful worker with the Rabbitohs, putting almost 80 years of his long life into the club. He was a foundation player in Souths Juniors in 1908. Photo courtesy of South Sydney District Club.

Souths needed four teams to make a competition in 1908 and there was a real struggle after two teams from Waterloo Oaks, and one from Redfern had been assembled. Perc Horne, a wonderful figure in South Sydney football all the way to his death at 99, was instrumental in getting the vitally needed fourth side. 'What did we do to solve the impasse?' he said. 'I left Waterloo Oaks (who were to be premiers for the first three seasons) and recruited 12 players from the drinkers at Abbott's Hotel — and there we were, ready to go (although a player or two short of the necessary 13 now and then). We called the Abbott's boys the Waterloo Centennial team (the next year they became Waterloo-Waratahs).' The team was also known as the 'Irish 13'. In 1909 Erskineville Kioras and Botany Methodist joined, providing a six-team competition. In 1910 four more teams joined from the strong churches competition. By 1914 there were 16 teams in three grades. The pioneers of junior football in the Souths district were

The genial Darcy Edward Thompson — first chairman of Souths Juniors. He started his football career with Kensington United before the War, then joined Fernleighs in 1946, contributing strongly in the progress towards the establishment of the new club in 1959.

an adventurous lot, joining the new game despite the Rugby Union hierarchy's decree that any player who turned out in the 13-a-side game would be declared professional and banned for life.

Souths Juniors began competition at the Sir Joseph Banks Ground, Botany, on April 25, 1908. The Rope Works Field and Booralee Park were other popular venues in pioneering days. Old-timers recalled some wild Saturday afternoons at Booralee Park, home ground of Botany Club. As a feature in the Juniors' Annual Report of 1971–72 reported: 'It was 80 minutes of mayhem followed by a dash into surrounding scrubland, carrying street clothes should the visitors win. Defeat made the Botany fans very angry indeed in those days. One afternoon a brawl broke out and didn't finish until the fence had been dragged down and a grandstand of types completely demolished. Open grounds also provided a special hazard to players, particularly wingers. A favourite trick of women spectators was to take an umbrella to the game. Many a winger was felled at full flight from an umbrella crashed to the head.'

The hard work of those early days mirrored what was to take place half a century later when the Juniors took their next great step — and set up a licensed club. Perc Horne, among others, worked day and night 'selling' rugby league to anyone who would listen in the early years of the century. He remembered: 'In those days and nights, transport was scarce, money was scarcer and if I wanted to get anywhere, I had to walk. The result was that I was dog-tired each morning after the long 'hard sell' meetings the night before. But we were getting results. More and more clubs were becoming interested and, most importantly, adopting the new code. That was my reward.' By 1911 rugby union had faded from existence in the district. Champion players had begun to emerge as they would in an endless stream in the years to follow … and so it began.

By the time George Wintle had his first taste of football in Souths Juniors in the early 1930s, the competition was long-since established, on foundations of granite. Wintle played, briefly, with Kensington. His memories of happier, earlier days stuck with him: 'My whole life has been football, first as a player, then as an official. The era when I kicked off — the early '30s when we travelled all over the place on the back of a flat-top truck to play, when we changed in dog boxes beside the oval and showered under the one hose — sound a bit primitive today. But we had a hell of a lot of mateship then.' Wintle recalls a fiery game in 1934 refereed by George Bishop, ex-Australian test hooker who went on to become a top grade referee, in which Bishop had him under suspicion for belting an opposing player. 'I didn't do it … he got the wrong man,' said Wintle. In a lively aftermath to the match Wintle's sister clobbered the referee with an umbrella. Around the time that the young Wintle was enjoying his brief career in the juniors, the grounds being used were: Lauriston Park, L' Estrange Park, Mascot Park, Booralee Park and Shepherd's Bush Ground at Mascot. By the time he was 18, George Wintle was an official within Souths Junior League. Meetings in those days were held in the old Boot Trades Hall in Botany. In 1953, he became secretary.

Old programs that exist in the magnificent Tom Brock Collection of South Sydney records and memorabilia held by the University of NSW give captivating glimpses of long forgotten days in the 'Juniors'. A program from season 1940 invites football fans to attend the weekly 50–50 dance at Paddington Town Hall, and carries an impressive advertisement for The Hotel Hampton Court (Kings Cross) — featuring 'a public shoe shine platform' and 'modern vapour bath service'. A 1948 program boasts: 'Every Sunday — hard, clean fast football will be played on the Redfern Oval.' A 1946 program carries advertisements for Spruso — 'for the hair', Joel's London Tavern Hotel, Redfern, and Aeroplane Pure Fruit Jellies.

In the memories of the many people who generously offered their time in the making of this book, the 'energy' of George Wintle was a recurring theme, although so too the great work of a coterie of quieter figures around him. In the period leading up to the purchase of Bell's Ballroom, he is recalled as a tremendous worker. As John Riordan and John Ireland noted in interviews, a favoured and recurring memory is of George pushing a trolley of pies (or ice creams) around Redfern Oval, where huge crowds of 10 000 or more would gather on the big occasions. 'Scotts pies, they were,' says Wintle. 'They'd deliver them hot.' Members of Wintle's family were often there, pitching in, too. All of it was honorary. George Wintle was secretary of the Junior League at no pay. In his working life he was a foreman at General Motors, Pagewood.

A 1957 Juniors program poses the question: 'Where else would you get daylight to dusk football, close finishes, fisticuffs, foot runnin' etc for one and six? We have made arrangements to serve pies, peas and hot Bonox this Sunday.' In a 1958 program George Wintle gives himself a pat on the back: 'We have a good catering business for sure — you can bet your bottom dollar that no individual could run it like us.'

From the sale of pies and ice creams and raffle tickets at Redfern, Coogee and Matraville, Wintle and his fellow travellers accumulated the money that made the dream of a club become a reality. The canteens were well run and highly successful. At Redfern there was a store where the club would hold 1 000 bottles of Coca-Cola, and 1000 ice creams, plus count-

BOOKS, BOOKIES AND A GOOD TIME

Forty years after Tom Adams had first signed on the dotted line to become a foundation member of South Sydney Juniors he was still around the place — still heavily involved. In a narrow alcove on the first floor Tom ran the library 19 hours a week — surrounded by more than 3000 books. The Juniors has had a library for members for much of its existence — and the popularity of the quiet room with its carefully-arranged books has never dimmed. On Tom's opening hours, there was always a steady stream of traffic — with considerable demand for this new title or that, that Tom had added to the collection 'at the right price'.

A former player with Brothers club back in the early 1950s Tom Adams was right at the coalface when the work began in '57 towards the opening of a licensed club. He remembers clearly the struggle to rustle up the necessary 250 members that would put the club in the ball park for a liquor licence. 'We got to 234 ... the 16 extras were bodgies,' he reveals, a twinkle in his eye. Adams recalls how the Commonwealth Bank at Mascot had knocked back the club's initial approach for a loan to support the purchase of 556A Anzac Parade — but that the Rural at Kingsford had come good with the necessary money. And he remembers the modest start upstairs at the old Bell's Ballroom — with no licence, but the chance of getting a drink on the quiet anyway. He can picture still Leo Wintle, George's father, in charge of the cigarette and tobacco kiosk, over in one corner.

In his younger days Tom was something of a firebrand who reveals today that he was barred from the club on a number of occasions. 'Nothing too major,' he says. 'Just little things that happened ... the rules were pretty strict.' After one such 'outing' he was back in the club having a first sip of beer when Don Wintle, George's brother, approached him. 'Last time you were here you wanted to fight me,' said Don. 'Now's your chance.' Next thing the pair were out the back of the club and into it. The result: Tom Adams was barred again.

He and George Wintle had what could fairly be called a 'prickly' relationship. Tom remembers: 'George once wrote in one of his newsletters, 'If Mr Adams walks down that side of the street, I'll walk down this side.' The pair were protagonists in an amazing and, in hindsight, hilarious confrontation one day in the early '60s when Tom Adams arrived at the club for work. At that time he was working as a barman, upstairs. Says Tom: 'You had to bundy on downstairs, in the foyer. I was on 6 o'clock shift, and arrived at the club at 5.57. 'Mr Adams, you're late,' said George Wintle. 'No I'm not,' I said ... 'I start at 6 o'clock.' 'Union rules are that you have to be here five minutes before the start of your shift,' said Wintle. That was absolute bullshit. I felt about this big ... as was his way Wintle had bawled me out before everyone in the foyer. 'Where do I bundy on?' ... I said ... 'and it'll bloody-well be for the last time!' Eventually Wintle told me to get off the premises and when I wanted to sign myself back into the club (as a member) he told me I was incorrectly dressed. I was in a bow tie, white shirt and cummerbund. So I went down the road to a mate's place, borrowed a suit, and came straight back up to the club. I headed upstairs to the bar where I was supposed to be working … and sat on the other side of the bar and had a few drinks with Steve Ryan (club director and George Wintle's brother-in-law).'

Tom Adams has many colourful memories of earlier days at the club:

Of the resident SP bookie 'AJ', to whom a blind eye was turned despite the strict rules of the club.

The big plaster dog that once stood in the foyer. Tom recalls how a mate of his, 'Kenny', had been barred after trying to take the dog out of the club one night. 'I was just taking him out for a piss,' Kenny explained.

Of old Mick Christie who ran the snooker room. 'A good old bloke,' says Tom. 'He used to call out the names for the tables … 'Mr Smith' … 'Mr Robinson' … 'Mr Adams' … but whenever he got to a difficult for-eign-sounding name he'd say … 'Mr whatever-your-bloody-name-is!'

Tom Adams calls George Wintle … 'a dictator' … 'obsessive' but despite their differences, pays him due accord. 'He ran a tight ship … without George the club wouldn't have started.'

---

less tins of Smith's Crisps in their shiny packets. From each item sold would come a profit of a penny or two. And from those countless sales came the club …

The Juniors' Annual Ball helped with the fundraising too. In 1959 it was 25 shillings a head — with lobster, chicken and ham on the menu. The venue was the Randwick-Daceyville Police Boys' Club, and 'pretty hostesses' would be on hand. A feature of the night was large ice cream cakes — made in the colours of each club.

Kensington and Mascot clubs were driving forces in the progress towards establishment of the licensed club. Berkley Burns, secretary of Mascot club 1955–63 and one of the 'originals' at the Juniors, estimates today that he personally nominated around 60 (of the 246) foundation members — with George Wintle's brother Don working equally effective-ly in the big roundup. Burns's links with Mascot club — and the South Sydney Juniors way of life — go back to the war years. He recalls early days when the 'B' grade games were played every Saturday at L'Estrange Park. 'There was never an afternoon without a brawl,' he says.

'They were lively times … it was 'on' every week.'

Today when he looks back George Wintle calls Lionel Bowen, the man who found himself at the heart of the birth of a club that all the energy and hard work produced, 'A good bloke … the best I know.' And Bowen in his turn recalls the favourable reaction of JJ Brown when Wintle went to see him, offering 8 000 pounds of the Junior League's money for the Bell's Ballroom building. 'I like the look of this fellow,' Brown told Bowen. Brown agreed to do business.

Lionel Bowen also has a colourful memory of the new club's first annual meeting in 1960. 'They invited me along … they'd done well that year,' he said. 'They were allowing the wives of members in and it got so crowded that many of the members finished up on the stairs … with all the ladies upstairs, seated. There was a move to exclude all women from the meeting, but George jumped up and took the mike. 'We wouldn't have a club if it wasn't for the women,' he told them. 'There's no way I'll accept that motion.' It got one vote.'

George Wintle knew the Bell's Ballroom building well. He remembers as a boy being taken along to Rechabites' meetings on the top floor — the Rechabites being total abstainers (from alcohol). Wintle recalls that most of the attendees were employees at the airport, at Mascot. The Rechabites' link with the club is a wry one. It took the Juniors two years to obtain a liquor licence — and until then the new premises were 'dry' … well, officially, at least.

In George Wintle's crisp memory, unfazed by the stroke that laid him low in the 1980s, Bell's Ballroom had stood on the site for '30 years or so', before the Junior League bought the building. The club was incorporated as a company in September 1957. The Grand Final day program of 1957 spoke proudly of the ambitions held for the newly-purchased building in Kingsford:

'Our plans for 1958 are mighty — we have just paid a very substantial deposit on a building worth 32 500 pounds. We have our Articles of Association, our plans and our initial membership, and go to court within a few weeks for a provisional liquor licence. Our new home for the South Sydney Junior Rugby League Club Ltd is at the corner of Anzac Parade and Wallace Street, Kingsford — known as Bell's Ballroom. Our plans are huge — we intend to provide modern club facilities for our members — to plough back into the district the profits derived from our bar and poker machines. The top floor will comprise a magnificent lounge with a view of Botany Bay and surrounding districts that is unsurpassed. Building and games room, indoor bowls, kitchen, snack bar and good bar appointments will make the Club something to be proud of. We have promised Council our fullest support for worthy causes and already have plans to assist the women athletes going to the Empire Games in Wales in July, 1957. A limited number of applications for membership forms are available: the entrance fee is one pound one shilling [$2.20] and yearly subscription two pounds two shillings [$4.40].'

A circular sent to the 246 foundation members in December 1958 and signed by George Wintle throws light on the ongoing story of the 'early days'. It reads: 'I am directed to advise that alterations and renovations to club premises have reached a stage where many facilities can be used by members. A full sized bowling mat has been procured, and is now in operation. This is an added amenity to the table tennis, darts, hookey board etc. We have an appeal before the Licensing Court, relative to our liquor licence application at the moment, and this should be finalised by March 13.'

At the beginning, the Juniors had only the upstairs for their use — and no liquor licence, or licence to operate poker machines. The licence took two years to come — granted finally in 1959 after a couple of earlier knockbacks. Fired by GMH in 1959, Wintle was given the job as 'clerk of works' at the new club, at 20 pounds a week, the money kicked in by supportive clubs in the Juniors; he was also made a director on the first Board. The men who took the step with George Wintle as the club's first Board of Directors in 1957 were: Darcy Thompson, Oscar Nilson, Steve Ryan, Jack Kelly, Ern Coupland, Tom Craigie — devoted South Sydney football men, all of them. The first chairman was Darcy Edward

The Board of Directors and senior staff in 1962. Back row: Olive Hambly, office administrator; Steve Ryan, deputy chairman; Tom Craigie, director; Ern Coupland, director; Jack Kelly, director; Dorothy Ryan, supervisor.

Front row: George Wintle, secretary-manager; Athol Knight, director; Darcy Thompson, chairman of directors; Tim Wallace, director; Oscar Nilson, assistant manager.

Thompson, a committed worker for the cause from the South Sydney Fernleighs. Darcy Thompson had started his football career as a lad — with Kensington United. At 16, he joined the Army, and during his two years in uniform served overseas with Australian forces. After his discharge he returned to football — and in 1946 joined Fernleighs. A genial and popular man, he is remembered with affection by old-timers left at the club. 'A terrific bloke,' says Tom Adams. 'They were good men … they used to control it well,' says George Wintle. 'It took us a two-year battle to get a licence. We fought and fought over it. We spent plenty of time in court … and it got so familiar I used to bring in morning tea for the bloody magistrate. So, originally when we opened, we couldn't serve alcohol, although there was bowls and dancing on the top floor … but no beer … well, officially anyway. We had a band, and we paid them the minimum. But the place was very popular, right from the start. We started to make money the minute we opened.' Pressed, Wintle revealed that well, yes, it had been possible to get a beer at the Juniors in the years 1957–1959. 'I used to 'pinch' a car from work [General Motors] and go and pick up the beer of a Monday. I'd get bottled beer from Britten's pub

Mascot Juniors F-grade premiers of 1957, which supplied a number of South Sydney grade players, including an international and club president, George Piggins (seated, third from left). Photo courtesy Berkeley Burns (Middle row, far left).

at Darlinghurst, and we'd sell it at two bob [20 cents] a bottle. We'd buy it at one and ninepence.

'Right at the start (on the granting of a licence in late 1959) we bought poker machines; I used to even have them positioned on the dance floor so they could play them out there … on the floor. We used to wheel the machines out onto the floor at certain times and call out the names of members. If your name was called out you'd get five free pulls on the machine. The jackpot was five pounds [$10]. We were strict on dress from the start. Men could wear shorts with long socks — but only till 8 o'clock.' Forty years on, John Riordan paints the scene as he remembers it: 'The dance would be in full swing and all of a sudden George would stop the music. 'Machine No. 39 is not being played!' he would announce.

'They were ancient machines, compared with what the club has today. We had 246 members (all men) to start with at the club and from memory, 12 poker machines at the beginning, doing our business with a bloke named Joe Gardiner from Ainsworths. Membership was one pound [$2] a year. Gradually the number of machines grew. We had penny machines at the start, and sixpence and one shilling; not too many two-shilling machines.'

When the newly-licensed club opened its doors on December 19, 1959 — it was still primitive indeed compared with the 'pleasure palace' (or 'Pokie Palace' as George Wintle would now and then refer to the club) that was to grow on the spot in the year ahead … but Souths Juniors' very own club, all the same. At that stage it was still just the one floor — upstairs — a situation soon remedied when the lessee downstairs (whose name was Krueger according to George Wintle's memory) was bought out. Bell's Ballroom was no more. At the start, in '59, the beer was carried upstairs by hand, the kegs lugged laboriously to the cool-room created next to the small upstairs bar. Tooheys was the brand in the first place. 'Tooths wouldn't deal with us,' huffed George Wintle. Cigarettes were a problem, too. 'They wouldn't supply us … the tobacco companies,' said Wintle. 'We had to buy cigarettes under the lap.' Wintle was the club's first secretary-manager, working six days a week, and Occa Nilson its first supervisor. Hawk-eyed, Wintle patrolled the door much of the time — a habit he maintained just as enthusiastically later on when the club grew, as in those exciting early days …

At the beginning the club opened its doors at 10am … and there was one barman. Extra staff came in at night. 'They worked damned hard, I'll tell you,' says Wintle. The hours were 10am–11pm through the week, and 10am to midnight on Saturdays.

The club at Kingsford ran pretty much a parallel path with Sydney's other 'mega-club' — the St George 'Taj Mahal' at Kogarah. Saints had opened a club as far back as 1952, on the intersection of Rocky Point Road and the Princes Highway. It was a basic meeting place with two poker machines, a couple of offices, a stage for the band and one long bar. The move 'down the road' to what had once been Prince Edward Park, to the spot where St George Leagues Club stands today, came in the early 1960s. On July 1, 1963 the 'Taj Mahal' was opened. Total cost was around 800,000 pounds ($1.6 million).

Prior to the developments of the 1950s and early '60s — and notably at Kingsford and Kogarah, social clubs in Sydney were few and exclusive. A study of the club scene in Sydney prior to 1950 which is included in the extensive papers of South Sydney club's late and much admired historian, Tom Brock, notes: 'Membership fees were high and admissibility limited, while the amenities, broadly speaking, were limited to bar facilities, dining rooms, billiard rooms and in some better clubs, steam rooms and swimming pools. Membership in these clubs was wholly for men, women being tolerated as visitors on occasions in a restricted area, such as the dining room. This type of club had little attraction for the average man and was too expensive for the worker.'

In the later years of his life the memories of the starting days at Souths Juniors remain strong, if fragmented, in George Wintle's mind. He recalls a bad period when thieves got in twice in a short time and took the takings of the day. And he remembers a spotty bunch of youngsters with their father in tow, who got changed in the office before performing. They were the Bee Gees. Without prompting, George repeats an unprintable story about the group's appearance at the club.

The Juniors banked with the Rural at Kingsford — the name, and the bank now long gone. For 20 years George Wintle lived in a semi-detached house adjoining the bank's premises at 313 Anzac Parade. As the money rolled in, secretary-manager Wintle would make the trek to the bank from the club when required. After the robberies he hired Armaguard to look after him on his journeys.

Gradually things changed at 'the club'. Like Topsy, the modest premises of 1957 just grew. A dining room and snooker tables appeared on the top floor; indoor bowls mats were purchased — 60 footers — and laid down for the enjoyment of members. When membership was up to 500, Wintle would go each week and buy $500 worth of presents from a shop in York Street — blankets and beachware and towels — using them for promotions within the club.

As the accompanying year-by-year profile of the development of Souths Juniors so clearly shows, the club's generosity as a benefactor to causes many and varied was in place right from the beginning. George Wintle remembers with particular pride the purchase, at a total cost of $20,000, of a hyperbaric tank — a high pressure chamber — in 1964, designed for the use of the Prince Henry Hospital, and transported in a slow journey from Wollongong. In 1971 the club played its part in opening the Hyperbaric Unit at Prince Henry — the only Hyperbaric Chamber to be established in a public hospital in Australia. Later the tank purchased by George and the club was transported across to the Prince of Wales Hospital, Randwick. 'It's there today, saving lives,' says George Wintle with pride.

Chairman Darcy Thompson (in front) and George Wintle with the hyperbaric tank purchased by the club in the 1960s for the use of the Intensive Care Unit at Prince Henry Hospital.

CHAPTER 2

THE KING OF CLUBLAND

The formation years at Souths Juniors, which can be judged to have ended on December 31, 1966, were extraordinary. At their heart … always … was the bespectacled, crew-cut, unbelievably energetic figure of secretary-manager George Wintle, a man driven … by some restless force. Wintle neither had nor has any pretensions about his standing in the eyes of some. 'Yeah, I met some opposition,' he says. 'Some didn't like me. I was tough. I insisted on a standard of dress. 'If you're going to come here … you'll be dressed up,' I said to them.' Claire James, over many years a wonderful servant of the Junior League, of which she reluctantly became treasurer — a position she held for 20 years — remembers Wintle as a 'hard taskmaster'. Wintle built a dynasty, with members of his family progressively added to the staff. In 1963 he told columnist Ron Saw: 'Some people seem to think that the name should be changed from the South Sydney Junior Leagues Club to the Wintle Family Club. Or to George's Nightclub … well, let 'em think what they damn well please. Some members here call me Der Feuhrer. They can call me what they like. This club is my life and I want to see it grow still bigger and still richer.' Having laid down hardline rules at 'his' club, Wintle believed in doing a good deal of the policing himself. Most often he would be found at the Wallace Street end entrance door, checking out the clientele…

Arguments and even more at the door were not unusual as the strict Wintle code was applied. 'I remember one day I was on the door ... watching people come in,' he said. 'It was after 8 o'clock and this fella came along, still dressed in his gardening clothes. 'You're too late, dressed like that ... you can't come in,' I said to him. Next thing we were out the front of the club, fighting in the gutter. He didn't get in. But it turned out he was a friend of the Police Commissioner's and he reported what had happened — and said I assaulted him. As a result, the local sergeant told his men to keep a close watch on me. And they did, the buggers.'

Wintle tells what is surely one of the great stories of club life — of barring at the front door the woman who was to become his second wife. 'Yeah, I met my second wife (Sylvia McGaurr) at the front door,' he says. 'And I told her she couldn't come in. She was wearing a tennis dress. I barred her. Two years later we were married.' Sylvia Wintle, 20 years his junior, died in the 1980s and George, stricken by a stroke, has lived the years into old age alone, in an (extremely) modest housing commission flatette in Botany. To visit him in the late 1990s is to realise starkly that George Wintle reaped no great financial rewards from his seven years at the helm of South Sydney Junior Leagues Club. Forgotten by many, and sadly in not much contact with his family — he was the father of six children in his two marriages, the first (to Ellen) lasting from 1940 to 1966, and is grandfather of one — he is a struggling figure.

But George Wintle's eyes sparkle when he talks of the club he built, and of the battles he fought. He remembers long, hard, happy days of earlier years. 'I was first in and last to leave,' he says, indicating absolutely

Claire James started work in the club's accounts office in 1964, beginning a long and fruitful association with the Juniors. With a smile in 1999, she recalled early days: 'Peyton Place had nothing on this place.' Photo courtesy of Ern McQuillan.

no regrets, remembering how the media had quickly tagged him 'King of the Poker Machines' and 'The King of Clubland' as profit returns grew at the club. But he snaps and snarls when names such as George Hansen (ex-South Sydney club treasurer), an old foe, or Wally Dean, the ex-barber from Redfern who became his bitter enemy at the Juniors, are mentioned. Of Hansen he says: 'a mean bastard and a dead-set villain.' Of Dean, with whom he engaged in titanic struggle through the period 1965–67 he says little that can be printed today. 'I did one thing in my life that I regret,' he says. 'I gave Dean 100 pounds to further his campaign when he was going for City Council. He got on, too. He treated me disgracefully.'

Another legendary Wintle story is of his brush with famous jockey Athol George Mulley. Wintle tells it this way: 'I was up at Forster, looking at the property we eventually bought as holiday flats and I got a phone call at the airport. It was the club. 'What's the matter?' I said. They told me that George Mulley had brought his trainer [sic] into the steam room and they were occupying all the seats. I said, 'bugger George Mulley!' 'Kick him out.' I barred him.'

The story hit the newspapers in a big way — as did many of the events of George Wintle's life in clubland. 'MULLEY OUT — Banned by secretary', screamed the *Daily Mirror* headline. The paper reported on September 15, 1965 that George Wintle had:

- banned Mulley on the jockey's first visit to the club;
- rebuked famous ex-jockey Fred Shean, who had been in Mulley's company.

George Hansen, South Sydney club treasurer in the 1960s. George Wintle thought little of him. 'A mean bastard and a dead-set villain,' said Wintle.

It was reported that Wintle had charged Mulley with 'using the club to the detriment of others'. It emerged that Mulley had been originally refused admittance because he was not 'dressed satisfactorily' (he was wearing a roll-neck shirt). Mulley had subsequently borrowed a dress shirt from a friend and been allowed entry. One bone of contention seems to have been that Mulley and Shean spent some considerable time — 'over several hours' — in the steam and sauna rooms. Mulley called Wintle's claims 'ridiculous' and declared he wouldn't be bothered with the club again. 'As far as I am concerned the ban can be permanent,' he said.

The Wintle vigilance extended to all areas of the club. When a bloke named Norm Coleman came to the club in the 1960s boasting that his version of 'The Grip' had the poker machines beaten, George was there watching. According to reports Coleman pulled nine jackpots before Wintle moved in on him. 'I've had a report,' he said 'that you were pulling the machine too hard.' 'Not me,' said Coleman.

MULLEY OUT
Jockey in club dispute

Banned by secretary

ABOVE: *Jockey Athol Mulley hit the headlines in the Sydney* Daily Mirror *(itals) one day after clashing with George Wintle at the club. Mulley was accused of 'using the club to the detriment of others'. 'I don't think I'll ever be bothering with the club again,' said Mulley.*

LEFT: *Athol George Mulley and the greatest horse he ever rode, the mighty Bernborough.* Photo courtesy of Ern McQuillan.

'I'm told you damaged the mechanism in the machine you were playing,' Wintle persisted.

After further debate, Wintle had the last word: 'I'll have to ask you to leave the club.' The punchline came a day or two later when Coleman received a letter from Wintle informing him that he had been suspended until further notice.

Lead slugs were another problem for the Juniors during a period of the mid '60s. Addressing the problem with a wry touch, Wintle wrote in the club report: 'You reckon you've got troubles with snails in the garden.

Where the poker machines never stop whirring

HARDLY a week goes by without the South Sydney Junior Rugby League Club and its spokesman, Mr George Wintle making the headlines.

This week the club announced that its 93 money-spinning poker machines had earned a profit of £135,849 in the nine months ending in March.

I went to see what all this activity was about.

As the lively club news-letter noted, gross takings from the machines now are about £780,000 a year and turnover is nudging £1 million.

Mr Wintle is a dynamic secretary-manager who likes to talk about the club's money.

He knows where every penny is going. In fast, executive-style language, he cites projects and benefits by the hatful: extensions will cost £140,000, be completed in October; in 12 months beer should be down to a shilling a glass; "the sky's the limit here."

As virtual boss of what is probably Sydney's most successful poker machine palace, he looks after the interests of some 5,500 members and thousands more in the area who use

George (we'll go on...

THE TARGET IS £1 MILL.

George Wintle and money-spinner.

The Sun-Herald story of 1963 captured the colourful feel of the Wintle days at the Juniors. 'Hardly a week goes by without the South Sydney Junior Rugby League Club and its spokesman Mr George Wintle making the headlines,' the story began.

You reckon you could use pounds and pounds of snail killers. Well, it ain't nothing to the slugs we're getting through our machines.'

Claire James (known affectionately within the club as 'Snow' or 'the old girl'), who had started in the accounts office back in 1964, chooses 'colourful' among other words in her description of the period from the mid '60s to the beginning of the Henry Morris era. 'Peyton Place had nothing on this place,' she said. In early days she remembers the club as a male-dominated workplace — 'a bastion of maleness'. 'There was just one female supervisor,' Claire remembers. 'The Board Room was known as 'Cowards' Castle'.' And she has a lingering memory of a realisation hitting George Wintle a day or two after the swimming pool opened. 'Can anyone swim?' George spluttered to the staff. 'Get to the swimming pool in case anyone drowns!' For all of the down times ('there was a lot of hatred between the opposing forces in the club'), Claire James's early-days memories of the Juniors are overwhelmingly fond ones. 'It was a real club back then,' she says. She recalls, however, that the antagonism even extended one year to the annual Christmas party when two kids fought over the issue of whose father was 'best'. And she is sombre when she recalls the day that George Wintle left, in 1966. The pair met in a corridor. 'I've just heard you're leaving,' said Claire. 'It's true … they're forcing me out,' Wintle responded.

It was a fact of the Wintle era, that a new tussle was often just around the corner. For a time in the 1960s it seemed the Juniors could have ended up as the club with no beer. The hotel industry took serious umbrage at the plan to reduce beer prices within the club, the move possible via supplementation of the bars with poker-machine profits. While the hotel industry stamped its foot, Wintle declared: 'As long as there is no law against it we will sell beer as cheaply as possible.'

At times the club, invariably via Wintle, flaunted its wealth. On his purchase for 25 000 pounds of *Stella*, the 50-ft, American-designed blue water cruiser, Wintle declared to the world: 'If Reg Ansett can have a directors' meeting in the biggest aircraft in Australia then we can — and should — have a directors' meeting aboard the biggest cabin cruiser on Sydney Harbour.'

The solidifying of the Juniors' absolute commitment to junior football in the district came in 1961. In March that year George Wintle announced that the Leagues Club would take over in entirety the promotion of the junior league — and had budgeted 5000 pounds for the step. Wintle said the club would guarantee the Junior League finances, accept responsibility for Sunday ground charges and provide equipment. The club would also provide each team with a set of guernseys, socks, numbers and footballs, plus provide a medical benefits scheme (7 pounds a week for injured A graders; 6 pounds B grade; 5 pounds C grade; 4 pounds D grade and one pound 10 shillings E grade), and provide tours (to New Zealand and Queensland … the beginning of a tradition, with Souths' junior sides roaming the country and beyond in the years ahead). Souths Juniors' commitment to the immense junior league never faltered from that day.

Library clippings files leave no doubt that George Wintle and/or Souths Juniors were regularly and

George Wintle in the news again — this time in the Daily Mirror, *talking big about the club's prospects. This article in 1965 prompted a terse* Mirror *editorial. Snapped the paper: 'One is justified in asking whether this vast gambling establishment is entitled to call itself a club. It is more like a miniature Las Vegas.'*

Club's target...

● GEORGE WINTLE and one of his machines today.

£5 MILLION A YEAR!

"Our poker machines will be turning over £5 million a year by 1968," Mr. George Wintle said today.

Mr. Wintle, controversial manager of the South Sydney Junior Rugby League Club, yesterday announced the club's net profit of £332,488.

The announcement of the record profit prompted an outcry against poker machines from clerics and community leaders.

Mr. Wintle said that two years from now the club should have 40,000 members. It now has 18,000.

The club's 1965 poker machine turnover was £2½ million.

"If we can't double our profits and turnover by 1968 I should turn in my card and leave the business," said Mr. Wintle.

Armed guards

Mr. Wintle was interviewed at the club while a staff of five counted £7000 takings from 187 machines.

Two armed guards stood by as the sixpences, shillings and two shilling pieces were fed to electric sorters which ejected them in neat stacks.

Mr. Wintle said the club

the Australian and State Governments £220,000 in taxes.

Mr. Wintle said his salary as club manager was £50 a week, plus the use of a Chevrolet.

"I could probably get twice that if I wanted to ask for more — but who needs it?" he said.

Mr. Wintle refused to be put on the defensive by the storm of criticism. If anything, he was indignant.

"These so-called critics obviously represent a very small part of the community," he said.

"There are about one million club members in this State — and the numbers are constantly growing."

He denied charges that the clubs were draining the economy or ruining homes.

"I personally do not

mediately to help the family out," he said.

"Our machines pay back 96.8 per cent of everything that's put into them and our jackpot payout alone is £4000 a day.

"Let us say a club member spends an average of £5 a week on our machines," Mr. Wintle said. "He is getting full value for the money.

Worth it

"He can play squash, or have a workout or a swim at our pool free.

"The women take part in free exercise classes. It would cost them a fortune if they used one of the commercial gymnasiums in town.

"The members have cheaper food, cheaper

Mr. Wintle pointed out that the club's dining room lost almost £35,000 — an indication of how cheap the meals were.

Community leaders, expressing alarm at the huge and growing poker machine profits, said poker machines were disrupting the State's commercial life and seriously threatening the stability of family life.

Bad debts

The secretary of the NSW Retail Traders Association, Mr. J. B. Griffin, said there was a desperate need for a severe limitation on the use of poker machines in the public interest.

That was illustrated by the extraordinary profit of £332,000 from poker machines on a gross of

referred to frequently by the clergy," Mr. Griffin said.

"The coincidental proliferation of bad debt write-offs of many business houses is undoubtedly a major by-product.

"What is not known is the consequent degree of suffering of the small tradesman who, because of his customers' compulsive playing of poker machines, has to carry his unpaid accounts."

The secretary of the Housewives Association of NSW, Mrs. K. Adami, said today the worst feature of the poker machine craze was the fact that women "were becoming worse than the men."

"The women are not paying their household bills and are getting behind

The Club's luxury cruiser Southern Belle *with a backdrop as spectacular as Sydney can provide. In the mid 1960s the* Belle *enjoyed the reputation of being one of the finest craft on Sydney Harbour — with its weekly cruises immensely popular.*

very often controversially in the news in the period of the Wintle reign (1959–66). In late 1965, for example, the club industry generally — and the Juniors specifically — were under fire for promoting the 'evil' of gambling. The Rev Alan Walker, superintendent of the Central Methodist Mission, described poker machines as 'the most despicable form of gambling that exists'. 'They are undermining the economy of the community through failures in hire purchase payments and the collapse of companies. At the Lifeline Centre we are discovering many cases where marriages are being wrecked by poker machines.' In late 1965 the *Sunday Telegraph* ran a major feature story in which Kingsford shop owners, most of them anonymously, attacked the club, claiming it was absorbing all available money in the area, and destroying their businesses. Wintle hit back, declaring that the club had in fact given an impetus to business in Kingsford because of the number of people it drew to the district. A bank manager told the paper he did not think critics of the club would want to be quoted because 'King George would get hold of it and put it in his

GREEN AND GOLD MEMORIES

In 1963 Souths Juniors helped the NSW Rugby League out of a hole by financing a team in the inaugural year of the Inter-District competition. Kingsford, a team built almost entirely on Souths Juniors (Laurie Myers from Easts was an exception) performed with great distinction throughout the competition's kickoff year after being a late entry. Captained by Tom Cocking and coached by Clem Kennedy jnr, Kingsford grabbed its own niche in rugby league's history — beating Guildford in the final at the Sydney Cricket Ground.

Souths Juniors Leagues Club voted to form, and finance the side after the NSWRL were 'one short' for their new competition, which eventually grew into 'Second Division' and then the 'Metropolitan Cup' of today.

Inner-city clubs were not really wanted in the competition which was designed to spread league's appeal through the growing Western Suburbs, plus re-introduce it to the Universities — but the Juniors reacted swiftly to the late call when another side was needed. The team had just a week and a half to get together, and prepare for the season ahead. The Kingsford boys were paid 10 pounds ($20) a game.

Kingsford wore green, with a gold yoke on chest and shoulders. Some notable members were Tom and Ray Cocking, hooker Stewart Tinker from the 1958 President's Cup team, second rower Norman Green, five-eighth Graham Creer, Bobby Hough, President's Cup captain of 1958–59 and winger Alan Heiler, a first grader with the district side in 1962. The selectors were: Jack Kelly, Jack Duggan, Wal Stigg and Athol Knight. On Final day, August 31, the Kingsford team was: J Hynes; L Myers, B Speechley, R Hough, R Lopresto; T Heiler, J McCarthy; W Hales, R Christie, N Green, F Browne, S Tinker, T Cocking (capt).

Kingsford played only two years in the League's new second-tier competition, which became 'Second Division' in '64. In the second season (1964) they missed the semi-finals by two points. At the end of it the decision was made that the club would leave it at that — with George Wintle influential in the decision. Kingsford's life in the Second Division was a short chapter in the diverse story of the Juniors — but a happy one.

Tom Cocking — captain of the Juniors-backed Kingsford side which won the NSWRL inaugural Inter-district (later Second Division) competition in 1963.

The deep sea fishing boat Jackpot 1 *on Sydney Harbour, the* Southern Belle *astern.*

newsheet'. (Wintle ran a lively weekly newsheet in the 1960s. The 'Weekly Newsletter' carried the tag 'priceless' and was never shy at hitting back at critics of the club — in Wintle's typically robust fashion.)

Wintle's subsequent declarations to the media were powerful defences of the club industry. In the heated atmosphere of November 1965 after the Juniors had announced a net profit of 322 448 pounds, he was pictured on the front page of the Sydney *Daily Mirror* alongside a poker machine. '£5 MILLION A YEAR!', screamed a huge headline alongside a story in which Wintle predicted poker machines at the club would be turning over 5 million pounds a year by 1968 (turnover had been 2.5 million pounds in 1965).

The story revealed Wintle's passionate belief in the club, and his role in it. It read, in part:

'Mr Wintle said the club employed 250 people. It supported several charitable projects, including a £45 000 youth centre and an old people's home. It paid the Australian and State governments 220 000 pounds in taxes. Mr Wintle said his salary as a club manager was 50 pounds a week, plus the use of a Chevrolet. 'These so-called critics represent a very small part of the

*community,' he said. 'There are one million club members in this state —
and the numbers are constantly growing. I personally do not know of one
single hardship case at this club caused by gambling on our machines — and
if I did we would probably act immediately to help the family out. Our
machines pay back 96.8 per cent of everything that's put into them and our
jackpot payout alone is worth 4000 pounds a day. Let us say a club member
spends an average of 5 pounds a week on our machines. He is getting full
value for the money. He can play squash or have a workout or a swim at our
pool free. The women take part in free exercise classes. The members have
cheaper food, cheaper liquor — and can see a first-rate nightclub floorshow
without cover charge. Isn't that worth a fiver a week?'*

*On the occasion of the 1968 World Cup,
the Club hosted the Great Britain touring
team aboard the Southern Belle. Powerful
front rower Cliff Watson looked the part
when he took the wheel.*

On page 6 of the same edition, the *Daily Mirror* railed against the Juniors,
poker machines and the club industry in an editorial:

'The South Sydney Junior Leagues Club, with its 18000 members
and its waiting list 'a mile long', possesses 187 poker machines which were
mainly responsible for its gross revenue of 798815 pounds this year. In
other words this so-called social club took something like three-quarters
of a million pounds in hard cash from its gambling members. One is justified in asking if this vast gambling establishment is entitled to call itself a
club at all. It is more a miniature Las Vegas. Nothing better illustrates the
extent to which the poker machine evil has gripped this state. There is

NO TIPPING PLEASE

In an early edition of the 'Weekly Newsletter', editor George Wintle left no doubt where the club stood on
the question of tipping. He wrote:

'Obnoxious. Helps create a special privileged class of people, the giver and the receiver. Also makes
commodities dearer. We will not tolerate tipping. Staff have received strict instructions in the matter. We ask
members and visitors not to offer tips, and we say that if it continues it can only result in two actions, dismissal of staff and suspension of membership.

'Your staff is well looked after. Have to work because it is not a rest home. They get staff drinks and
supper.

'DON'T OFFER TIPS PLEASE.'

A lone swimmer does his laps in the club pool — a source of health-giving exercise and enjoyment for countless members over the years.

ample evidence that poker machines have beggared many families ... The time has come for the Government to take another look at the problem and try to devise a method to control the unbridled spread of poker machine gambling.'

Via his fearless approach and an obviously keen sense of the workings of the media, Wintle, and the Juniors became Sydney's best known — and most widely publicised — club through the colourful '60s. Any journalist short of a story knew that he would only have to pick up the phone to George — and there'd be some news. 'I'm good newspaper copy,' he said once. Ron Saw once called him a 'never-ending vocal jackpot'.

After the club had announced a profit of 105 287 pounds in 1961, he invited two of the Juniors' most strident critics — the Rev Alan Walker and the Rev Bernard Judd — to visit the club. They declined. Around the same time secretary-manager Wintle sparked further controversy after a *Mirror* story which claimed that members of South Sydney Juniors were to be told they were not 'pulling their weight' unless they played the poker machines. George Wintle told the paper that members could 'make' 100 pounds a year from the club by not playing the 'bandits'. Some members were eating subsidised meals every night at the expense of the poker-

THE 'GRANDEST' POOL

It was in typically colourful terms that George Wintle in early 1965 announced continuing progress on the swimming pool which has been a centrepiece of club life at Souths Juniors ever since. In the 'Weekly Newsletter' of February 18, 1965 under a headline, 'THE POOL' (Progressing very well and will be opening soon), editor Wintle wrote:

'The best half-sized Olympic Pool in Australia. 'Ow about dat!'

- Size: Dead length, 25 metres, width, 32 feet, allowing for five maximum racing lanes. Depth 3ft 6ins to 6ft 6ins.

- Capacity, 86 000 gallons water, maintained at a temperature between 70 and 76 degrees.

- Lit underneath by 18 special waterproofed lights, each costing 100 pounds.

- Approximately one mile of ceramic tiles went into the pool structure, surrounds, dressing rooms.

The rules were clearcut:

- 'Smoking and drinking will not be permitted in the pool surrounds or gallery.'

- 'Persons using pool must shower, with plenty of soap and water (and not in costume) before moving out into the pool. It is obvious that we must keep the pool and surrounds absolutely clean and spotless.'

In the March 4 edition of the 'Weekly Newsletter' as the pool's opening approached (the following Friday), Wintle described the club's new addition as: 'the grandest indoor swimming pool in the whole dog-gone continent of Orstralia. Why, even in Texas, they've nothing like the pool in the Pokie Palace. After lunch ya can don ya 'swimmers' — OF COURSE AFTER YOU HAVE HAD A SHOWER IN THE RAW AND ATTENDED THE POWDER ROOM.'

ABOVE: *The club's weekly newsletter of February 18, 1965 trumpeted the wonders of the new pool ('progressing very well and will be open soon'). Wrote George Wintle: 'The best half-sized Olympic pool in Australia. 'Ow about dat!'*

BELOW: *The pool — a haven for 35 years for the get-fit brigade.*

machine players. This would be explained to 'erring' members in the club's 'Weekly Newsletter'. The story continued: 'Mr Wintle admitted there was the 'odd bod' who wasn't putting the 'odd bob' through the machines. 'But education being such a wonderful thing we will keep plugging along until we bring these people into the fold,' he said. Mr Wintle's expressions drew a storm of protest from church authorities.'

Unrepentant, George Wintle listed the club's positive attributes in 1961:

'For a joining fee of three pounds three shillings and two pounds two shillings (associates) a year, members enjoy:

A subsidised dining room — a chicken dinner costs 6 shillings.

Extensive and palatial premises at Kingsford. Work is in hand to double the space within six months at a cost of 60 000 pounds.

Participation in the club's squash, golf and indoor bowls clubs at reduced rates for courts and green fees etc.

Entertainment, including a Saturday night dance with local artists and a band and a 2 000 pounds organ which is played on other nights.

Poker machines — eight in 1959 and 41 now ... with the 'best jackpot in town' — (20 pounds for two shillings).'

The club, as it was in 1963 — an artist's representation from the front cover of the sixth Annual Report.

In a bold move in September 1963, the club bought Una Voce, a holiday resort at Lower Portland on the Hawkesbury River. After the club had offered 20 000 pounds ($40 000) the property went to auction. Passed in at that figure, further negotiations continued — and finally the deal was done at 25 000 pounds ($50 000). Wintle reported in the 'Weekly Newsletter': 'It is proposed to finance the proposition with a bank overdraft. At the present time it's very doubtful if we could pay cash for a 3-course dinner.' Thirty-six years later Una Voce, by then virtually rebuilt, remained an important facility for the members of Souths Juniors.

Sun-Herald journalist James Hall visited George Wintle at the club just before that purchase, in July 1963 (by then the 41 poker machines had become 93) and profiled him revealingly:

There were some famous faces in a Coogee 'B' grade side of 1959, the year of the club's opening — left to right, back row: Nick Moraitis (manager/co-coach — bound for later fame as owner of Might and Power), K O'Shea, Jack Coote (Ron's brother), B Glanville, Merv Cross (later first grader with Souths and Easts followed by a distinguished medical career), K Killorn, G McGonachy (coach). Middle row: F Gilbert, N Hughes, A Neill, B Flynn, N Scott. Front row: W Purcell, Paul Cross (ball boy — later first grade winger with Easts and Balmain), J Carroll, Jack Cross (treasurer).

'George (we'll go on calling him George, since everybody else does), 48, medium height, crew-cut, rather terrier-like in dark-framed glasses, puts in about 100 hours a week at the club. He tries to find time to have dinner with his family each night in Maroubra — the only place, incidentally, where he drinks — 'I could get drunk every night otherwise'. He doesn't smoke. For what he calls a 'labour of love' he gets 40 pounds a week plus a 10 pound allowance under the terms of his 20-year contract. Also on the weekly 1600 pound payroll are 108 permanent and casual workers. They include his sister, Dorothy Ryan, who holds down the No 3 job as supervisor, his brother Don, a steward, his elderly aunt who comes in to make morning tea and his father, 70-odd, who works at the change counter on Friday, Saturday and Sunday nights.' (Additionally George Wintle's brother-in-law Steve Ryan was a director of the club at that time and had been since the club's foundation.)

Wintle's working schedule was genuinely in the vicinity of 100 hours a week. He would start work at 7am seven days a week — by helping empty the voluminous buckets of coins from the previous day's bounty. When time was called late in the evening, he'd still be on the job. 'Why shouldn't I have been?' says Wintle. 'I was well paid.'

For Hall, Wintle spelt out the 1963 philosophy: 'We don't allow bad

THE WINTLE PHILOSOPHY

In an open letter to new members in late 1963, George Wintle effectively set out the Souths Juniors philosophy. The letter, published in the club's four-page 'Weekly Newsletter' of the time is a valuable insight into Wintle — and the way he viewed the club into which he had put so much energy and hard work.

'We are justly proud of our club, its friendliness, its sociability and its grand people. We sincerely hope by your acceptance (as members) that you will join the many good folk who spend enjoyable times here. On the sporting side we have Ladies and Gents' Bowling Clubs, Golf Clubs, Squash Club, Fishing Club, Tennis Club and Snooker Club — a fully equipped gymnasium for ladies and gents. Associates and members' wives have the use of the gym under an instructress on Mondays and Tuesdays. Male members under instructor Wednesday and Thursday. In each instance ladies can bring teenage daughters, men can bring teenage sons and for our Golf Club members we have a driving range on the roof. Every night there is some activity — bowls, billiards, euchre, rummy. Thursday night, oldtime dance, Friday night dance, Saturday night a cabaret with floor show, Sunday night a dinner dance and floor show. We have purchased two large blocks of flats at The Entrance for members for holidays. We have also purchased a large guesthouse on the Hawkesbury River.

'Of course we have quite a few regulations, but these are only made to maintain the decorum we desire. Dress is a very important factor, and in the evening members and guests are required to be attired as follows: Gents — clean

From very early days the club always provided a variety of attractions for members. Here, in a pic taken for a Club journal in the '60s, a lady bowler 'puts one down'.

shirts, slacks and shoes; no thongs or crew-neck sweaters. Saturday nights we like a nice suit or good sports coat, white shirt, tie etc (no monogrammed jackets or blazers). Sunday after 1pm, no tee shirts. Ladies during daytime — no shorts or matadors. After 6.30pm, frocks. Sunday night after 6.30pm — men: nice material type shirt (short-sleeved knitted, Banlon or woollen shirts not permitted, irrespective of whether a jacket is worn or not), clean slacks and shoes. All male members and visitors at all times must be cleanly shaven.

'This club is not a pub — members must not abuse the privileges by coming after hours with visitors. No boisterous behaviour is allowed, and at all times, members who bring guests must remain in their company and if the member leaves — so must the guest. Tipping of staff is not permitted. You are allowed to bring two guests normally, but permission can be obtained for any additional guests by contacting the secretary. Associate members are not permitted to bring male guests. You are permitted to bring one guest for dinner at the club price. Any additional guest you bring must pay a minimum set charge.

'We sponsor sports for young ladies, viz: basketball, marching, hockey, tennis and a girls' club where physical culture and judo are taught. We sponsor rugby league football and tennis for boys. In conclusion may we offer you the opportunity to join a real club with a good atmosphere, one that you can be proud to show to your friends and family.'

ABOVE: A serene setting at Lake Tabourie — a club holiday cottage by the water, photographed in January 1968.

LEFT: In January 1964 there was a day never to be forgotten for South Sydney kids when the great Ken 'Muscles' Rosewell came to the Snape Park Courts to hand out some tennis tips. Ken is pictured with Cheryl Meyer.

Una Voce on the Hawkesbury — the way it was before its development into a more modern tourist hotel. The guesthouse-hotel has been an immensely popular amenity for club members over the years.

language in the place. And if anyone has too much to drink, we ask them to leave. Men are not expected to be too friendly with their women, either. I don't allow fellows to put their arms around women in the club. I'm not a puritan, but someone might walk in and get the wrong impression.'

Wintle had no doubts about his own value to Souths Juniors. 'I reckon I'm worth 20 000 pounds to this club,' he told the *Daily Mirror* in 1963. 'I have a 20-year contract as secretary-manager and there are still 17 years to run. If anybody thinks I am not fulfilling my job then I can be bought for that figure. This club has become a little empire, and I'm its nominal head.'

An apocryphal story concerning George Wintle emerged that same year. It is said that three members were eating oysters — at 5 shillings a dozen — in the club dining room. 'These oysters are beauties,' said one of them. 'Where do we get 'em from?' 'George's River, I think,' said one of the others. 'Gawd strike me!' said the oyster-eater … 'don't tell me he owns a river too!' True, or not — the story says a lot about George Wintle's standing at the club he did so much to build.

A headline in the 'Weekly Newsletter' of February 13, 1964, summed up the Wintle approach. It read 'Onwards, ever Onward' above a story recording the following news: 'We have taken an option and have sent a nice sum to hold it on three and a quarter acres of land at Botany, right on the Bay. Can't develop it immediately, but it will come, boy, sure as God made little apples. What's it for? Well, I'll tell you. A big bowling club. Yep! The biggest. Five greens, no less. Double storey clubhouse with a magnificent view of the water. Big car park etc. Land alone, 68,400 pounds. Phew! We have not got, but?'

The legacy of the Wintle era as George and his directors steered the club, brings the old man great pride, even today. He can reel off the achievements: the purchase of Una Voce and the second property on the Hawkesbury, the other holiday flats at The Entrance, Shelley Beach and Forster, the support of many charities, good causes and sporting organisations, bedroom accommodation for a dozen visitors, two car parks built on the old tram tracks, extensive, endless renovations, the swimming pool (a $260 000 investment in 1964), squash courts, the South Sydney Juniors Bowling Club at Botany, the fishing boat, the powerful ongoing support given to the Junior League, the tennis courts, the music, the floorshows, the bringing of world-class talent to Kingsford. The list goes on…

The view from across the river to Una Voce — popular holiday spot and a Great Escape for club members over so many years.

TOP: *Von, Maureen, Cheryl and Sue — from the Meyer family — summer holidays at Una Voce, 1967.*

CENTRE: *The view across the tennis courts from Una Voce on a late afternoon in May 1964.* Photo courtesy of the Meyer family.

BOTTOM: *Vonnie Meyer tries out the Una Voce bowling rink, 1964.* Photo courtesy of the Meyer family.

CLEM KENNEDY REMEMBERS ... LITTLE MAN, BIG HEART

Clement Michael Kennedy has a place forever in the story of South Sydney football — and Souths Juniors. A product of a Souths district school (Patrician Brothers Mount Carmel School, Waterloo) and the junior league (starting with Cleveland Street 'C' grade, 1938) the diminutive Clem could genuinely be said to have risen to great heights — as a footballer, and a coach. When he played halfback for Australia in the third Test of the 1946 Ashes campaign, scoring the only Aussie try of a losing Test, he was 5ft 4ins tall and weighed 9 stone 5lbs — at that one of the smallest men to ever pull on the green and gold. Between 1951 and 1966 Kennedy engraved his name indelibly in the storybook of South Sydney junior football — when he coached Souths' President's Cup teams to an unprecedented eight premiership victories, plus to the runners-up podium in 1959 and 1966. In all, he was coach of the team for 16 seasons.

Clem Kennedy, pictured in action in 1945. The Rabbitohs played the '45 season in jumpers of green with a red V, a style switch caused by the high cost of manufacturing striped jumpers under the restrictions of post-wartime conditions.

Clem remembers his days in the Junior League with great clarity. 'I went to Clevo (Cleveland Street) to night school and Joe Healey boss of Souths Juniors came there one night, looking for players. I had left school at the end of 1937, and in '38 I played C grade with Cleveland Street — an under-nine stone competition in those days. The rules were that you were allowed (to put on) half a stone after the start of the season. They were strict on it. The officials used to arrive with scales, and stop games that were in progress. They'd wait until the game had started, so they could catch the cheats.' Kennedy came to the junior league from a brilliant school

One of the greatest of Souths' Junior League production line, Bob McCarthy — charging into the clear at the Sydney Cricket Ground with skipper John Sattler in support.

career; he was halfback and captain in a dominant Mount Carmel side which was undefeated for four years and scored an astonishing 1200 points to 9. When his team thrashed Redfern in 104–0 in 1937, Clem Kennedy contributed five tries and 19 goals, for 53 points.

The War years, during which he served in New Guinea with the 39th and 53rd battalions, interrupted the Kennedy career — as it did those of many others. He had played first grade for Souths, as a 17-year-old in 1939. The glittering prizes came later, when the War was over and he had shaken off the effects of the malaria he picked up in the New Guinea highlands. By 1945 he was a NSW player, and in '46 came his crowning achievement in the winning of a Test jumper. Later wandering in his career took him from Souths to Cessnock (1947), Newtown (1948–49) and Grenfell (1950) — but in 1951, he was back 'home' at Souths Juniors, leading to his unprecedented run of success, beginning the following season, as coach of the President's Cup teams. 'They were looking for someone to coach the President's Cup side,' says Kennedy laconically.

As coach, Kennedy was a hard taskmaster. 'Yeah, I was a bit of a slave driver,' he says. 'My slogan was: 'If we can't outplay them, we'll outstay them.' The teams I coached were fitter than Souths' Firsts. At the end of any training session they were buggered. And everything I asked them to do at training, I'd do too. 'I'm going to keep you sprinting until I run last,' I used to tell them.

'We (Souths) were the first to start summer training as a President's

Cup squad. I used to start looking for players as soon as the Cup ended each year. It was the best time. I'd look most closely at C grade … when the general interest was in the As and Bs. And the blokes who fired in the semis … they were the ones. We'd pick a squad of about 30 — and work out regularly in the gym at the Juniors, down at Maroubra Beach — and elsewhere.'

Souths' President's Cup teams under Clem Kennedy were regarded as the game's 'State of the Art' in junior ranks. The teams of the '60s, loaded with budding stars (Bob McCarthy, Ron Coote, George Piggins, Paul Sait, Graham Wilson, Brian Hambly, Eric Simms, Gary Stevens among them) spread the message of good football on country and interstate trips backed financially by the growing Souths Juniors Club. 'We used to go to places where the game needed a kick-along,' Kennedy remembers.

There were extraordinary events. In 1962 Bob McCarthy and Ron Coote were both trialling for lock-forward in the President's Cup side. McCarthy got the nod — and Coote, bound for near-legendary status later in his

ABOVE LEFT: *The great fullback, goalkicker and graduate of Souths Juniors, Eric Simms, on his selection in the Australian World Cup squad of 1968.* Photo courtesy of Ern McQuillan.

ABOVE RIGHT: *One of the greatest of South Sydney players and one of the finest lock-forwards of all time — Ron Coote, ready for the '68 World Cup.* Photo courtesy of Ern McQuillan.

RIGHT: *From the ranks of the Souths Juniors Paul Sait developed into one of the game's great all-rounders, equally devastating as a backrower or a centre.*

BELOW: *They came through the ranks to become high achievers in the game — John Berne (left) and Gary Stevens, one of league's most robust tacklers of the post-war era. Pictured at Redfern Oval after a match in April 1976.*

career — missed out altogether, to Clem Kennedy's disbelief. It was in '62 also that Kennedy had the remarkable experience of coaching both teams in a junior representative match. When Western Australian Colts visited in '62, Kennedy was co-opted to coach the side. However, he was also coach of the Combined Souths 'C' Grade, chosen to play the visitors at Redfern Oval one afternoon. So Clem 'doubled up' — hopping from one dressing room to another before the game, and at half-time.

As Clem Kennedy built his President's Cup tradition in the early 1960s — so George Wintle and his fellow workers were building the club which would provide an ever-lasting backbone for South Sydney junior football. Kennedy says of Wintle: 'A great worker ... he did a hell of a lot. But so too did a lot of blokes ... Jack Kelly ... Athol Knight... 'Occa' Nilson ... Ernie Coupland ... Darcy Thompson ... Joe Power.'

Kennedy stepped down as Souths' President's Cup coach in 1967. No one argued the truth of it: that the little man with the big heart had made a monumental contribution.

SOUTH SYDNEY JUNIORS TO INTERNATIONALS

Alf 'Smacker' Blair

Ray Branighan

Ron Coote

Les Crowe

Steve Darmody

Denis Donoghue

Col Donohoe

Jim Dymock*

Howard Hallett

Brian Hambly*

Ernie Hammerton

Greg Hawick

Terry Hill

Keith Holman*

Harold Horder

Harry Kadwell

Clem Kennedy

John Kerwick

Eric Lewis

Bob McCarthy

Alf O'Connor

Frank O'Connor

Arthur Oxford

George Piggins

Bernie Purcell

Ian Roberts

Paul Sait

Craig Salvatori*

Jim Serdaris*

Eric Simms

Gary Stevens

Bill Thompson*

George Treweek

Jack Troy*

Benny Wearing

Jack Why

Percy Williams

* Indicates Souths Juniors who became internationals at clubs other than South Sydney.

PROBABLY A SOUTHS JUNIOR

Harry Finch

THE FOLLOWING SOUTHS INTERNATIONALS DID NOT PLAY IN SOUTHS' JUNIORS

Tommy Anderson

Jim Armstrong

Cec Blinkhorn

Tim Brasher

Arthur Butler

Billy Cann

Mark Carroll

Clive Churchill

Michael Cleary

Frank Curran

Les Davidson

Jim Davis

Terry Fahey

Herb Gilbert

Bob Grant

Johnny Graves

Arthur Hennessy

Bob Honan

Brian James

Jack Levison

Jim Lisle

Paddy Maher

Ted McGrath

Ian Moir

Ray Norman

John O'Neill

Denis Pittard

Jack Rayner

Eddie Root

Johnny Rosewell

John Sattler

Bill Spence

Elwyn Walters

BOB MCCARTHY REMEMBERS ...
'AND YOU'LL BE DRINKING ORANGE JUICE'

Bob McCarthy in full flight was one of the great sights of rugby league in the 1960s and '70s. Here big 'Macca' tests out the Eastern Suburbs defence with a typical charge at the SCG. In the background, famous South Sydney faces — Gary Stevens, John Sattler and John O'Neill.

'I started my career in football in Souths Juniors, with Chelsea Club. F grade, I think it was. The next year a club called the Cleveland Street Olympians disbanded and were taken over by Moore Park. They stuck with the old jumpers — the NSW country jumpers, maroon with the two gold 'Vs'. At Chelsea they used to give you a jumper and a pair of socks; the new club said they'd throw in a pair of shorts as well, so a few of us from around Redfern and Moore Park jumped ship and went across to Moore Park Club. We sort of got the new club going.

'I had four years in the Juniors — F grade with Chelsea, E grade with Moore Park, and two years in D grade. At Moore Park the deal was that if you played B grade, you got two bottles of beer. Now and then I played E grade in the morning and B grade later in the afternoon. I never did see the bottles of beer though. The A graders used to get two quid [$4] each. Redfern was the main game. You played Redfern on a Sunday if it was the main game for that grade. Otherwise you might be at Mascot Oval, Kensington Oval, Waterloo Oval, Alexandria Park, Snape Park, or Coogee Oval. I always hated Coogee. I don't know what it was; it was (and is) bigger than a normal ground, should have suited a bloke like me with a bit of speed. But I used to hate going there.

'It was in 1961 that there was talk that Souths Juniors were putting on a trip to New Zealand for the Flegg team. New Zealand? Fair dinkum, we were flat out raising enough money to get to Manly back then. We thought it was a pipedream. I played Flegg that year. Cootie (Ron Coote) was the captain — and we got beaten 7–5 by Manly in the semi-final … and they went on to thrash whoever it was in the final. Subsequently the rumours came true — and we got sent to New Zealand, to Christchurch — to play three matches there.

'We were all billeted out — and I was placed way out in the suburbs with a family, at the foot of a mountain. I remember sitting and having tea with them and looking out the window at the snow-capped peaks around. At home in Redfern when I looked out the back, all I saw was terrace houses. This was different all right. Next morning I was sitting back at breakfast, expecting that I would be picked up to go to training. But the lady of the house told me: 'No, they're not coming to get you — you've got to take the bike.' 'What bike?' I said. 'I can't ride a bike.' But I had to — for frigging miles, to get to the training ground. When I got there they were all sitting around the fence — and just burst out laughing.

'In the Flegg side, Ron Coote was at lock, and I was in the second row. But we both played lock in the Juniors and the next year (1962) we were both going for the lock forward spot in the President's Cup team. We played Balmain in a trial match at Mascot Oval — and I was running late. I had slept in. Cootie played the first half — and we were behind. I overheard one of the selectors say to the coach Clem Kennedy about me:

The grand final of 1971 done, and won — and Ron Coote helps a valiant rival to his feet, the St George warrior and captain Graeme Langlands. Coote presented the photo to Souths Juniors, bearing his personal message of thanks.

'No — get rid of him. We don't want him. He hasn't got any discipline.' A couple of the other selectors — Jack Duggan and Jack Kelly took my side. 'He's here,' they said. 'You've got to give him a go.' Clem Kennedy didn't want a bar of it. I was pretty p—— off and I just said to them: 'Look, don't worry about it … I'll go back to bed.'

'Anyhow, they played me — and I went out and scored three tries … had one of those games that footballers dream about. We thrashed them in the end. When the game was finished I was sitting with Cootie as they announced the side — just listening for my name. They announced it, at lock. You beauty … I'm in! I said to myself. I just presumed Ron was in too and I turned to him and said … 'well, we're in mate.' 'No I'm not,' he said. 'I didn't make it.' I argued with him for a bit — but it was true and there was a real scene when that realisation sunk in. One of the selectors was from Kenso (Kensington, Coote's home club), Wally Stigg — and he was furious and let them know it. I thought to myself: 'It's really hit the fan here.' The second row spots went to Barry Atkinson and Alex Penkilis, who turned out to be pretty solid lower grade players — while one of the best backrow forwards to ever play the game had to cool his heels until the next year. Anyhow — we won the Cup and I got 'man of the match' in the final played before the first Australia v Great Britain Test at the Sydney Cricket Ground … in front of almost 70,000 people.

'I got knocked out in the first tackle. A bloke hit me with his knees and I played the game pretty much on memory. Back in the dressing room afterwards my head was aching pretty bad. I went out and watched the start of the Test — and can remember seeing Billy Boston hurl Ken Irvine over the touchline. Then I was feeling so crook, I went home. 'Don't go to bed,' my father warned me. But I did — and I woke up with a shocking headache. Next day I ripped my knee playing for Moore Park … and was finished for the season.

'Later that year they put Cootie back in the team (preparing for 1963) in the second row and I was at lock — and we played the Illawarra Under 21s. Before the game Clem Kennedy pulled me aside. 'Macca, watch this fullback,' he said. 'What's his go?' I asked. 'He's got a big step,' said Kennedy. Early in the game the Illawarra fullback made a break, split our centres. I was 'sweeping' and I moved across to nail him. All of a sudden he went whooshka off one leg then bang off the other leg as we tried to round him up. 'Where is he … how did he do that?' I was thinking. Illawarra scored two tries, we kicked three goals and it ended up a 6all draw.

'Afterwards I walked off with the skinny fullback. 'Good game, mate,' I said to him. 'Yeah thanks … you played good too,' he said. The friendship between Graeme Langlands and Bob McCarthy began that day. Eleven years later we were captain and vice captain respectively of the 1973 Kangaroos. 1962 was my only year of President's Cup football.

'A few days after we won the Cup that year we had to go to the Juniors to get measured for our blazers. I walked in the door of the club down the Nine Ways end, and George Wintle was there. I was only 16 at the time — and I thought: 'Geez, I'd better tell Mr Wintle who I am.' But there wasn't too much got past George — and he already knew. 'I've come to get measured for my blazer for the President's Cup,' I said. 'Yes Mr McCarthy,' he said. 'And you'll just be drinking orange juice.' 'S—,' I thought. 'How come he knows?' So while the other blokes in the team were drinking beer and celebrating … I was sipping orange juice.'

THE YEAR WE SIGNED WES HALL

In the mid '60s, the South Sydney Juniors were responsible for a remark-able resurgence of cricket in the district. Chief benefactor was George Wintle, who listened sympathetically when Randwick Club official (and renowned Sydney sports journalist) Phil Tresidder, related the cricket club's problems. The club was faring poorly and worse still, interest in cricket was suffering through schools and junior clubs in the area.

The solution? Bring a famous overseas player in to inject new life and enthusiasm in the game. George nodded in agreement and asked the inevitable question: 'Who do you have in mind?'

The great man, Wes Hall, talks to starry-eyed youngsters about the secrets of bowling fast.

Tresidder said what about the magnificent West Indian speed bowler Wesley Hall, who had had Australian batsmen in full retreat a season or two earlier? George Wintle liked the idea. At that moment club director Athol Knight walked along the corridor and was asked what he thought of the plan. Just great, he said — and the invitation was on its way.

Wesley Hall accepted and in the spring of 1965 brought his wife to Australia — at the full expense of Souths Juniors. Accommodation was provided at the club.

Hall captained Randwick that summer and suddenly the Wicks were up and away — right through to the semi-finals, with a bunch of fine young players firing under Wes's exciting captaincy. They finally lost out to Cumberland, who produced a dead flat pitch to effectively curb Hall's ferocious pace.

Each morning of his stay, the West Indian giant appeared in the club foyer in his creams — and a sportsmas-ter would appear to whisk him off to one of the local schools where he conducted coaching classes. The big fella revelled in his role — and schools queued up to earn a visit. As the summer progressed, schools from outside the district pre-vailed on Wes for a coaching stint. Cricket was the big winner.

One of the young players who played under Wes, John Letson, wrote in the club's Jubilee Year Book:

'Undoubtedly the most notable of all Randwick's characters was Wesley Winfield Hall. Season 1965–66 was made memorable for Randwick thanks to the appearance of the great West Indian fast bowler as first grade captain. To say Wes had a wonderful influence on cricket in the district is to grossly understate the truth. Wes possessed a charisma that few had. A superbly proportioned athlete who would give the Cleo centrefold a magnificent lift, this wonderful man believed that his abilities as a batsman and wicketkeeper far outweighed his explosive attributes as a bowler. Wes started his cricket career as a wicketkeeper — and one of my favourite memories of season 1965–66 was Wes wicketkeeping, bare hands, for a couple of overs against St George at Hurstville after regular keeper Keith Edwards made a late arrival.

'The 'Coogee cutter' was born that season. Wes took 56 wickets despite missing two matches. And beautiful man that he was, every time he took a

Wes Hall at his new home, Coogee Oval, with (left to right), 'Occa' Nilson, George Wintle, Bill Beath (President, Randwick Cricket Club) and Fred Snell (Secretary, Randwick Cricket Club).

wicket at Coogee, he loved describing the late movement both in the air and off the wicket. The truth was, he was so quick that the ball didn't get a chance to move. But when the ball did hit the seam, it really deviated.

'One of his memorable performances was 7 for 20 against Sutherland — after Sutherland had dismissed Randwick for 80. Wes bundled Sutherland out for 53. That day he bowled at a furious pace. One ball rose sharply, hitting Gary Parker in the head and ricocheting down to the fine leg fence for four leg byes. Parker ran towards the square leg umpire with blood oozing from a head wound, and collapsed. Picked up and reassured by all including Wes's 'Sorry man', Parker uttered the immortal words: 'I'm not frightened by you, man. Get back and bowl again.' Parker then lapsed into semi-consciousness and was assisted from the field.

'Wes believed every mortal could catch and field like his idol Gary Sobers. As a consequence, players were posted to incredible positions, especially for Wes's bowling. Some great catches were taken — mainly out of fear of being decapitated. Wes's presence was an inspiration to the younger players and he captained Randwick with considerable efficiency. Hall's popularity became a byword in the district and the crowds flocked to see the Randwick team in action. Those were the days!'

Take a bow, George Wintle … and Souths Juniors.

Tresidder recalled that when Hall first bowled on Coogee Oval, beginning his enormous run-up from back near the fence, the ground was dry and sandy. The champion West Indian speedster found the going tough on the beach-like surface. There was general agreement that what the ground needed was a highly efficient watering system, to promote the growth of grass. On consultation, George Wintle and the Souths Board didn't hesitate — well realising that the junior league would gain a winter benefit from such an improvement, too.

During and after Wes Hall's visit testimonies rolled in from schools in the area for the enthusiastic work done by the West Indian champion. Typical was the following, from Randwick Primary School: 'The visit of such a talented and enthusiastic cricketer can do nothing but benefit the code of cricket in our area and indeed in the Sydney area. Congratulations are due to you and your club for such a forward-looking move.' From Patrician Brothers Primary School: 'Mr Hall's speech to the assembly after having presented the caps to our winning cricket team was truly inspiring and full of excellent advice for the youngsters.'

Renowned sports journalist (and ex-Souths junior) Phil Tresidder. He was instrumental in bringing Wes Hall to the district in 1965.

CHAPTER 3

THE END OF THE WINTLE ERA

History records the truth of it: that empires both rise ... and fall. And so it was at South Sydney Junior Leagues Club in the era that became known as the 'swinging sixties'. In an episode which resounded with dark deeds, fierce in-fighting, lobbying that would put Canberra in the shade ... and some seriously dirty pool, George Wintle's reign of iron-fisted command came to an end.

Somehow it seemed inevitable there would be a major collision one day involving George Wintle — a man who didn't just step on toes ... he stomped on them. As the '60s rolled on his enemies within the club's portals increasingly levelled the charge of nepotism at him as Wintle relatives dotted the club's payroll. He was accused of being a despot ... a dictator ... a megalomaniac. Among some members of the staff he was known as 'the Fuhrer' or 'little Hitler'. There was anger at Wintle's regular trumpeting in the press at this innovation or that made by his 'Pokie Palace' (a favoured Wintle term) ... or of how much money was rolling in. Columnist Ron Saw described him as 'The Bradman of big-noters' and observed later: 'His big-noting, including his refusal to listen to the demands of his directors caused him to be tossed out of his job.' In addition, Wintle's budding romance with a married woman, Sylvia McGaurr (whom he subsequently married) was widely frowned upon. And the other side of the coin was that the little gamecock of a man now headed a club which not only was a cash cow with significant assets and financial reserves, but one which also possessed not a little power and prestige around the place. A nice club to run.

'They were gunning for me,' says Wintle today when he reflects on the events that unfolded back in 1966. 'They sacked me while I was away on holidays in Queensland.' Despite Wintle's extreme antipathy now to the men who were to become the eventual powerbrokers at Souths, Wally Dean and the late ex-Test referee Darcy Lawler, he was in fact sacked in January 1966 and suspended from the club on a vote of the 'old' Board which did not include Dean and Lawler — a body headed by Darcy Thompson (chairman) and Wintle's brother-in-law Stephen Ryan. He was 51 years of age. In an ironic twist, just weeks before his sacking a survey of business undertakings in Australia had placed Souths Juniors first as a profit-maker — despite the fact that it had the lowest total assets and the second-lowest

est shareholders funds of the organisations considered. The club was compared with 50 other organisations, including television and radio companies, hotel and motel chains, theatre groups, bowling centres and other clubs. Notwithstanding, George Wintle was given the boot. 'When I left the club … when they sacked me, I was still secretary of the Junior League,' Wintle remembers. 'I was barred from coming into the club … the doorman barred me. For a time we [the Junior League] met in a different hall, in Rainbow Street, Randwick. All the delegates would come out of the meeting and go to the club. I'd go home.'

Wintle remembers well the day he drove South Sydney's venerable

A newspaper headline was never far away when George Wintle was at the helm. These two from the Sunday Mirror *(top) and* Daily Mirror *(below) signalled the end of an era — reporting on Wintle's resignation from the club in January 1967, and subsequent decision to leave Sydney. These were stormy days at the Juniors.*

New job for George

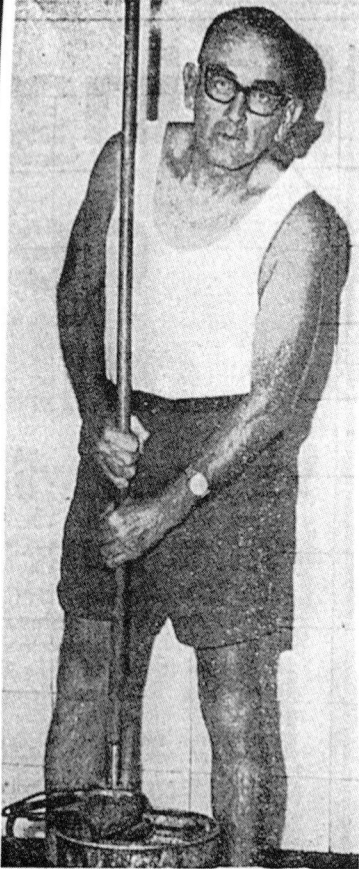

Mr. George Wintle, who amassed a fortune for the South Sydney Junior League's Club as its secretary-manager, is now working as a cleaner.

Wintle now a cleaner

Today our picture shows him as a part-time cleaner at the Jouralists' Club in Chalmers St., City.

Mr. Wintle was one of the founders of the South Sydney club and during his seven years as secretary-manager it grew fantastically, mainly due to huge poker machine profits.

But several months ago, he fell foul of the club's directors, who suspended him for six months.

He was not bitter or even embarrassed about his new position.

"I have to live and this is work just the same as any other job," he said.

"Any honest job is a respectable job and I can hold my head up anywhere.

"I have done nothing to be ashamed of.

Suspended by the club in 1966, Wintle took on work as a part-time cleaner at the Journalists Club, Chalmers Street. 'I have to live and this is work the same as any other,' said Wintle when the newspapers tracked him down.

official SG George Ball to St George Leagues Club. After his sacking Wintle had kept the Chevrolet that belonged to the Juniors. 'It turned out to be a bad move — but I invited George Ball out to St George Leagues Club one afternoon, and we went in the big car. When we came out of the club, the car had gone. They [the Juniors] had reclaimed it.' To replace George Wintle as secretary-manager the club appointed Mr RA Bob Laforest, a club industry professional — after 'Occa' Nilson had filled in for a time. In the one annual report signed by Laforest, that of 1965-66 (signed on September 28, 1966) there was not a single word of mention of Wintle or the 'troubles'.

In March 1966, the *Daily Mirror* carried a forlorn photograph of Wintle in singlet, shorts and thongs — and with a bucket and a mop. He was working as a part-time cleaner in the Journalists' Club in Chalmers Street in the city. 'I have to live — and this is work the same as any other job. Any honest job is a respectable job — and I can hold my head up anywhere.'

Onwards in '66 through one of the most extraordinary years in the South Sydney Juniors' history, George Wintle went to war to get his job back. Drama was never more than the next conversation away at the club, it seemed. Under suspension, and operating away from the club, which had been virtually his 'home' for seven years, Wintle was a relentless figure amidst a maelstrom of activity:

He successfully blocked a planned extraordinary general meeting of the club in May, via an Equity Court injunction.

He was backed by a petition of members calling for his reinstatement as secretary-manager.

He was on the receiving end of a writ, claiming $100,000 damages from his sister, Dorothy Ryan (known in the club as 'The Duchess').

He cashed an insurance policy to pay for 18,000 copies of a three-page circular headed 'A personal message from George Wintle'. The circular answered charges which had been levelled against him.

He was divorced (November) on the grounds of adultery.

He was disqualified by the district club (South Sydney RLFC) — for 'refusal to hand over books and vouchers and for his attitude in not acting on decisions of the district club committee'. The ban was tied to a stinging letter Wintle had sent to NSWRL Chairman Bill Buckley, critical of the Rabbitohs' handling of football in the district. Wintle was virtually on a war footing with the district club for most of the year. The ban placed on him ended his long years of service as secretary of the Junior Rugby League.

Souths Junior League stuck solidly behind Wintle, passing a unanimous vote of confidence in him and agreeing to pay him an honorarium of 25 pounds a week.

The Wintle support squad staged massive doorknock appeals from dawn till dusk in his support.

Any car within cooee of the club was pamphleted.

There was an unsuccessful move by directors to remove from the constitution the vital clause that dictates that four (of seven) members of the Board must be members of the South Sydney JRLFC Management Committee.

During one (of many) meetings at the club a group of more than 400 people gathered outside the club in support of Wintle.

A growing figure in the club's life by then was the stocky Walter James Dean, President of South Sydney Junior Rugby League, secretary of Alexandria Rovers, born and raised in the territory (at Alexandria) and a hairdresser by trade. Dean, 32, was steeped in the lore of the Australian Labor Party, and a passionate 'true believer'. His grandmother Rosie Day attended the first ALP meeting at Balmain in 1908 and was later a campaign manager for NSW Premier Jack Lang. Dean's father once campaigned for Bill McKell who went on to become NSW Premier and Governor-General of Australia. 'Now, am I ALP or what?' Dean asked a journalist cockily some years later.

Ironically, in view of subsequent events, George Wintle linked with the Dean-Darcy Lawler team in his bid to return to the Juniors as secretary-manager. As election night neared Wintle left no doubt about his thoughts on the old Board that had sacked him: 'They have to go,' he told

Darcy Lawler, pictured with his son Ted near the end of a notable, if controversial, refereeing career. Lawler's long career at the top included: 375 first grade games, 16 Test matches, 7 interstate games, 16 semi-finals, nine grand finals. Lawler was to serve for 27 years as secretary-manager of the Juniors, during a period of change, controversy and growth. Ted, a ballboy for Souths when the photo was taken, went on to play for the Rabbitohs.

the media. 'The way they're running this place it will soon be broke.' On election night in late November, Wintle supporters handed out more than 20,000 'how to vote' cards outside the club. The lobbying had been fiercer than anything even a Federal election could match.

The feisty Wintle was not beyond using the weekly South Sydney JRLFC football programs to further the cause. On a weekly basis, he fired off missiles. On the weekend of October 1–2–3 the program's major front page story was this: 'The annual meeting of the SSJRL Club will be held on Monday, November 7. The directors couldn't stall any longer. We wanted the meeting earlier but so many 'herrings were strewn' we couldn't make much headway. They are still casting 'fish' — suggesting candidates are ineligible, getting South Sydney District Club to upset our decisions, suggesting our boys are not bona fide etc. They haven't said much about the bowling club deal — why the rush to get the project going, an almost immature basis to crucify your money, a shameful attempt to make jobs for the boys — like the appointment of an assistant manager at $100 per week to assist a secretary-manager who does nothing and who gets, we hear $160 a week.'

On the departure of George Wintle, Darcy Lawler (left) and Wally Dean — in waistcoat and pork-pie hat — became the new strong men at the Juniors, pictured here on the day that teams from the Juniors made history in 1969 — winning all three finals of President's Cup, SG Ball and Jersey Flegg competitions.

DECIMAL DAZE

On the 14th of February 1966, the club wrestled with the great dilemma facing Australian society — the switch to decimal currency. A special brochure was produced to make life easier for patrons. Headed 'Decimal Currency and the Club', it read:

'On Monday next, the 14th February 1966, the Club will deal in decimal coin for the sale of goods. All cash registers in the various bars, snack bars and dining room will be altered to accept the new coins and prices of drinks, meals etc, will be displayed in decimal currency.

However, poker machines cannot be altered to accept decimal coins for at least two months, and it must be stressed that only coins currently in use are to be used.

Maintaining the existing good relations between members and staff may require just a little more patience and good humour than before, and the management requests members as well as employees to bear with any early problems.'

Added to the note was a price list, showing what drinks and other bar products would cost in the new currency. The list included:

Gin Sling — 40 cents

Scotch (1oz) — 20 cents

Brandy — 12 cents

Rum (OP) —18 cents

Wine (2 ozs) — 10 cents

Lemon squash — 10 cents

Beer (middy) — 13 cents

Beer (schooner) — 18 cents

Coca-Cola (can) — 13 cents

Tobacco (fine cut) — 59 cents

Bex (box) — 12 cents

Chocolates (1lb box) — $1.25

President Wally Dean congratulates Deane Wilson at a function in November 1970. Deane had raised most money for the Miss Australia Quest which was held in the club that year.

On behalf of the Lawler-Dean team Wintle made a raft of promises:

'We will prevent mates being looked after.'

'Our directors will not have dinners for mates and free drinks for all.'

'The cash will be under strict surveillance at all times.'

'We will stop the 'Dippers'.'

'You will be shocked at the things that are happening,' wrote George.

For some time in 1966, the weekly match program was akin to a political sheet. When a move to change the constitution within the Juniors was lost in August that year — a move designed to reduce the power of the football delegates, Wintle crowed the following Sunday: 'They were done like a dinner!' He railed against the Bowling Club, commenting 'it will be a bigger white elephant than the Chevron-Hilton'. He railed against Bob Laforest, the man who had replaced him in the club. And he hinted at dark and disturbing trends within the club's walls: 'We know all these acts which are bringing the club into disrepute — men arm-in-arm, odd types, SP betting.'

In early December 1966, it was announced that Wally Dean's pro-Wintle team had tipped out the incumbent Board (Darcy Thompson, Stephen Ryan, Thomas Craigie, Ernest Coupland, John Kelly, Tim Wallace and Athol Knight) en masse. In came Wally and his men (Dean, Ronald Ellison, Norman Christie, Leonard Hart, George Bell, Frank Kilcran, and Darcy Lawler). Lawler topped the ballot. When Darcy Lawler became secretary-manager (replacing the briefly reinstated George Wintle in 1967), Norm Christie (some time later) assistant secretary-manager and George

Bell left the Board, they were replaced by Messrs Jack Caldon, Mort Hart — and later, Arch Henderson. When the December 1966 result was announced more than 100 people cheered and sang outside the club.

Afterwards, Lawler announced that Wintle would be reinstated, probably as 'controller' of the club. 'He will be back by next Wednesday night,' said Lawler. At home at Botany, George Wintle told any pressman who cared to listen: 'You're looking at the brokest bloke in the world. I've got just enough money to pay the rent and I'll be mighty glad to get back to work.' Wintle declared he had used every cent he had — about $2000 plus a couple of hundred more dollars he had borrowed — in the cause of getting his job back. He had succeeded. And so it was after a year of sound and fury that George Wintle came back to the Juniors ...

A week or so later, the perceptive Ron Saw cast his gaze on the club and wrote:

'Last month, a new team headed by Darcy Lawler the referee and Ald Wally Dean (who, at 31 is the youngest alderman on the City Council) replaced the Old Guard. They got in by promising, among other things, a new deal (i.e. bigger payouts) for poker machine players, stricter supervision of cash and stocks and expenditure — and George.

At the opening of the new club foyer everyone dressed in their Sunday best. Wives of the directors posed for this special shot to mark the occasion, (left to right) Joan Lawler, Lil Christie, Aileen Henderson, Dawn Ellison, Kath Kilcoran, Dot Hart, Billie Cracknell.

'Last week, George came back. Not humbly, but swinging a scythe at the people who, he insisted, had been out to get him. In a few days he demanded the heads of:

Two floor supervisors.

His sister, Mrs Dorothy Ryan, who had worked directly under him and who, he said, had wanted his job.

His ex-wife, Mrs Ellen Wintle, who works six mornings a week at the club.

His son, a teenager, who picks up a dollar or two by working in the club office on a Saturday and Sunday mornings.

'So far, nobody has been fired, and the new directors are hoping, rather tentatively, for peace. All we need,' says Ald Dean, now club president, 'is time to settle and soothe George. The club needs him badly. What George needs is a manager. He keeps shouting that either his sister goes, or he goes.'

Wintle offered Saw some thoughts on Wally Dean: 'Wal Dean's a very immature young man,' he said. 'He needs me. I put him where he is and if he listens to me for a few more years he'll be a lot more than an alderman. He'll be the president of the biggest club in the world … I put Lawler where he is too … he's got a lot to thank me for. The club needs me back because it's been like a ship without a rudder. Now I'm back and I've got a job to do and I want to do it my way — the way they promised me I could do it. Either they're going to let me do it that way or they can find someone else.'

Saw asked the ticklish question:

'What about your sister?'

'She'll go,' he said darkly.

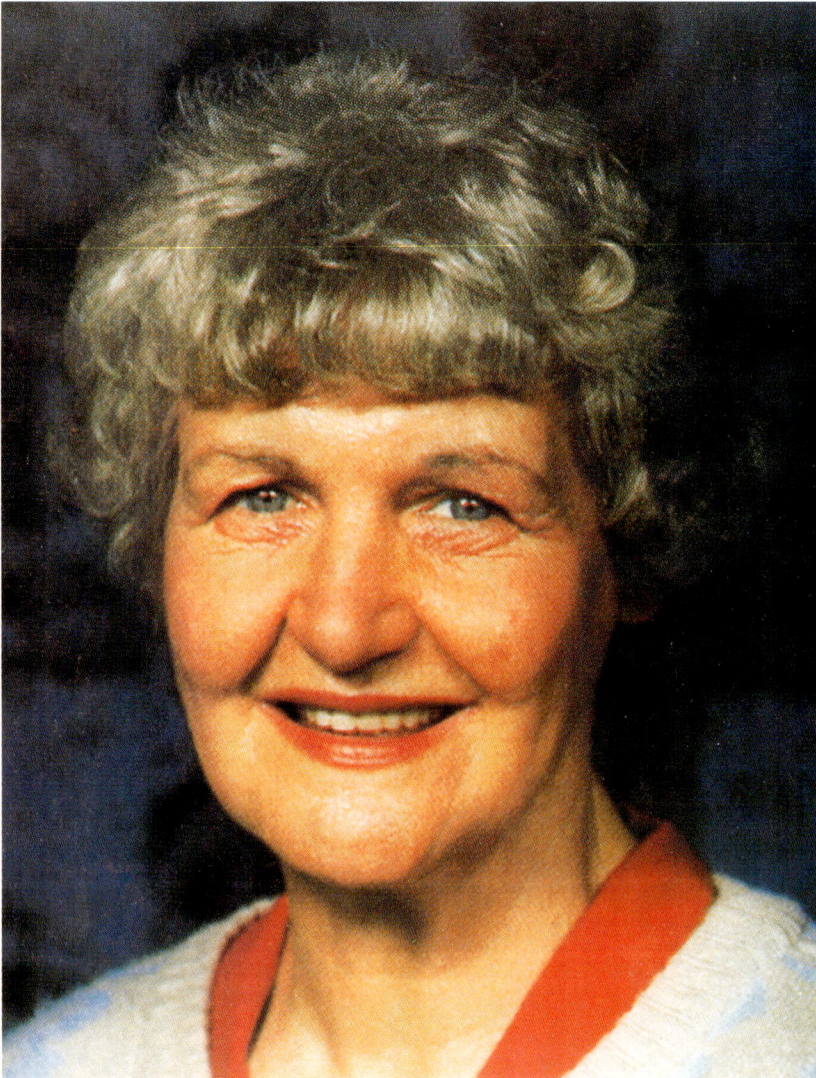

Joan Child a long-standing and loyal servant of the club — first as secretary to George Wintle, then as secretary to Darcy Lawler during the long years of his tenure. 'Hating' the job at first, Joan stayed at the Juniors for 29 years.

Wintle ended the interview with fateful words: 'Just give me time. Give me a couple of months and this will be the best club in the world. Things are beginning to hum again already.'

Within two and a bit weeks, George William Wintle was gone from the Juniors forever. On December 31, 1966, he sacked himself from his $200 a week job, and closed the door — for a time at least — on one of the most controversial careers in Australia's clubland history. 'I did it while I still had a bit of dignity,' Wintle explained. Of the new Board he had helped sweep into power he declared: 'I backed a loser. I thought they were right behind me but all too soon I found out they weren't. They didn't want to carry out their pre-election promises and seemed bent on stripping me of all authority. They said they would give full membership to women and they didn't. And they said they would dismiss several employees who were unacceptable to me —

Darcy Lawler had both supporters and detractors through his years as secretary-manager. Here the camera captures Darcy in relaxed and happy mood.

and they didn't do that either.' The last straw for George Wintle came when a steward he had sacked was reinstated by the Board. Defiant to the last Wintle declared: 'I'm nobody's puppet. A man cannot be boss unless he has complete control. They [the Board] are in power for 12 months and I'd be like a punch-drunk fighter if I kept getting knocked down until then.' It was a typical up-front Wintle gesture that he announced his resignation over the public address at a packed club on a Saturday night.

Next day Wintle declared he was getting out of town, packing the family in his Volkswagen van and heading north. 'They're opening a little place north of Brisbane called Bribie Island,' he said. 'They might need a motel manager or something. I hope so … anyway.' In fact, Wintle never

went to Queensland — for any length of time, anyway. Meanwhile club chairman Wally Dean issued a brief statement declaring that club directors could not and would not allow victimisation of staff by Wintle. 'It is the policy of this board of directors that the board should run the club — not an individual. Every time we made a decision he didn't like he'd walk out on us with a threat to resign.'

The roller-coaster ride of the George Wintle era at Souths Juniors was over, or at least appeared to be. Darcy Lawler promptly stepped down from the Board, and became the club's new secretary-manager, beginning a period of service that stretched for 27 years. The first edition of the match-day program the following year, April 15–16, lists Darcy Lawler as honorary sec-

The young Henry Morris — his contribution in bringing stability, good management and growth to the Juniors in the years after the 'Troubles' was to be beyond measure.

retary of the Junior League. Wintle's memories of it all more than 30 years later were bitter ones: 'Dean organised everything,' he says. 'They tried to keep the secretary there (Bob Laforest), but I wouldn't stand for it. I said, 'No … I want my job back.' So I got my job back and he got the sack … and a lot of money. But I could see the way the club was going. I made a decision with my late wife … I remember telling her: 'I can't put up with this.' She just said to me — 'well, get out'. So I did … on the 31st of December. I got nothing … certainly no golden handshake.' During his seven years at the Juniors the club had gone from nothing — to the richest club in Australia. Membership had increased from 246 to more than 19 000.

Things only got worse between Wintle and the club he helped build. He claims today that at that time he was on the receiving end of bomb threats … that a bomb would be put in his car. And on the night of July 2, 1967 he ended up in gaol, after being arrested by police when he returned to Sydney with his wife after a cruise aboard the liner *Canberra*. At issue were two charges of false pretences laid against him by South Sydney Junior Rugby League Club. Furious at charges he declared 'trumped up … absolutely no substance in them' he was later released on $2 000 bail, using his house as a surety. George Wintle fumes still at being held overnight in a 'dirty old cell' at Central Police Station.

Three months later George Wintle appeared in Central Court charged with obtaining two cheques (one of $1 044.05, the other of $2 604.68) from the club with intent to defraud. In court, Wintle's solicitor Mr JF Richardson said the two charges had been 'actuated by malice on the part of the [South Sydney Juniors] Board out of certain allegations made by Mr Wintle. They are simply an attempt to discredit him.' On October 26, 1967, Wintle was acquitted. Mr JA Letts, SM, said he could not be satisfied beyond reasonable doubt that there was intent to defraud. The magistrate commented that there was a mass of evidence that suggested that the club was not well run. Wintle walked free, to begin a new life, but not before dropping a writ on the club for $250 000 damages, declaring his good standing in the community had been eroded. Five years later, the club settled out of court for a fee that was never publicly disclosed. Confidential papers held in the club's archives solve that particular mystery. As a result of his Supreme Court action against the club, George Wintle in November 1972 was given the sum of $15 000.

The distance that quickly grew between Wintle and the Dean-Lawler team he had supported was clearly evident in an editorial comment penned by Darcy Lawler for the 'Weekly Newsletter' in October 1967. It read, in part:

THEY CALLED ME 'LITTLE HITLER'

A 1966 story in the old Sydney *Sun* newspaper gave the clearest insight of all into the philosophies of George Wintle — and what made George tick. The story was typical Wintle — Boots 'n' All — and published under the headline: 'They called me 'Little Hitler'.' The story appeared in the midst of the club's most turbulent period, with an unprecedented power struggle still underway, and founder Wintle out in the cold, but fighting for a continued working life at the Juniors. Following is an abridged version of the *Sun's* story, told in George Wintle's own words:

'I have been told on odd occasions that I ran the South Sydney Junior Leagues Club like 'a little Hitler'. Perhaps I did. But I'd do it again if I had the chance. You've got to have discipline; you have to make hard and fast rules and stick by them. You have to set a high standard and then you'll find people move up to that standard …

'To run a big club the right way, you can't have segregation. You can't have women barred, or pushed away into a dungeon-like corner. When we decided at the Juniors to admit women associates, I made it a rule that they should be the wives of members over 21 or spinsters, widows or divorcees OVER 40. To some, it seemed a strange rule. But I didn't want the club to become a 'pickup place'. I hoped the inclusion of women associates would bring decorum — and it did.

'Any club has to set a high standard and maintain it religiously. You won't find a high standard in a club that caters for the drunkard or the poker machine addict. The drunkard doesn't have a place in club life. Neither does the poker machine addict — because he isn't interested in the fuller life a club

can give. He is concerned only with pulling the handle, win or lose …

'Shorts are permitted in the club during the daytime. But at night a member or his guest has to have on a decent pair of long trousers and a shirt. And that doesn't include jeans. Desert boots are barred too. In the dining room, of course, a coat and tie are compulsory. Suits and ties are compulsory through the club on a Saturday night. This even applies to the blokes playing billiards …

'Although the club has a swimming pool and gymnasium, members are not permitted to carry a towel through the club. It has to be carried in a zippered bag. And the rule says that a member or his guest can't come in unshaven.

'Grog has been the downfall of many publicans and a club manager has to be careful too. You can't afford to have a drink with every liquor firm traveller who comes in. I drink very little anyway, and my entertainment expenses while I was at the club would have been about 10 shillings a week. At the South Sydney club the stress isn't on liquor. Schooners are not sold after 6.00pm on Saturdays and not at all on Sundays. And only 8-ounce goblets are sold in the dining room.

'I have heard from time to time the story that I used to stand up during the club dance and advise members that several poker machines were vacant and that the dance would not go on until they were being played. It just did not happen. Most members realise that the club facilities come from the machines. And they have a little flutter from time to time, if for no other reason than their conscience's sake. But this doesn't mean they are going to throw away the gas money.

'I had no way of knowing which members never played the poker machines — and no way of knowing if a member was losing money he needed, either. A member might be on a salary of 100 pounds a week. Am I going to go up to him and say: 'Are you sure you can afford to lose those two bobs?'

'I made it a rule that there was no tipping at the club. It applied to the members as well as stewards. It's undignified for the steward in the first place. Both the steward and the customer involved faced suspension for the practice.

'At the South Sydney Junior Leagues Club we had an annual turnover of two and a half million pounds [$5 million]. I have a lot of evidence that this turnover gave people a fuller, richer life. And no evidence at all that it made beggars of them.'

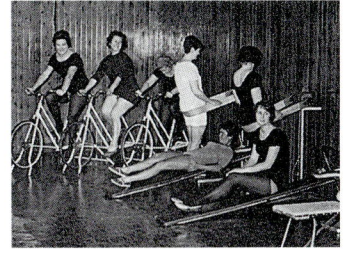

The Juniors gym as it was in the mid 1960s.

'It has been the present Board's policy not to enter into 'dirty' politics each week. However due to the lies and mis-statements edited in a 'rag' called 'The Clarion', which unfortunately has been infiltrated into this club and certainly is an insult to members' intelligence, this editorial is certainly warranted.'

Lawler savaged the previous management methods used at the club, commenting: 'The Club's supervision until this year has been a 'one man show' — and frankly it is too big a business to be controlled by one person.' Lawler observed that in the club's storeroom 'procedure and system' were unknown words and that it was 'truly a miracle that no-one had been poisoned' considering the state of the beer pipes.

He concluded: 'Members, I could write a book on what our Directors have had to do to guide the club back to its high standing.' It was a solid bucketing of Wintle — and his methods.

In early November 1967, the 'Weekly Newsletter' reported that a writ had been served on the club by George Wintle, claiming $250 000 in damages. Lawler wrote that he and present Board members had been subjected to a 'great many sinister remarks'. The bitterness evident in 1966 was still clearly within the club. Wrote Lawler: 'We have read in a biased local paper in the district — which would not accept a paid advertisement from the Junior League Committee — that there is a mass of evidence suggesting that the club is not well run, a statement that is false. The amount of rubbish served up to members outside by other groups would keep a bushfire alight for a week.'

Thirty years down the track, Henry Morris shoots straight on his opinion of the treatment George Wintle received in 1966. 'They double-crossed him for sure,' says Morris. 'It's a damned shame what happened to him. George was like all of us … he had his faults and his sins. But his heart was in this place … and they did a terrible thing to him.'

Morris has no doubt that one of the 'sins' for which George Wintle paid the penalty was his inclination to boast of the club's achievements in the press. 'He used to talk too much about how much money the club was making through poker machines — and he drew the attention of the government. George liked the spotlight … and he promoted the club with great enthusiasm. The fact is this: if it wasn't for George, the club wouldn't be here. He brought in his family to work in the place … that sort of thing … but I have absolutely no doubt he ran it 'straight'. He wouldn't be living the way he is today (a struggling existence in a small bedsit) if it had been any other way. In my view he was, and is, as straight as a gun barrel. In the long view of the history of the club he will be remembered the way he should be … as the man who started it all.'

Supporting Wintle, Morris got caught up in the maelstrom. 'I backed George,' says Morris today. 'And because of it I faced expulsion from the Junior League. I was secretary of Botany United at the time — and the club fought against the motion put to the Junior League that I be kicked out. Darcy [Lawler] had always wanted me expelled from the Junior League.'

The year 1967 was a horror one for Wintle. Midway through the year he was in the headlines yet again when named as a co-respondent in a divorce suit — and subsequently ordered to pay $1 000 damages to a wronged husband, Arthur Millard McGaurr.

In the wake of all the trauma, Wintle and his (now) wife Sylvia, close enough to flat broke, worked for a time at the Aurora Hotel, in Surry Hills. He left after receiving a death threat and the pair went into hiding. It is rumoured that the 'heavies' who were sent to the hotel to give Wintle the word received their instructions from inside the Juniors. In one of his last published interviews in 1983 Wintle told the *Sun-Herald's* Barbara Muhlvich, 'People thought I must have amassed a personal fortune working at the club because it had been going so well. It had a $4 million annual turnover. The fact is I only got my wages, nothing else. I might be an arrogant, conceited bastard at times but I'm not a crook. I don't rip off anyone.'

Battling to make ends meet, he worked at various odd jobs — he drove a taxi, ran a beach kiosk at Clovelly and worked as a cleaner — before finally returning to clubland. When Wintle took over the Maroubra Seals Club it was $80 000 in debt, and losing $500 a week. After five years of the Wintle touch, the club was booming — making a $200 000 annual profit on fully-owned premises worth $1million. He moved on to other clubs — to Cronulla-Sutherland Leagues, Port Hacking Rugby Union Club and Botany RSL. In 1973, there was some welcome good news for him when the life suspension imposed by South Sydney District Club in 1966, was lifted.

A friend, Maxine Driscoll, remembers George, irascible as ever at Botany RSL. 'I was in my first year working at the club when he took over as treasurer,' she recalls. 'The club was just in the red, but George turned that around. As soon as we saw his car of a morning the call would go up … 'he's here!' … 'he's here!'. I was at the front desk and honestly I would dread him walking through the door. I used to wonder, 'what's he going to do today'. I can still see him stopping to pick up a piece of paper from the front path. He'd come bustling in … 'get this path clean,' he would demand. Then he'd be off upstairs and all the supervisors would be running around in a flap. 'What about these ashtrays … they're dirty!' 'You've got to look after your members,' he'd say. And when he finally went home we'd all look at each other and say: 'Phew! Thank God he's gone.' With George it never changed — he would always be trying to make the club as good as it could be for the members. It was his main interest always … the members.'

In his late 60s he was still planning, working to make this club or that function more efficiently. In 1979 he took over the Eastern Suburbs Catholic Club, burdened with $1 million in debt, and with fewer than 1 000 members. Wintle set out to woo the local Catholic population of 40 000. He stood outside churches on Sunday mornings and handed out

Even 30 years on, the club on Anzac Parade was still a big part of George Wintle's life — and of his memories. George would recall with some bitterness the circumstances of his departure in the '60s — but with pride and enjoyment the formative years that had gone before.

'support your local club leaflets', he visited all local parish priests, he nego-
tiated with church leaders. Eventually the club was re-named the
Southern Cross Sporting & Social Club — and Wintle in 1983 enticed
Sydney's first VFL Club, the Swans, to use the club as its home base.

He was 68 then, but the move was typically Wintle: bold, innovative,
energetic. The stroke that laid him so cruelly low in his retirement years
was a bitter twist in the life of a man of such verve. But his story in the
world of the clubs remains a truly remarkable, if controversial one … and
so too that of the turbulent years of the 1960s when at ultimate personal
cost, he put every fibre of his being into the building and fostering of the
'Juniors'.

WHISPERS WEEKLY

The period between George Wintle's sacking from the club (January 1966) and the voting in of the Dean-Lawler Board late in the year developed into a monumental slanging match between the opposing forces. A bitter Wintle led the campaign against the establishment via a news-sheet — named first 'Wintle's Whispers' and then 'The Facts'. In typical fashion the ex-secretary-manager lashed out at those he believed had brought him down. And in the club's 'Weekly Newsletter' the establishment hit back. Caught in the middle was the Junior League, doing its best to make it 'business as usual' despite the almost daily distractions. Probably never before or since has clubland had such a boots 'n' all battle.

Following are excerpts from some of the newsletters still held on file by Tom Adams in the club's library:

June 30, 1966: 'Another rag (after 'Wintle's Whispers') has appeared containing erroneous information and entitled 'The Facts'. This rag purports to be signed by G Wintle … he still persists in living in a dream world.'

July 14: 'The rag called 'The Facts' is still being distributed in the 'toilets' or stealthily by hand under front doors or in letter boxes. The lead writer of this 'poor seller' is running out of ideas and his limited public must be getting tired of reading the same old 'jazz' all the time. One cannot help wondering how Wintle, when employed as secretary-manager could extol the virtues of your directors each year — and now turn so completely about face and be so loud in his protests about what they did and what they are doing. Wintle is a man of such high principles that he continues to reside in a property belonging to you without ever having paid rent since he moved in.'

July 21: 'It would appear from Issue 5 of 'the masterpiece' — 'The Facts' that some of the home truths are hitting Wintle where it hurts (his supreme ego). Members can now see him in his true colours as never before. Your directors say: 'Little Caesar is dead, let's bury him!' The Football League must surely be realising that having Wintle as 'honorary paid secretary' is like having a 'tiger in your tank'.'

July 28: 'Despite an undertaking not to print any more issues of 'The Facts' Wintle, showing his true colours as always, has produced Issue No. 6. He must surely be an embarrassment to his solicitors — he is just a pain in the neck to us. 'Little Caesar' has the effrontery to state that your Directors started the legal battle. Any executive of any firm dismissed from office for the reasons that he was, would have had the good sense to bow out quietly — but not this character.'

August 4: 'Two weeks from Thursday will be the day that every realistic member will be able to get rid of this Wintle character once and for all [this a reference to the vote on changing the constitution of the club]. Every member that he has insulted, abused and rode rough shod over for years will be able to show their appreciation. For the Directors to vilify and malign Wintle is a shocking thing according to him, but assuredly he must write his rubbish with tongue in cheek. These two words — vilify and malign are, and always have been, the main words in his limited vocabulary.'

September 29: 'Your Directors regret the inconvenience to all members through certain individuals distributing handbills outside the club. Your Board of Directors have no wish to become involved in a name-calling fight with Wintle. However he persists in spreading rumours and lies. Rumours have been freely circulating that the former secretary-manager (the late Mr O Nilson) had been dismissed from his position prior to his death. This is a deliberate LIE.' (The highly regarded 'Occa' Nilson, foundation director and fine worker for the club, had died only a few weeks before this reference. Occa Nilson had been appointed assistant-manager of the club in 1959, and had been appointed secretary-manager for a time on Wintle's departure in early 1966. On his death, president Darcy Thompson said of him: 'We all wish to pay tribute to him for his honest, loyal and conscientious services to both organisations.')

November 3: (An editorial under the heading, 'At last the truth has come out') — 'The Junior League candidates for directors say they will ask Wintle to come back as secretary-manager of the club. For so long these people have been bleating that this dispute has nothing to do with Wintle. How ludicrous can a dispute become? Your present directors — league men who have devoted a lifetime to Junior League in this district — dismissed Wintle for his irresponsible conduct and blatant disregard of the Board's instructions.' (The editorial goes on to talk of a letter sent by George Wintle to NSWRL

The Board of Directors 1966–67 — minus chairman Wally Dean. Left to right (top row): Ron Ellison, Frank Kilcran, Norm Christie; (bottom row): Len Hart, Mort Hart, Jack Caldon.

BOARD OF DIRECTORS

CLUB DEVELOPMENT

It is most pleasing to note that your Club has enjoyed a prosperous twelve months and despite heavy taxes, profits and membership subscriptions are at an all time high. Notwithstanding the heavy increases placed on your Club per medium of Supplementary Poker Machine Tax and Licencing Fees none of these has been passed on to the members.

In addition to this as the figures below indicate, the Club has advanced considerably during the administration of current Board of Directors.

Net Profit for 30th September, 1966	$ 99,722
† Net Loss for 31st December, 1966	$ 13,220
* Net Profit for 31st March, 1967	$135,787
* Net Profit for 30th June, 1967	$109,423
Net Profit for the year	$331,712

* Indicates Profits made after present directors occupied office.
† Indicates legacy left by previous administration.

President Bill Buckley — describing it as a 'highly defamatory and scurrilous attack on Mr Buckley and other responsible league officials.' The editorial also refers to a Wintle's scheme to build a 100-bed hospital for the aged as 'hare-brained'.)

November 17: 'Next Monday evening at 8pm is the Annual General Meeting, and we hope that after it is held there will be no further pestering of members outside the club. Your Directors deplore this irresponsible behaviour. Wintle doesn't care what happens to the club or its members as long as he gets his photo in the paper. This type of childish selfish behaviour cannot be tolerated by respectable and responsible members.'

On Wednesday, December 7, 1966 the election battle was fought — and won comprehensively by the Darcy Lawler and Wally Dean-led challengers. Final voting was as follows:

Darcy Lawler 2435	John Kelly 2173
Wally Dean 2410	Stephen Ryan 2145
George Bell 2392	Darcy Thompson 2113
Norm Christie 2387	Tom Craigie 2085
Len Hart 2365	Percy Pardey 2078
Ron Ellison 2358	Fred Robinson 2066
Frank Kilcran 2335	Pat Hennessy 2013.
(all above elected)	

The old order had been swept from office — among them the club's inaugural president Darcy Thompson. The Junior League-backed ticket had gained a stunning victory. On the night of the annual meeting the new Board met and made various decisions and pledges, including:

Suspensions lifted on G Wintle and Ron Ellison.

All associate members prior to Dec 31, 1965 to be invited to accept full membership.

Immediate steps to be taken to improve service, civility and cleanliness.

George Wintle was back. But for the man who had been the Juniors' driving force it was a pyrrhic victory. Within a month he was gone — forever.

SOUTH SYDNEY JUNIOR RUGBY LEAGUE CLUB LIMITED
WEEKLY NEWSLETTER
"THE BEST FOR THE BEST"

No. 148 New Issue (290th Issue).   THURSDAY, JULY 21, 1966   Registered Under the Newspaper Act, 1898   PRICELESS

Cub Reporter ..

PART FACT— .

PART FICTION

Was bailed up on Monday night by staff members, Vawdon and Glanville. "See us before you go, Johnno, and we will give you a couple of items for your column," they wailed.

Suffering catfish! With a little luck there may be room to sign my name to it, and that's about all. Here, read the couple of items and weep. On Monday, August 8th, at the Coronation Hall, Mascot, a social dinner will be held for male members of all our intra clubs. Dinner will start at 7 p.m., and when concluded first-class entertainment will go on non-stop till we be thrown out on time.

Being a born stickybeak, I for one intend to find out what form the entertainment will take. How about you? Tickets are only a dollar a head, and may be obtained from the secretary of your intra-club.

Staff members have only to see Messrs. Vawdon, Glanville or Don Wintle, but be prompt. A full house is expected.

Lady intra-club members have not been forgotten. Soon we hope to be able to announce a similar type of function for the girls. What a night that will be, go go boys, squeaky baritones and what else have you? Wow!

+ + +

The second announcement concerns your little monster, sorry, male offspring. Although the cricket season has not yet begun it is hoped this year to enter two junior sides, in addition to our adult A and B teams. One side will be for lads under 14, the other for boys under 12. No doubt your boy will be keen to represent his dad's club, so if you are interested, contact Mr. F. Robinson at 20 Jenning St., Matraville, or J. Glanville at the club. Mister Glanville may be easily recognised, if you don't know him personally. His vital statistics are 40-40-40, but don't let on I said so. He'll slay me!

+ + +

Final plug is for the blokes who dunk their thumbs in your beer, our worthy stewards. Now they have taken up football, they are seeking victims far and wide. This time they are journeying to far off Tamworth to play the local boys.

How about kicking in for a one-way ticket and keep 'em there. I'm all for it! How about you?

Roy Johnson.

SPECIAL NOTICE

The Cricket Club will be holding their annual meeting in the Club on Sunday, 31st July. All members and intending members invited to attend. Time, 10.30 a.m.

Place, Function Room, first floor.

EDITORIAL

It would appear from Issue 5 of the "masterpiece" — The Facts, that some of the home truths are hitting Wintle where it hurts (his supreme ego). "Methinks he does protest too much," for members can now see him in his true colours as never before. Your Directors say "Little Caesar is dead," let's bury him!

Wintle has now undertaken, through his solicitors, that he will not publish any further circulars in relation to his dismissal and this dispute. Members may notice that he takes this view after receiving some of his own medicine.

The main thought this week and for the Special Meeting for members to consider is why Wintle is throwing back somersaults to try and get reinstated. Could it be that he hopes that the Club will meet his enormous legal costs when the cases finally catch up with him. As we mentioned last week the club is inevitably committed to meet its own costs, thanks to Wintle, but surely it would be stretching the bounds of reason to expect a hand out from the members for his own personal costs.

The Football League surely must be realising that having Wintle as "honorary paid secretary" is like having a "tiger in your tank," and he is certainly not helping their cause with his vituperative comments. Your Directors are anxious to help the Junior Football League, but they would like the Executive of the League to help themselves by getting rid of Wintle.

Wintle raves about the proposed Outdoor Bowling Club. We would like to point out that this was one of his ideas, but we can assure all members that this project will be handled with common sense, and the development of the Bowling Club will be a gradual one, not $750,000 as Wintle seems to think.

For the Special General Meeting on Thursday, the 18th August, 1966, your Directors will refresh your memory as to their reasons for dismissing Wintle when you receive the envelope containing the meeting notice. Please exercise your right as a member to vote by proxy as indicated if you are not able to attend the meeting. Vote "FOR" the first resolution and "AGAINST" Nos. 2 and 3. It is up to you to put "paid" to this nonsense once and for all on the 18th August, by attending the meeting or using your proxy vote as your Board advises.

THE SMOKO . . .

It's on Monday night! We know it's right for you to all be there
To smoke your fags and eat the food, and also drink your share.
It's not a lot of trouble, and it's not a great expense,
And if you are not coming then you haven't any sense.
You know it's right on Monday night, it's just the place to go,
So if you don't attend this "do," you'll miss a damn good show.
It will be quite a friendly night, when you all meet in good cheer;
In fact we'll guarantee you'll have the brightest night this year.
There'll be lots of happy moments to make you forget your strife,
So make sure you get there early, with a leave pass from your wife;
Just be there on the eighth next month at Mascot's large Town Hall,
Where members of the intra-clubs will meet for good of all.

Howard Keyvar.

TENNIS CLUB DANCE

To celebrate the holding of the first annual tennis championships at Snape Park by the S.S.J.R.L.C., a gala dance will be held at the Clubhouse, Snape Park, on Saturday, 6th August, commencing at 8 p.m.

All members of the Tennis Club are eligible to attend. Admission free. See notice board, Snape Park.

✦ Ladies' Day

LADIES' DAY will be held on TUESDAY, 16th August, 1966, so keep this day free because it promises to be a bigger and better day than ever.

We have a great line-up of artists for you and the show will be compered by JOHNNY LOCKWOOD, comedian.

The Star of the Show, return by popular demand, is BILL NEWMAN.

SHANDA, Magician, and the star of Tokio Night,
and
GO GO GIRLS.

Invitations will be forwarded within the next few weeks.

Senior Citizens' Centre

In the past Associate Members of our Club have kindly given their free time voluntarily in assisting us to run the Senior Citizens' Centre. Without their valuable assistance we could not have managed.

Again we are calling upon any Associate Member who can assist us on this project. If you have a free morning or afternoon to spare, would you please contact Miss Sandra Wunsch, Monday to Friday, 10 a.m. to 5 p.m.

SUPER JACKPOTS

Super jackpots, as from Friday, if not struck before, will be:

2/-		
	1	£220
	2	$360
	3	$420
	4	$320
	5	$200
	6	$220
	7	$300
	8	$240

1/-		
	1	$150
	2	$60
	3	$70
	4	$90
	5	$90
	6	$60
	7	$70
	8	$60
	9	$70
	10	$80
	11	$90
	12	$80
	13	$80
	14	$100

6d.		
	1	$35
	2	$40
	3	$50
	4	$70
	5	$35
	6	$120
	7	$30
	8	$55
	9	$55
	10	$45

Four-reeler poker machines are for members and associates only. Visitors are not permitted to play four-reelers under any circumstances.

THIS IS YOUR CLUB!

No. 2

By virtue of our membership we are entitled to and may, if we desire, devote ourselves to or partake of the many varied aspects of Club life offering. All these things are ours for the taking. They are organised for us, in part by the various committees that make up the interclub groups which in turn receive all the help and support required from the management and Directors of the Club, who in their wisdom are very conscious of the importance of such bodies, for therein lies the future growth, prosperity and success of the Club as a whole. The past, present and future support of the Junior Football League is another major consideration of the Club, this being the only group not part of the intraclub structure, but receiving singularly greater sponsorship. We have all this, and the future holds promise of more.

Our rights to continued freedom and protection from adverse publicity could be in jeopardy, so we are charged with the responsibility of supporting the management and Board, who have so ably and conscientiously worked for our benefit.

We must protect and preserve this group, whose very existence and effectiveness is being threatened by an individual whose actions have always been, to say the least, questionable.

BARRY DUNN REMEMBERS ... THE WAY WE WERE

'I remember the building way back before George Wintle came on the scene. The KC Club (the Kensington Club) it used to be called — and there was a big sign out the front. It used to be let out for weddings and functions. George Wintle was the driving force behind getting the Juniors established, no doubt about that. He was a very hard bloke, but pretty fair to his staff. My mother worked at the club for about three years after it started, as a librarian, and I know firsthand that George had a lot of time and concern for his staff. But if anyone was doing anything wrong he wouldn't muck around — he'd get rid of them straightaway. There was a generous side to George though. For example, there were more than a few times when my mother was putting a few bob through the sixpenny (five cent) machine — and George would pass by and drop a few more coins into the tray. He had some charm about him;

'George was smart enough to know that if the women liked the club, they'd bring their men along too. He was the right man at the right time, in the right job. It's good that he's back 'onside' with the club these days — we welcomed him back ... after the other mob had pushed him out. He's such an important part of the story here. He was never off duty — he would be here day and night. There was barely a moment you wouldn't see him here. He'd be down at the door and in those days you had some really tough blokes coming to the joint. George would be looking them over and saying: 'Not in.' 'Not in.'

'The dress code in the early years was very strict. In those days you had to have a collar and tie on to come into the bloody place! Many years ago one of our President's Cup selectors was Wally Stigg who was with Kensington United. Wally arrived at the club one day with his Kenso blazer on — a Bermuda jacket with a dragon on the pocket. George met him at the door. 'Mr Stigg, I'm sorry you are not allowed in,' he said. Wally was heading through the door, and George repeated his warning. Wally Stigg's response was to rip the pocket off the coat. 'Now it's a Bermuda jacket ... is that okay George?' he said.

'I've had an association with the club virtually since it opened its doors. I'm not a foundation member — but I was a club delegate, right from its beginning. I have lived most of my life in the area. I was a not-very-good footballer and played cricket for Randwick. In 10 years coaching with Maroubra, I coached 11 premiership-winning sides ... two in the one year. Before the club was developed, when I first started with Maroubra, it used to cost us 20 pounds to put an A grade side into the competition down to 12 pounds 10 shillings for an H grade side. We used to have to pay for all gear, plus training facilities. As delegates we met at the Coronation Hall at Mascot, then the Griffiths Hall, then at the tennis courts down at Snape Park. Finally we came back to the club for our meetings — and we've been here ever since. I've been on the Board here for 22 years, and deputy president for 21 of those years.

'There have been some changes all right over the years, and a lot of credit goes to those early directors listed in the annual report. And we have been through stormy times, too. There was a period during the Royal Commission when I wondered if whether there would be a club anymore. But we rode through the storm. There were some bad times ... times when we had crims hanging out at the club. And we had plain-clothes police looking for the crims. I remember them grabbing a bloke in here one night — they had been after him for weeks. Those days are long behind us now — and thank goodness for that.

Barry Dunn was there at the beginning (1959) and in 2000 was still a strong figure at the Juniors as deputy chairman — his story and memories spanning the entire period of the remarkable story of the 'Juniors'.

'I remember when Judge Head made an appointment to come out and see the club during one of the hearings. Darcy Lawler said: 'Let's get everything spic and span' — and he had cleaners and painters and all these people running around smartening the place up.

'Politics were a reality in the club during that time. At one stage I shifted to Martin Road Centennial Park for a short time — and they passed a rule on the Board about 'residential qualification' which meant that I couldn't stand for committee. I wasn't too popular with blokes like Darcy Lawler and Wally Dean — but when I got onto the Board Darcy (CEO) had to change his views a bit. I still wasn't his No 1 boy by a long shot ... and for sure he wasn't mine.

'The club was founded for the propagation of Junior League in the South Sydney area, and for the benefit of other sports and charities. And in my time here the amount of money poured into the Junior League — and Souths senior club too — and into charities and into other sports is unbelievable. It runs into millions and millions of dollars. I think we have 33 intra-clubs

OPPOSITE: *This, of course, is what it's all about — youngsters playing and enjoying rugby league, their opportunity provided by the unstinting support of Souths Juniors.*

today — that's how widely the club caters for individual interests. It has always been a 'members' club' — a place where a man can take his wife and children out for a safe and enjoyable and relatively inexpensive night. We spent $1.7 million this year supporting the Junior Rugby League. That $1.7 million supports more than 140 sides. That's ground hiring costs, provision of jumpers, shorts, socks for all players, insurance and the provision of all training facilities, lighting etc. And we give the clubs $200 per team. Out of that sort of set-up you're going to get talent — and one of my good memories is the trip to New Zealand with the Flegg side back in the '60s. We didn't know it then — but in that team were three future internationals — Ron Coote, Bob McCarthy and Eric Simms.

'But the clubs still work to raise their own money — and the competitions still depend a very great deal on the voluntary workers. My wife Dawn is just one of many; she has worked at the kiosk at Redfern Oval for 22 years now. For all the money and work that we put in as a club — the competition must still have its foundation of voluntary workers, people prepared to give up their time.

'Over the years the licensed club has had (and has now) many loyal and long-standing employees. Once a year we host a '20-year luncheon' — for people who have worked at Souths Juniors for more than 20 years. The numbers are up to about 580 now. We have had some tremendous staff — people who love the place, and just don't leave.

'Something that has never been much publicised is the number of young people we've helped put through university. A percentage of our casuals have always been uni students; if they're at university for four years, they know they have a job here for four years. I think you can say fairly that the club has had a total community involvement for all of its 40 years.

'The area was South Kensington originally until it was re-named Kingsford after Sir Charles Kingsford-Smith — and the club has always had a connection with the racing fraternity. Old Norm Christie who was on the Board of Directors for a short time before being appointed the club's assistant secretary-manager tells the story that in early days George (Wintle) encouraged him to do a little SP-ing in the club. But the way Norm used to relate the story the pair of them had a blue — and George gave him up to the coppers. George would probably tell it differently.

'"Colourful' is a word that has been used to describe our history at Souths Juniors. I think it does the job.'

JOAN CHILD REMEMBERS ... THE CLUB I GREW TO LOVE

'I started at the club in 1965, employed as secretary to George Wintle. There was a lot of turmoil at that time, effectively a struggle for control of the club, and George was only there for about another four months after I started. I hated it at first — just didn't fit in. Things were so difficult then in that atmosphere ... some days I'd wait at the bus stop and think: 'Oh no, I can't stand another day.' Gradually I worked myself into the way of things. Life got better — and in the end I stayed 29 years!

'I remember Bell's Ballroom (from which the club grew) quite well. Actually my sister Margaret had her 21st birthday party there. It was just a basic dance hall ... the way they were in those days. It was a big room with a wooden floor, and seats all around the perimeter, a bandstand at one end.

'I went from my job at Johnson & Johnson to the club, answering an advertisement in the *Sydney Morning Herald*. At Johnson & Johnson it had been mainly shorthand and typing, and I was looking for some variety in my work. I certainly got it when I came to Souths.

'They were troubled and uneasy times (in 1965). I think we on the staff were all for George, but some dirty things went on. I can remember when the election was coming up proxy votes, supporting George, being thrown into the waste-paper basket. When the coast was clear some of us would retrieve them and make sure they were registered.

'For all the problems, I enjoyed the brief period working with George Wintle. I felt as George's secretary that I was doing the sort of work I should be doing. He had his friends and he had his enemies ... some loved him, some hated him. He was just like that. He had these strict dress rules — no blazers, men had to wear a tie after 7 o'clock, long socks with shorts — those sort of things. And there's no doubt he put pressure on people to play the poker machines. After a show he'd get on the mike and say: 'Now, go and put your money in the poker machines on the way out.' But he was a man who looked after people who couldn't look after themselves. The older ladies going to bowls ... he'd always make sure they had a lift home ... that sort of thing. He was a caring person. After George left — the first time — I was secretary to Mr Nilson (Occa Nilson) for a while and then to Bob Laforest (who replaced George Wintle as secretary-manager for a time in 1966).

'Then Darcy Lawler came in on the ticket that George ran — and he was appointed secretary-manager. I became Darcy's secretary — and was with him all the years he was here. He was a hard, tough sort of man — but he had a good sense of humour. Darcy made his rules — then was pretty inflexible on them. I remember one year a New Zealand doorman at the club who wanted to go home for a reunion for which members of his family were coming from all over the world. It was Christmas — and Darcy had a strict rule that the staff couldn't have holidays at Christmas. He wouldn't let this man go — and in the end the doorman resigned, so that he could attend the reunion.

'Wally Dean? Well, I always thought of him as a loveable rogue. He was the sort of fellow who if he had a dollar and he thought you needed it more than he did, he'd give it to you. He was generous … and flamboyant. Once I recall he was on stage in the auditorium and I noticed he had odd socks on. I pointed it out to him. 'That doesn't matter,' he said. 'As long as you noticed!'

'I was called to give evidence at the Royal Commission (into licensed clubs). That was a tense period at the club … we had a few of those here. I was really pretty 'new' in the place and I really didn't have much idea of what was going on. There were a lot of rumours going around — but I must say that I never saw anything untoward. In the early days I didn't go to the Board meetings to take the minutes.

Joan Child and Darcy Lawler — the club's 'engine room' for more than a quarter of a century.

I heard some stories … that's about all. But even during the difficult times the club continued to grow. We were always up with the top club. Since Henry [Morris, chairman] came in things have been pretty stable.

'We have always had good shows at the club, and that has pulled people in. Not that they liked paying for it when we put a 'cover' charge on some years ago. I remember we had Pat Boon here at one stage — and there were only about 200 people at the show, in a 900-seat auditorium.

'There have been some great shows over the years. Howard Keel and Kathryn Grayson stick in my mind … I remember there was a bit of a problem because Kathryn was in love with Howard and he wasn't reciprocating. So many good shows … I remember when the African

The genial Oscar 'Occa' Nilson — a strong figure in the club's beginning, and growth.

Ballet were here they were invited to come up for the intra-club cabaret after their show and it turned out to be a wonderful night. We were all dancing together — the Ballet members, and the staff.

'During George Wintle's time, we had Lovelace Watkins as special guest act at the club. I remember the first time I met him. He said to me, 'What's your name?' … and I said 'Joan'. 'And what shall I call you?' I asked him. 'Just call me Love,' he said.

'Darcy Lawler used to have a party for us at Christmas in earlier days — and there'd be dancing and singing. At one of them I remember one of my shoes flew off when I was dancing and shot past Darcy's head. Another year, all the girls got into neck-to-knee costumes … olden days garb. Darcy said to us: 'I'll bet you a week's pay you're not game to go around the club dressed like that.' Well, we'd all had a few drinks — and off we went, prancing around. When we got back and asked Darcy for our week's pay he had his answer ready for us: 'I said a WEAK pay.'

'Workers at the Juniors have built something of a tradition of long-service. These days we have a 20-year luncheon. When an employee reaches his or her 20th year of service he or she is invited to the lunch — and is presented with a gold watch. The numbers at the annual 20-year lunches are up to about 60 now; even after you leave the club you are invited back.

'I think for all its years the club has been a community centre for local people. When I first started and I'd come to work at 9 o'clock there'd be people waiting out the front — to get back to their own poker machines. I used to think: 'How awful to be doing that.' But I gradually realised that the club, and even the favoured poker machine, were like old friends to people. Some of them were lonely people with not too many things to fill their days. At the club there'd be friendship and warmth and safety — plus the chance to use so many facilities, in and out of the club … the squash courts, the gym, all the intra-clubs, the holiday flats, the movie days.

'The kids' Christmas parties have always been a big event. Like lots of

Joan Child in the 1990s. 'I don't believe anyone could ever question the fact that the club has made a wonderful contribution to the entire district over the years.'

others, my grandchildren attended them ... and they're fully-fledged members of the club now.

'I think the club has been fortunate to have a good and generous man at the helm these last 24 years in Henry Morris. Generosity has always been the way of Souths Juniors — so many organisations, hospitals, clubs in the area are supported by the club — and Henry has certainly kept that tradition going. I don't believe anyone could ever question the fact that the club has made a wonderful contribution to the entire district over the years.'

THAT'S ENTERTAINMENT

Topline entertainment has always been part of the way of things at Souths Juniors. In earlier days bands and artists performed almost every night on what is now the ground floor, and on the first floor. A new dimension was added in May 1968 with the opening of the auditorium. There were two shows nightly, Thursday to Sunday. The first show in that year was an extravaganza — 'The Pat Gregory Ice Show'. Many of the world's top entertainers came to Souths Juniors in the years that followed. Almost every leading Australian 'act' of the last 40 years has appeared at the club, plus countless overseas stars who have come from Las Vagas … Paris … London … New York … to take their place on stage at the 'Juniors'. The Leslie Uggams show holds the record for most musicians and singers employed — 27. Neil Sedaka used 23 musicians and singers and recorded an LP live in the auditorium. For the major musical productions — of which there were as many as three a year some years — the club employed as many as 40 people. The list below is only a sampler — but an indication of just how much world class entertainment has been a way of life at the club.

Many of the world's top entertainers of the passing years found their way to the club at Kingsford including the famous English comedians Norman Wisdom (below) and Warren Mitchell (below right).

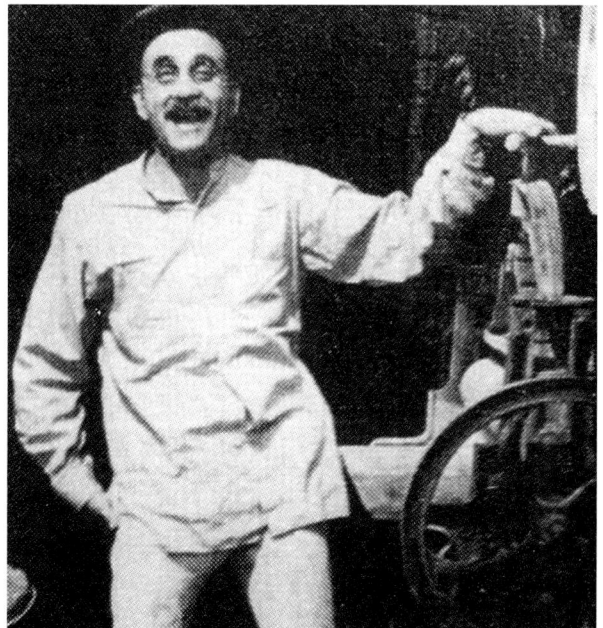

OVERSEAS STARS

Jerry Van Dyke

Kathryn Grayson

Frankie Lane

The Bachelors

Johnny Ray

Eartha Kitt

Matt Munroe

Steptoe & Son

The Bee Gees

Lonnie Donegan

Marcia Hines

The Duke Ellington
Orchestra

Rich Little

Neil Sedaka

Max Bygraves

Norman Wisdom

Frank Gorshin

Harry Secombe

Dick Emery

Reg Varney

Ricky May

Warren Mitchell

Acker Bilk

Mike and Bernie
Winters

Howard Keel

Leslie Uggams

Donald O'Connor

Al Martino

The Inkspots

Cilla Black

Winifred Atwell

Dorothy Lamour

Morgana King

Danny La Rue

Vic Damone

The Drifters

Glittering international stars of the calibre of Jerry Van Dyke (below left) and Max Bygraves (below) brought the crowds flocking to the Juniors — virtually transforming the club into the entertainment heart of Sydney.

MAJOR SHOWS

BELOW: Entertainment at the Juniors came in all shapes and sizes, all styles — Pat Gregory (below) was Australia's skating star and her extravaganza, 'The Pat Gregory Ice Show' was the first show to entertain Juniors' patrons in 1968.

FAR RIGHT: (above): Johnny Tillotson and (bottom) the mellow-voiced John Rowles (with guitar).

Annie Get Your Gun

Paint Your Wagon

Les Ballet Africain

Chinese Dalian Acrobatic Troup

The Bulgarian Dance Company

The Best of Broadway Musicals

Bottoms Up Revue

South American Nights

South Pacific

Guys and Dolls

Tokyo Revue

The Cherry Blossom Revue

The Leningrad Music Hall

Black and White Minstrel Show

Showboat

AUSTRALIAN STARS

June Bronhill	Frank Ifield	Johnny O'Keefe
Jon English	Julie Anthony	The Deltones
Judy Stone	James Morrison	Billy Thorpe
Col Joye	Barry Crocker	Slim Dusty
Kamahl	The Seekers	Normie Rowe
Graeme Bell	Doug Parkinson	

LEFT: *It wouldn't be Showtime at the club without the glamorous ballet. Over the years the faces changed — but the quality? Never!*

BELOW: *A Juniors' promotional poster of the 1990s — providing a snapshot of the breadth and variety of the entertainment 'packages' provided for fans.*

CHAPTER 4

'KICK BACKS' AND PAY BACKS

The 150 000-word report of the Moffitt Royal Commission into allegations of organised crime in NSW clubs, delivered in August 1974, ultimately foreshadowed the end of Wally Dean's highly controversial tenure as chairman of Souths Juniors. It ended also a turbulent and riotously 'colourful' period in the club's generally buoyant history. Justice Athol Moffitt was scathing in his published findings, noting that Dean and an associate, the former champion oarsman and ex-detective Murray Stewart Riley (a bronze medalist with Merv Wood at the 1956 Olympic Games) 'can be said to have organised plundering of clubs by improper and apparently criminal means'. In a stunning report he described Dean as a 'grasping, dishonest man who continues to hold office' and who had shown 'a ruthless inclination ... to achieve his dishonest purposes'. Dean had engaged in 'sinister' activities, said Justice Moffitt. He examined Dean's connections with other people involved in the Royal Commission's enquiries. Among these were Leonard Arthur McPherson, who was described at the enquiry as the 'Mr Big' of the Sydney underworld, Murray Riley, who was sought as a witness but never found, Lionel Arthur Abrahams, a company director and entertainment agent and Joseph Dan Testa, an American alleged to have links with the Mafia. Mr Justice Moffitt said: 'There are grounds for suspicion that any crimes of Riley and Dean are of the organised crime variety for the additional reason that there are

real grounds for suspicion — short of positive inference — that there are organisational connections between Riley and McPherson and Dean, and between McPherson and Testa and the other group of local criminals who entertained Testa here.' (The Royal Commission was told that Testa, an alleged member of a Chicago crime syndicate, visited Sydney in 1969, went on a hunting trip with Leonard McPherson, was entertained at parties, taken on a Harbour cruise and to a city nightclub.) The judge said Dean had had links with McPherson over many years and had associated dishonestly with Riley. The activities of Dean, Riley and Abrahams within the operations of Souths Juniors took up some 20,000 words of the Moffitt Report. The section on Wally Dean was headlined, 'Dean's activities and exploitations in SSJ (South Sydney Juniors)'.

(The Mafia reference in the Moffitt Report recalled a rather extraordinary item that appeared under Darcy Lawler's name in the club magazine in late 1972. Under the heading 'A word from Darcy Lawler' the secretary-manager wrote:

Proud in his Australian gear, Ron Coote meets prospective stars of the future at Redfern Oval. The cycle continues.

'The management of South Sydney Juniors is greatly concerned at allegations of Mafia infiltration into leading social clubs. Charges of corruption are being given widespread coverage in press, radio and TV and there have been repeated suggestions that foreign involvement exists. Because of these alarming, but as yet unfounded reports, your Board of Directors demanded an immediate and full enquiry. In my six years with the club as secretary-manager in which most of the current Board of Directors have officiated, I can refute any overseas interest in any phase of our operation.')

A *Sun-Herald* investigative article published years later (1987) reported the following:

'In December 1971, police officers interviewed an anonymous source. According to police interview notes, this person alleged that 'a man called Wally Dean … and a man called Riley have been to the States with the Mafia' … ')

The Moffitt Report continued: 'Within SSJ, by devious means, Dean used his position as president to enter into business dealings with the club or to receive money from persons with contracts with the club. In evidence he made many concessions which demonstrated, on analysis, exploitation of the club and abuse of his position. He is shrewd and made concessions only, it seems, where he was aware of what could be shown by documents available or possibly available. It is reasonably clear that the records of Garson Enterprises Pty Ltd (the vehicle and cloak for many improper dealings) … were not 'lost' but were most likely looked at and dealt with by Dean in some way. It is likely that the documents were interfered with. Some cheque butts certainly were. The documents were mysteriously 'found' in Dean's office when pressures were applied by my enquiry concerning their disappearance.' Dean was in the witness box for almost 14 hours at the Commission.

Mr Justice Moffitt referred to Dean's activities in forcing a Mr Martin of the All Clubs Cleaning Company and Coronet Carpet Company Pty Ltd — which he described as the apparently reputable cleaning contractor for Souths Juniors at about $3 500 a week — to pay a 'kick-back, dishonestly extracted' to Dean of $150 as 'public relations officer'. 'Dean's duties were a sham and the weekly payments a kick-back dishonestly extracted,' the judge said.

The report continued: 'Dean received money from Kay Constructions Pty Ltd allegedly for work done for it, shortly before that company received a very lucrative construction contract without any other tenders being called for.

'Dean was a director of and, it seems received wages from, Tracy Burns Pty Ltd and this company supplied fancy goods to the club.

'The club discontinued its wrestling contract. The contractor owned the ring. The club was starting boxing and its minutes show the club was looking to buy a ring. Dean bought the ring himself for $1 500 and, under the name of H & D Sports Hiring Service, hired it to the club at $60 a week. After three years … the ring was sold to the club for $3 000.

'W.J. Dean and Son Supply Co. sold novelties to the club.

'A club contractor was induced by Dean to hire Dean's taxi truck in supplying the club.

'Design and decor work for some $5 500 was carried out for the club by Aesthetic Arts Pty Ltd and at that time Dean, Sinclair (William Charles Garfield Sinclair, later convicted in Bangkok of heroin trafficking and subsequently acquitted on appeal) and one Green were directors or shareholders, but this was invoiced to the club in the name of Green. (Dean, reportedly had a $150 per week arrangement with the company

Greg Hawick, who went on to perform great deeds as one of the finest of rugby league's post-war five-eighths, was a distinguished 'product' of the Junior League. Photo courtesy of South Sydney RLFC.

which provided props and sets for the Juniors entertainment program.) There were numerous other dealings between the club and this company, either in its own name or using one of the other various firm names.

'Garson Enterprises received the contract to furnish the Sky Lounge of the club. The figures from the relevant books show a payment to the company of $35 094 and expenditure in purchasing the furniture at $17 640. The company was not in the furniture business and no other tender was obtained.'

In December 1973, with pressure mounting in the midst of a fiery election campaign Wally Dean told the club's annual meeting: 'I have reported that I have no business interests within the club in the past 18 months, and I signed a statutory declaration to this effect. The reports in the press relate to the period prior to 1968.' At the same meeting in response to a question from the floor as to whether 'McPherson' was a member of the club, chairman Dean responded: 'There are lots of McPhersons on our register, however I presume you mean Len McPherson and he is definitely not a member of our club, and has never been a member.' In interviews for this book, however, there was impeccable confirmation that McPherson was linked to the club for a lengthy period, and that he used to meet Darcy Lawler in the church across the road from the Juniors. The signal for the meeting would be a phone call from 'Mr Day' (McPherson's code name) to Lawler. McPherson was apparently on some sort of contracted arrangement to 'look after' the club … keep out crooks etc. The arrangement was apparently in place through much of the Lawler era.

The young Bernie Purcell, in 1955. He was, and is, a Rabbitoh legend — a man who came through junior playing days to find fame at the highest level.

BEATING THE BANDITS

In the days when poker machines were 'one-armed bandits' Souths staff needed to be eternally vigilant to nab the shady operators. There were various methods used to 'beat the bank'. In 1972 club management was alerted to a syndicate of poker machine manipulators who were working the club — all of whom were non-members. The club's 'Weekly Newsletter' reported: 'When a jackpot is pulled this nefarious group endeavour to solicit an unsuspecting member to sign for them and may occasionally even offer a little reward for the trouble.' Members were advised: 'If by chance you should be approached by these parasites, help yourself and your club by reporting this malpractice to the nearest supervisor immediately.'

Another trick used was the insertion of a long steel rod (very thin) through the hinge section of machines with side-hinge opening. The modus operandi was this — when an ace came up on the first reel, the rod would go in to lock the reel. The perpetrators were then playing for aces two and three — with the odds greatly reduced. In one period at the club in the '60s there was evidence of a dozen machines being tampered with in this way — although no indication of how much success the villains had had.

In November '73 the club's 'Weekly Newsletter' fired a shot across the Commission's bows, taking serious offence at 'uncorrected' evidence concerning the furnishing of the Sky Lounge by Garson Enterprises. Darcy Lawler produced a detailed fullpage statement on page 1 of the newsletter, for and on behalf of the Board.

During the Royal Commission the head of the security firm guarding the club revealed that three fictitious names had been added to his list of employees. The admission came from Robert Harold Dalby, owner of Adept Security — who cited 'tax evasion' as the reason behind the ploy.

On the replacement of the former entertainment agent Richard Gray (in October 1971) at the club, by Lionel Abrahams of Top Artists Promotions, the Commission found there was 'great suspicion' concerning its propriety. 'Large sums went to these 'agents' in the order of something just under a million dollars annually,' the report said. 'With Dean's history of extracting money from others and what he could out of the club's business and with the relations that existed between Dean, Riley and Abrahams, and the cash dealings of each, it is almost impossible to think Dean would go unrewarded in respect of the vast payments.'

A major investigative report published in the *Sun-Herald* in 1987 and based in part on the book *Drug Traffic: Narcotics and Organised Crime in Australia* by Dr Alfred McCoy and in part on work undertaken by renowned journalist Evan Whitton reported: 'South Sydney Juniors had a large budget for entertainment:

'$770 000 in 1970 and $945 000 in 1971. Its booking agent was Mr Richard Gray. However, in 1970, Riley, with a partner, established a booking agency called Arcadia Top Artists. In August 1971, Gray was involved in an after-hours brawl with Riley, his partner and Dean. Gray sustained severe injuries and his dismissal as the club's booking agent. Arcadia then won a virtual monopoly on agency work and Riley made over $50 000 a year as his share of the profits. Dean had no official position in Arcadia Top Artists, but his future wife, Carol Dunn, was temporarily employed there.'

Some of the stories emanating from the club in that shadowy period almost defy belief — such as an employee being knifed in the arm one night by a well known Sydney crime figure … because he would not toe the line.

Justice Moffitt's 1974 investigation into it all continued at vast length and unrelentingly … focusing at a further point on the links of Riley, Dean and Abrahams to the Motor and Mariners Clubs, as well as Souths Juniors. (Wally Dean was secretary of the Associated Motor Club for a time in 1970.) The Moffitt conclusions were scathing:

'Many of the activities, but particularly those of Dean and Riley, are of an organised variety. Some can be said to be organised plundering of clubs by improper and apparently criminal means.' The *Sydney Morning Herald*'s State Political Correspondent, John O'Hara, reported further: 'He [Justice Moffitt] found an 'appearance' of criminal conduct by Walter James Dean, 'obviously with the co-operation of others, including the secretary [Darcy] Lawler, in extracting, by virtue of his office, in predatory fashion, and by devious and grossly improper methods, money from South Sydney Juniors and other clubs.'

The McCoy-Whitton article also linked Wally Dean with Sydney's largest baccarat school, at 33 Oxford Street, Darlinghurst ('The 33 Club') — reputedly a haunt of 'showbusiness personalities, prominent lawyers, and knighted businessmen'. The claim was made publicly that Dean at one stage was paid $600 a month for 'promotion' at the 33 Club.

Murray Riley, linked so closely to Dean in the Commission's finding, later served 10 years for attempting to import $40 million worth of marijuana to Australia, after being sentenced in 1978. Arrested in England in

1990 for alleged involvement in a $93 million computer fraud, Riley subsequently 'disappeared' after escaping from Aldington Gaol in Kent. He had been convicted and sentenced to five years gaol for plotting to defraud British Aerospace. On the question of his earlier links with Souths Juniors, there were published claims in the 1980s that after he (Riley) was deported from New Zealand to Australia in March 1967, he became the club's poker machine supervisor, allowed to appoint a number of phantom assistants whose salaries went directly to him. His association with the club seems to have finished in late 1973. At the Board meeting of October 11 that year Darcy Lawler reported that Riley had asked for leave of absence for three weeks commencing from September 4. As he had failed to recommence work after the three weeks had elapsed, Lawler had sacked him. The Board endorsed the secretary-manager's action.

Denis Donoghue, another in a long and distinguished line. Front-rower Donoghue won premierships with Souths, played Tests for Australia — and went on to become president of the Rabbitohs in further premiership-winning years.

Many of the more serious revelations came — then and later — as a vast shock to members who had continued to enjoy the club's burgeoning facilities through the 1960s and into the '70s. In some ways (but obviously not all!) the members were better informed than ever before, mainly via the impressive Souths Juniors Magazine (News — Views — Happenings at your club) which kicked off in March 1969.

In Vol 1, No 1, secretary-manager Darcy Lawler wrote proudly of 'the biggest club in the world (in excess of 38 000 members, with a net profit of $500 000 plus the biggest premises in the world and … tennis courts, bowling greens, holiday flats, guest lodge, golf course, fishing vessel, sailing vessel, luxury cruiser'. The cover photo of edition 1 was a beauty — of some mighty mites in action in the juniors. The wordy caption inside

captured the feeling: 'This photograph, taken by our staff photographer, is, we feel, all of the human interest that one could wish to capture in the 'little fellows' playing the greatest game of all — rugby league.'

Within edition 1 was news that the 'Wilma Colvill of London Charm School' had 'proved a wonderful innovation' for ladies in the club — and members of the 'popular Souths ballet' were fetchingly photographed in gingham tights. The gals became the 'Souths Juniors Lovelies' in a later edition of the magazine. The Wilma Colvill Charm School offered ladies free of charge some tips in deportment, make-up, hair care, hand-care and wardrobe planning.

Darcy Lawler nominated a post-war Souths side composed entirely of products of the junior league: Eric Simms, Jack Troy, Brian Moore, Bob Honeysett, Len Brennan, Greg Hawick, Clem Kennedy, Ron Coote, Paul Sait, Bernie Purcell, Denis Donoghue, Ernie Hammerton, Bryan Orrock. No Bob McCarthy? In late 1969 came news that chairman Dean had been appointed to South Sydney Council.

The magazines that remain on file at the club are a mine of information. Under poker machine rules (1969) it was noted that only three minutes were allowed 'in the powder room or obtaining change at the change desk'. Darcy Lawler chided late-leaving members, writing tersely of 'demonstrative and noisy people leaving the club' and 'the raucous yelling and singing of the inconsiderates'. And the club sent hampers to the 'boys' in Vietnam. On Mondays the entertainment was 'Terry Dear's New Faces', on Tuesdays, wrestling, on Wednesdays (with boxing on alternate Wednesdays), popular dance music. Forthcoming attractions included Kathryn Grayson and Howard Keel and 'Mr Versatile', Nelson Sardelli. In the press it was reported that in attracting a dazzling array of talent the club was already challenging ritzy nightclubs the Silver Spade and Chequers in the entertainment business.

In many ways the club was living up to an ambition that Wally Dean had quoted in his colourful way before he became chairman: 'When we get in, we'll be kicking golden footballs!' Regular mention

BELOW: *Cheeky stuff from the Souths Juniors Ballet — glamorous as ever and dressed (almost) to kill.*

OPPOSITE, TOP: *Fight night at the club as a couple of willing scrappers take a glove for the entertainment of members.*

OPPOSITE, BOTTOM: *A last minute check by a staff member, as yet another showtime nears in the (old) auditorium.*

SOUTHS JUNIORS BALLET

was made in the magazine of the club's slogan: 'The Best for the Best.' Through the late '60s and early '70s life was very much 'going on' at the club notwithstanding the storm that lay ahead.

Life was often eventful, although there were events that the magazine chose not to mention:

Darcy Lawler's 'catch' of a man named John James Warren as Warren tampered with poker machines at the club one night. The secretary-manager subsequently found himself in the headlines when it was revealed that Warren was alleged to have murdered two Sydney men in 1966.

The brief closing of the club on a November evening in 1970 when 600 workers went on strike to protest over the club manage-

THE WAY WE WERE

ment's sacking of four fellow-workers. Between 4 000 and 5 000 people who had come to see the Howard Keel Show had to be turned away.

The club's unsuccessful battle in 1970 to stage a pantomime (Cinderella) for the enjoyment of the children of the district — a plan stymied by the strict application of the licensing laws. The panto was to have starred Little Pattie and children, who would have entered the club by special rear steps, would have been given Christmas gifts, free chips, sweets and soft drinks. 'Clubs Can't Play Santa Claus' read the *Mirror's* large headline on the story.

In the eventual aftermath of the publishing of Justice Moffitt's report in 1974 — although with no haste — Wally Dean was eventually left with no choice but to step down as chairman of the Juniors, to be replaced, briefly, by long-serving director Len Hart. Earlier, in '74 (on January 30) Dean had been re-elected chairman of the Board after a long and bitter struggle for power. A reform group led by Bill Sheedy and Ray Vawdon campaigned vigorously to unseat Dean and his fellow directors. In the final count the retiring Board members (Messrs Dean, Hart, Henderson, Cracknell, Shannon, Johnson and Kilcran) were returned with more than a 1 000 vote majority, with 6 000 proxy votes supporting the incumbent Board proving vital. The previous month, the annual election of Board members was ruled invalid by the NSW Equity Court over the use of proxy votes. It was claimed that 'bunny girls' were used to secure votes. Pictured with a celebratory beer in hand after being re-elected Dean said: 'This Board has made the club the biggest in the world with a $50 million turnover in the last seven years.'

The election was a boots 'n' all affair (see following chapter). Darcy Lawler railed to the annual meeting of December 1973: 'There have been many adverse press reports and there were even suggestions that the ballot box from the recent elections had been confiscated and taken to the police station. This is a slur on my character and on my accountant Mr Murphy, and we have taken out writs against the papers concerned.' (Long-serving accountant Cliff Murphy was regarded as a great contributor to the Juniors' cause. Henry Morris has called his contribution 'magnificent'.)

Years before the gathering storm of 1973–74, in May 1967, some five months after he had quit Souths for good, George Wintle had dropped bombshells galore in a hard-hitting overview of the Sydney club industry — a forerunner to the eventual Royal Commission.

Wintle went public declaring: 'The graft and corruption in clubs would shock you.' He added that the amount involved in expenses by committeemen and directors of licensed clubs 'would stun you'. Wintle said he knew of one club where free meals for directors and their friends in one month amounted to $1 200. Said Wintle: 'They drink special Scotch whisky. I know one fellow who has a better office than Dr Coombs of the Commonwealth Bank. Only recently a chap told me about food-stuffs he went to sell to a certain club. A director said: 'I'll pay you for 25 cases, but only deliver 24; I want the other one'.' Wintle called on the Government to protect club life. 'It is big business now and there should be more stringent regulations, particularly covering the financial side of it.' Wintle said he believed wrongdoing was becoming 'the rule, rather than the exception' in clubs. 'I am ashamed of it,' he said. Approached by a newspaper, Wally Dean declined to comment on the claims.

Described years later in one newspaper as having been one of the 'movers and shakers' of Sydney life, Dean disappeared from public view for lengthy periods after his naming in the Royal Commission and subsequent exit at the Juniors. In 1977 he was declared bankrupt in the Federal Court, owing $10 042, an order subsequently extended to 1986. In 1978 the papers carried reports of his arrest on the Gold Coast over $2 000 in unpaid fines. Dean involved himself with the football club the Gold Coast Pirates in his time in Queensland. The eventual re-appearance of Wally Dean in Sydney came not long after police revealed they had 'strong information' that he had become the victim of an underworld killing. Three years later *Sun-Herald* reporter, Nancy Berryman, found him at work in Maroubra, earning $100 a week as a part-time barber. She wrote of his fall from grace: 'Now Dean says he can't get a job, and can't get back into the Australian Labor Party. The ALP expelled him in 1974 for breaking a party pledge. He resigned from South Sydney Council without ALP approval.' Dean maintained in the interview he had done nothing wrong. 'I've never been involved in drugs and I've never had any convictions.' He claimed he was the only person to have suffered from the findings of the Moffitt Royal Commission. 'I've been made a scapegoat. There hasn't been one person arrested or charged by the Crown over that Royal Commission.' He described the Royal Commission as 'a joke' – 'a piece of political propaganda'. He admitted then, as later, that businesses in which he had had an interest prospered with Souths Juniors as a preferred client — but insisted everything was legal and fair. Dean had been back in Sydney then (1981) for 10 months after living for several years on the Gold Coast under an assumed name.

Eastern Herald journalist, Darren Horrigan, described the former chairman colourfully when he unearthed him 10 years later (1991): 'When the city clubs were at their peak, Mr Dean was the boss of Sydney's biggest. He frequently carried a gun and was often accompanied by a bodyguard. At different times president and chairman of the South Sydney Junior Rugby League Club, an alderman on both the Sydney and South Sydney Councils, an Australian Labor Party numbers counter and a man with many powerful friends, he was, in the traditions of the Irish Catholics in Australia, someone to know (wink, wink).' Horrigan reported that in the wake of the 1974 Royal Commission, Dean had 'lost his self-esteem, his energy and many people he regarded as friends. Most hurtfully of all he lost his ALP membership. This was when Wally Dean virtually disappeared.'

Tough, confident, and widely described by some associates as 'an affable man' (Sydney journalist Warren Owens tagged him a 'rogue'; another interviewee for this book called him 'good hearted' and 'a loveable rogue'). Dean was still on the front foot, notwithstanding all that had happened. Henry Morris, who had known him for years, told of the good qualities of a complex character: 'Actually, Wally had a heart of gold,' said Morris. 'He was a bloke with feeling; if he could help you … do you a good turn, he would.'

In the interview with Owens, Dean's own views were tinged with bitterness: 'The biggest mistake of my life was running around with ex-policemen,' he said. 'There's plenty I could say about some bloody coppers running around Sydney now … I just want to go for a job on an even footing with the next bloke, without the whispers haunting me. I want a fair go.' Says ex-Mascot secretary Berkely Burns of him: 'I'll tell you what … he was

OPPOSITE: *The Souths premiership squad of 1969, runners-up to Balmain: Back row, left to right: Arthur Branighan, Gary Stevens, Bob Honan, Kerry Burke, Bob Moses, Ron Coote, John O'Neill, Mike Cleary, Ray Branighan, Paul Sait. Front row: Elwyn Walters, Brian James, Bob McCarthy, John Sattler (capt), Denis Pittard, Bob Grant, Eric Simms.*

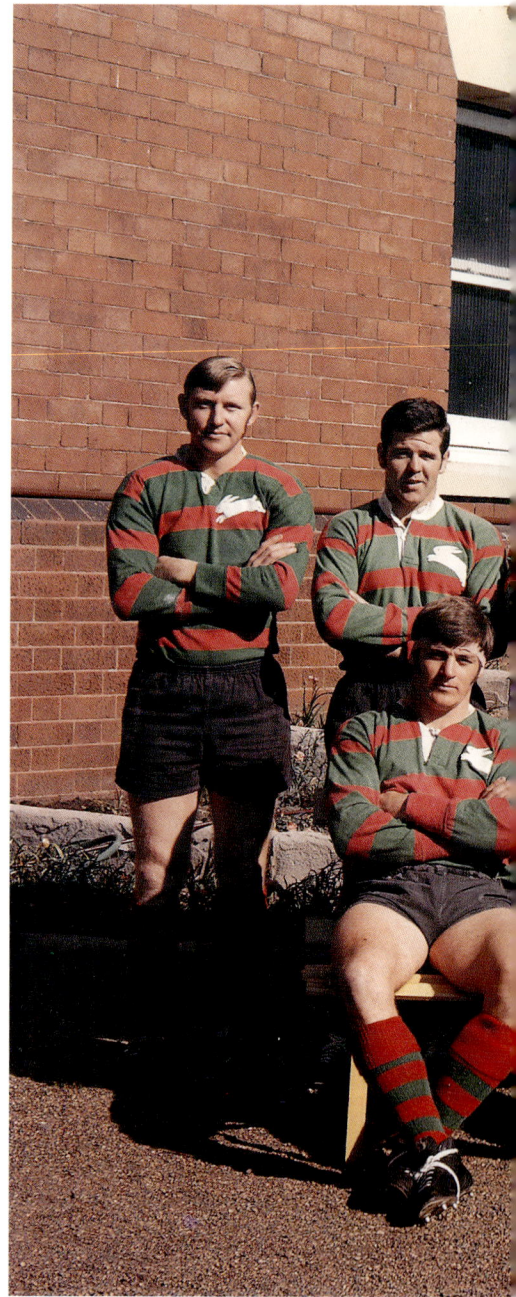

a good-hearted bloke. I could name a couple of blokes that he saved over the years. There was always something happening around Wally. He used to say: 'If a cat had kittens … they'd blame me."

His passion for the football side of the operation — in which he had his beginnings — never dimmed. In 1969, Wally Dean wrote with some pride: 'South Sydney Junior Rugby League has given the senior South Sydney football club a $130,000 present. Souths three grades are studded with products from the Junior League, but the sum mentioned is a

reasonable estimate of what the five [sic] big guns — Eric Simms, Ray and Arthur Branighan, Ron Coote, Paul Sait and Bob McCarthy — would be worth on the transfer market today. We are proud of the impact these men have made in the senior ranks. The development of these players is testimony to the fine organisation that is the South Sydney Junior League, and to the support it gets from the licensed club ... Driving through the district on any Saturday, Sunday or holiday as some 4 000 youngsters play organised football — and one feels satisfaction in knowing that his or her club has played a leading role in making it possible.'

Noted Sydney sports scribe, Geoff Prenter, in recalling a story about the enigmatic Dean in 1999 — labelled him 'a bloke with a heart as big as himself ... for all his faults'. When Prenter was a young journalist on the Sydney *Sun* he ran into a spot of financial bother. 'I bumped into Wally at a function at the Juniors and happened to mention my plight to him in conversation,' said Prenter. 'He was there in his pinstripe suit ... looking like one of the 'Mob'. He asked me how much money I needed — and I told him around two thousand pounds. 'Meet me outside the Sebel Townhouse next Thursday,' said Wally.'

'I was there on the appointed day — and in my mind's eye I can still picture the black stretch limo pulling up across from the hotel, its windows darkened. One of them lowered an inch or two and a finger beckoned me. 'Get in the back,' said a voice when I went over to the car. I was pretty shaky I can tell you. I wondered if I'd written something that had upset Wally and his pals. But Wally was in the back of the limo, amiable as ever. 'Good to see you Geoff,' he said. 'We're just going down to Primo's (a fancy restaurant at Elizabeth Bay) ... come along with us.'

So Prenter joined Dean and some others, long forgotten, at a luncheon at which, according to the journo — 'nothing was spared'. Eventually Wally got around to the subject at hand. 'Geoff, about this 2000 pounds,' he said. Prenter picks up the story: 'I honestly didn't know what was to come ... I presumed it would be some kind of dark scheme. But in fact Wally offered me a very kind deal that couldn't possibly have been more legitimate. 'We're thinking of bringing out a magazine,' he said. 'We'd like to offer you a contract to edit the magazine for us; hopefully it will help you out of your problem, too.'

Leading Sydney sports scribe Geoff Prenter had dealings with Souths president Wally Dean and labelled him: 'A bloke with a heart as big as himself ... for all his faults.'

Says Prenter today: 'I was relieved … and greatly appreciative at the same time. The whole thing sort of summed up Wally Dean. Probably he had ambitions to be a bigtime 'heavy' … but he was never going to be that. He was too kind … I know that he helped plenty of people.'

Walter James 'Wally' Dean whose presidency of Souths Juniors represented one of the most colourful and controversial periods in the history of Sydney clubland.

The benevolent side of Wally Dean shines through in such items in the archives as the 'Weekly Newsletter' of February 8, 1974. With NSW country districts suffering bad flooding, the Juniors dug deep. And in Dean's frontpage message to members, there is a sense of real pride. '$2000 Special Appeal for Flood Relief Fund' read the large type. 'Juniors well to the Fore.' The item continued: 'The Directors and Management wish to thank members who got whole-heartedly behind their suggestion to aid this worthy cause and we take great pleasure in announcing that the magnificent sum of $2000 has been forwarded to the appeal.'

When in his 60s, bespectacled, with his hair thinning, the enigmatic Wally Dean came back to the Juniors after the lost years — in the late 1990s. He would visit the club from time to time — now just a face in the crowd — the days when he was 'the boss' long since gone. Viewed from a detached perspective … and whatever the full truth of it, the aftermath of the Wally Dean era was not a happy time for South Sydney Junior Leagues Club. The club's name was dragged through the mud and very publicly. Down the track — in 1975 — lay the payoff, the truly shocking day when the club lost its licence because of all that had gone on … or seemed that it might have.

SLICES OF LIFE AT THE JUNIORS

ALBERT CLIFT

Albert Clift's career in South Sydney's junior league competition was by any standards brief — and modest in achievement. Albert played for St Peters Surry Hills, and in June 1922 was called up to Souths Thirds. In first game of the 1923 season he badly dislocated a shoulder. Each time Clift tried a return to the field after that he would dislocate the shoulder. Finally he retired — and it was from that point that his great contribution to the South Sydney cause began. Albert never stopped working for the club in some way or other. He was Souths timekeeper for 36 years and behind his house in Mascot built an amazing 'Souths Museum' full of footballing treasures — one man's priceless gesture to the club he loved.

BOB McCARTHY — A MEMORY OF GEORGE WINTLE

'I remember a day in 1963 when Judy (later Mrs McCarthy) and I were sitting on the hill at Redfern one Sunday afternoon, watching the Juniors. George Wintle came around with one of those big old ice cream bags. 'Can I get you something Mr McCarthy?' he said. 'Aw, no … I'm pretty right thanks George,' I said. 'How about Judy … would she like an ice cream or something?' said George. Well, Judy didn't want an ice cream, but she said to him: 'You wouldn't have a chocolate there, would you?' George didn't have any chocolate but he asked Judy what she wanted — 'just a block of chocolate'. 'Don't worry … just get it next time around,' she said. But George was off like a shot. 'Mind that,' he said — and left his ice cream bag with us. Then he walked all the way around to the other side of the ground, to the shop — and came back with the chocolate. As I paid him the two bob, I thought: 'How good a worker is this bloke?' There was no way George was going to lose the sale.'

BOB McCARTHY

'I remember being at the door of the club one day when a well-dressed woman came in. 'Excuse me lady,' said George. 'Would you mind straightening the seams of your stockings. You know it's very, very ladylike to have your seams straight.' George used to watch the main room like a hawk. If you weren't playing the poker machines he'd be just as likely to say: 'Joe Bloggs, do you like this club?' The bloke would invariably answer 'yes'. 'Well, if you like the club,' George would say, 'would you mind playing the poker machines?' He didn't mind embarrassing someone — but his motivation was honest enough. George knew that if people played the poker machines the club would thrive. If they didn't it would struggle.'

ABOVE: *Bob McCarthy, who rose through the Juniors' ranks to stardom, evades the tackle of Great Britain's Jimmy Thompson in the third Test of the 1970 series, at the Sydney Cricket Ground.*

IF YOU'RE GOING TO PLAY BILLIARDS …

When the new billiard room was opened in the club in the 1960s — there were rules set down, just as there were everywhere else in George Wintle's Juniors. George's rules for billiard players, set out in the news-sheet were:

BELOW: *The club billiard room, over which George Wintle imposed strict rules in the 1960s. Included was — 'don't act the lair … it's a gentleman's game'.*

- Don't smoke over tables. Ruin a cloth and it's 70 quid.
- Don't place beer glasses on table edge and don't drink over tables.
- Don't misuse the cues by trying to straighten them over your knee or the back of your neck.
- Don't lean cues against walls. Place in rack.
- Don't swear or behave offensively.
- Don't gamble. We are licensed to have poker machines, not to bet on billiards.
- Don't hog the table.
- Don't act the lair. It's a gentleman's game.

FLOWERY WORDS

The licensed club's passion for the junior football it so staunchly supported, never flagged. The club magazine of October 2, 1970 noted: 'Our junior league grand finals were played last weekend at Redfern Oval and the weather man was not very kind to us. But despite this, the standard of football was what you would expect from Souths Juniors — higher than self-raising flour.'

Comedian Lucky Grills was a popular figure in the immense passing parade of the 'shows' at the Juniors over the years.

THE WAY WE WERE

If only things had stayed this way ... In February 1971, the costs of drinks in the auditorium were:

- Beer (10 oz) — 18 cents
- Fancy drinks — 45 cents
- Liqueurs (1oz) — 36 cents
- Scotch (1oz) — 36 cents
- Scotch (1/2 oz) — 13 cents
- Whisky (Aust — 1oz) — 19 cents
- Whisky (Aust — 1/2 oz) — 11 cents
- Vodka (1oz) — 18 cents
- Vodka (1/2 oz) — 10 cents
- Gin (1oz) — 17 cents
- Gin (1/2 oz) — 9 cents.

NOW, THAT'S TALENT!

Sunday Sportsmen's Mornings were popular at the club for a time, allowing the boys to gather for a beer and some fun.

The entertainment for one such show in November 1971 was:

Johnny 'Rubber' Craig, the Duo Andelos, Herbie Marks, Maria Venuti, Lucky Grills ... and 'the remarkable talents of Simone & Monique'. There was no further explanation.

YOU'RE NEVER TOO OLD TO BE A JUNIOR

In an edition of the club newsletter in 1970 it was noted that an application to join the club had been received from a Mrs Bourke of Bathurst, who had family in Maroubra. 'This in itself doesn't seem remarkable,' noted the journal editor, 'but when you hear that the lady in question is 102 years old, that really stops you in your tracks. The directors in their wisdom decided to bestow honorary membership on the grand old lady. Director Frank Kilcran did the honours and made the presentation, after which she replied, 'I am now going to have a go on the pokies." It was a story with a happy ending: Mrs Bourke struck a $24 jackpot!

ABOVE, LEFT: *Equipped with all the necessary gear, and coached by men who know their stuff, youngsters playing in Souths Juniors learn about the game and its culture the right way.*

LEFT: *They tread where Churchill has trod … and Rayner, Coote, McCarthy and all the rest. Youngsters running out for a big game at Redfern follow the footsteps of Rabbitoh history.*

ABOVE: *The great Johnny 'Chook' Raper. Perc Horne tipped very early that Ron Coote would replace him as Australia's top lock forward.*

OPPOSITE PAGE, TOP: *Cilla Black was one of the many big stars who made the trek from England to the club at Kingsford.*

OPPOSITE PAGE, BELOW: *The Kessler twins, looking very '70s' — a glamorous and popular act.*

THE RIGHT STUFF

In 1965, when he was 74, the man who did more than anyone to get Souths Junior League off the ground in the early days, Percy Horne, cast an eye over the talent in the juniors, and gave his verdict. Perc's words could probably have applied to any era of South Sydney junior football — although history has proven the period of the early to mid '60s very special indeed for the district. Perc declared there was 'excellent timber in the young saplings' then playing in the juniors, and declared:

'There are some amongst them who will be spoken of in the future as outstanding players,' he said. 'They have everything that they need to take them to the top. They have ability and most importantly, opportunities for being coached by men who are great footballers in their own right and through their own abilities.' Among the promising players, Perc pointed to Bobby McCarthy — 'with the potential to go to the top' — and Ronnie Coutt [sic] — 'an outstanding player who in the future will take Johnny Raper's place at lock forward'. 'There are many others in who I have the greatest faith,' said Perc.

The old man offered final words of advice to the crop of young players: 'League is a grand career for any young man. But there are two main provisions for success. You must train hard, because to play league properly, you must be supremely fit. You must have a job, not only in case you fail to make the grade or are forced out through injury but as a standby when football days are over. Then, if your form holds, the world is your oyster.'

THAT'S ENTERTAINMENT!

It was never a cheap operation to get the 'right' people to fill the auditorium on show nights. A glance at the records for 1973–74–75 indicates the immense costs involved, even then — almost a quarter of a century ago. In 1973 top-priced acts included Max Bygraves ($21 500), Dale Robertson and Joe Fingers Carr ($17 500 weekly), Jerry Vale ($17 000), Mexican Fiesta ($19 500), Sounds of Young Hawaii ($14 000).

The weekly rates for some of the top artists in 1974 included Frank Ifield ($10 500), The Minstrel Show ($13 500), Dorothy Squires ($12 000), Norman Wisdom ($17 500), Max Bygraves ($21 500).

In 1975: Howard Keel, four weeks ($60 000), Frank Gorshin, four weeks ($62 000), Bottoms Up, six weeks ($105 000), Kessler Twins, four weeks ($40 000).

In 1976: Dick Emery ($24 000 per week), Cilla Black ($31 000), Jane Powell ($17 000), Frankie Howerd ($16 000), Brian Henderson Bandstand with stars ($10 000).

The deal signed with Top Artists Promotions for 1975–76 to provide entertainment for the club was of $650 000 a year, 'or such further amount as may be agreed by the Board of Directors of the club'. At the time of the 1974 entertainment salaries listing in Board minutes, secretary-manager Lawler had his salary raised from $343 weekly to $400; assistant secretary-manager Norm Christie went from $241 to $300.

COUNTING THE CASH

'Fountains of Gold' — another chapter in the ongoing saga of the gaming machines that have been part of the Juniors' story since the beginning. Over the years the machines have played their part in enabling the club to provide brilliant amenities for members — and vast support to local community organisations.

In evidence given to the Metropolitan Licensing Court in November 1975, when the club's licence was under threat, Souths Juniors' solicitor, Cliff Murphy, gave a revealing insight into procedures for collection of poker machine money in that era. Murphy told the court how the machines were cleared every day at the close of business. 'The first step for the last couple of years has been remove the drawer from the bottom of the machine where the money has fallen — and to pour it into a plastic container — which is resting on a set of scales. The money is weighed and the individual weight of every machine — the whole of the 454 throughout the club — is recorded. There are at least three persons as witnesses; the person who removes the money, one girl who sits directly in front of the machine to accurately assess the weight, and one other. After the individual recording has been

made the money is poured into a lockable cash tin as they move from one machine to another. As the cash tin becomes filled, the lock is slammed home and it is delivered under the eye of a guard on a trolley to the cash room, where once again the whole cash tin is weighed and its weight recorded before it is put into a safe and locked up for the night. The following morning the principal cash room employee enters the cash room, invariably under the eye of or in the company of a guard, and he opens the safe and removes the cash tins for counting, but as he removes each box from the safe he individually weighs the box and records it on a separate sheet, different from the sheet that was prepared the previous evening by a different employee. He records the weight of every box that is removed from the safe.' Murphy told how the weight sheet was later compared with the weight sheet from the previous evening.

Think of a sport — and you'll find it at the Juniors. Here the Karate class is pictured in full swing.

INTRA-WARS

Two of the intra-clubs — Bridge and Karate — were at loggerheads in 1973. Problem was they both used the intra-club room on the same night — the Bridge crowd the carpeted end and Karate the parquetry end of the room. Noise from the Karate crowd upset the Bridge-ers to such an extent that they officially complained to the Board. Darcy Lawler subsequently forwarded a letter to the Karate Club requesting that their members practise as silently as possible. The matter is not mentioned again in club minutes.

POKIE RORTS

On Thursday, March 15, 1973, seven poker machine mechanics were apprehended for illegally taking money from machines. Police were called and the offenders were charged.

CHAPTER 5

THE STRUGGLE WITHIN

The period from late 1973 to May 1975 when Wally Dean stepped down as chairman, was a watershed in the history of Souths Juniors. To draw on a weather analogy, the conditions were 'cyclonic' much of the time. The challenge mounted to the incumbent Board in 1973 by a reform group determined to change the way of things at the club led to a furious battle for power. On the return of the Board after the first round of elections on November 30, December 1 and 2, the reform group challenged the outcome in the Equity Court — and eventually had the result declared invalid.

Seething with rumour and turbulent feelings, and seriously polarised by the battle, the club's membership group was asked to vote again (12,648 voted) — on Tuesday, January 29. Again the sitting Board of seven, led by Wally Dean, was returned to office. Again the reform group, led by Denis Leslie Ryan challenged — before Justice Holland in the Equity Court. Wally Dean, his star waning, polled lowest of the seven incumbent Board members with 6760 — but was still clearly ahead of the reform group's Ryan who was next on 5646. Frank Kilcran topped the ballot with 8627 votes. A motion was passed to destroy the ballot papers in the wake of the election — this apparently in defiance of a court order restraining the club from damaging or destroying the papers …

Within days the matter was back in court, with a barrister, Mr FS McClary QC claiming in the Equity Court that the destroyed

papers concealed 'significant irregularities' and were burned after a motion passed at a 'stacked' meeting. McClary claimed there was evidence of fraudulent malpractice and false voting. Meanwhile, there were sensational headlines:

KILL THREAT TO CLUB CHIEF — shouted a major story in the *Daily Mirror*. The story read: 'Threats have been made against the lives of Darcy Lawler and Wally Dean, the two leading figures running South Sydney Junior Leagues Club. Mr Lawler, the club's secretary-manager, early today received an anonymous call threatening to 'blow your head off' after the announcement of the club's disputed election results. Overnight, the *Daily Mirror* switchboard operator received two other calls, threatening to 'blow up Wally Dean's house' and to 'blast Lawler out of office.'

Lawler told the paper: 'Some cur rang me at about 5.30 and asked if the old committee had won the election. When I replied they had won easily, this man said, 'I'll blow your head off.' 'Lawler told the *Mirror* that his wife had also received threats during the power struggle at the club. The secretary-manager left no doubt where his loyalties lay: 'The [old] Board have made this the best-run club in Australia, and possibly the world,' he said.

Darcy Lawler — 'Some cur rang me at about 5.30 and asked if the old committee had won the election. When I replied they had won easily, this man said, 'I'll blow your head off'. Feelings at the club ran at white heat at times during the 1960s and '70s.

Henry Morris tells another story reflecting just how tough and dirty it got at times back then. He remembers the time that a car belonging to Johnny Willis — a member of the group opposing the establishment at the Juniors, was blown up. 'He was a beautiful bloke, Johnny,' says Morris. 'He'd run for everything bar Miss Australia. I wish I had a tenth of his personality. Well, in the midst of all the dramas someone blew his car up … and it made the papers, of course. They were tough times. I think most of us knew who was responsible.'

It was to be another nine months before the elections of late January 1974 were eventually ruled to have been valid. During a 25-day hearing, 85 witnesses were called — and the judgment exceeded 100 pages. Mr Justice Holland found that the club had discharged its responsibility and that a new election was not justified. The judge found that Denis Ryan had failed to establish his case which included claims that the election was invalidated by fraudulent malpractices, false voting, bias, intimidation, wrongful admission of votes, wrongful use of company's funds, misconduct and other improprieties.

More drama followed. At a meeting in late November Wally Dean recommended that the participants from the reform group involved in the Equity Court action, should be cited to appear before the Board to show reason why they should not be expelled from the club. More headlines followed as the press got wind of the move and quizzed Darcy Lawler. The five men involved were Messrs Vawdon, Ryan, Dyke, Sheery and Ford. Reported the *Sydney Morning Herald*: 'The five men told a *Herald* reporter on Thursday night after they had been escorted from the club, that they were banned from the club pending a decision on their expulsion.'

Meanwhile, Wally Dean was re-elected chairman of the Board, unopposed, notwithstanding the events of a significantly traumatic year, and the sitting Board members returned to office, despite a further challenge by some members of the 1973—74 reform group. The Reform Group candidates Merv Colbron, Bob Dyke, Denis Ryan and Ray Vawdon promised 'better club administration' and campaigned on a number of grounds:

- an increase in the financial support given to clubs in the Junior League;
- a better deal for poker machine players in the Juniors;
- improved standards of catering;
- a review of the club's heavy expenditure on entertainment (which was up around $1.2 million pa).

It was in early 1975 that Henry Morris was asked to the accept the position of caretaker director — the first small step towards his long and fruitful reign as club chairman.

Remarkably, the minutes of the 1974 annual meeting at which the incumbent Board hung on to power make no mention of the Moffitt Royal Commission Report, of which the club's activities had commanded 20 000 words. The cloud hanging over members of the reform group and their ongoing memberships of the club eventually lifted with a decision that 'no further action be taken' settling the matter at the Board meeting of January 30, 1975. This meeting also signalled the end for the 5 cent poker machine in Souths Juniors. Darcy Lawler told the meeting that the 5 cent machine was 'no longer a paying proposition' — and it was agreed that the 50 5 cent machines would be replaced by 32 of 10 cents and 18 of 20 cents.

And it was on that same night in January that Henry Morris took the first small step that led eventually to his long and productive reign as chairman of the club. On

FROM LEFT TO RIGHT: *Ossie Rae, Ron Ellison (behind), Les Haggett, Wally Dean, Darcy Lawler — a photo from the mid 1970s.*

Brian Shannon's announcement that he had made the decision to retire from the Board for reasons of ill-health, Morris was asked to accept the position of caretaker director. Henry Morris agreed, the move rubber-stamped by his letter of acceptance in the days that followed.

In the early months of 1975 the club was under considerable pressure, with members of the Board systematically subjected to long 'grilling' sessions by members of the licensing police. Transcripts of many such interviews exist in the club archives, and they leave no doubt that the club's directors were 'put through the wringer' in the interviews conducted at Police Headquarters, College Street. The interrogation of Wally Dean by Detective Inspector BD Taylor makes intriguing reading. To most questions the club chairman gave a two-word answer — 'no comment'. The final exchange is this:

Taylor: 'Well Mr Dean, it would appear to me that you do not intend to answer any questions. Is that the position?' Dean: 'I believe I have the right to answer questions or not — as I see fit.'

Taylor: 'I can see no good purpose in pursuing these matters further. Are you prepared to read and sign this record of interview?'

Dean: 'I will read it.'

Wally Dean's days as chairman had probably always been numbered since Justice Moffitt's scathing judgments in his Royal Commission papers. They were changing times at the club: in October 1974, Lionel Abrahams who had headed up the entertainment recruitment for the Juniors, resigned. In mid-May the next year, Dean called a meeting of the directors, at short notice. Thanking them for attendance at such short notification, Dean tendered his resignation as chairman of South Sydney Junior Leagues Club, citing 'pressure of business and family commitments'. He said that the decision had been a difficult one and he trusted that the club would continue to prosper in the future, as it had done in the past. He then handed Darcy Lawler his letter of resignation.

The final minutes-note on the Dean Years is brief — in no way conveying the sense of drama that must have existed in the room that night. It reads:

'The directors thanked Mr Dean for the work, time and effort he had put into the club during the past nine years and they hoped that his future private and business life would be happy and successful. Mr Dean left the meeting at 6.25pm.'

And that was that. With Darcy Lawler in the chair nominations were called for chairman and then, vice-chairman. Long-serving Len Hart (chairman), a safety officer at the Total Oil Refinery, and Frank Kilcran (deputy chairman) were duly elected, unopposed. Viv Wemyss was telephoned from the Board room and asked if he would accept the position of caretaker director. He told the conveyer of the request, Darcy Lawler, that he would be honoured to take the position.

With the Licensing Board investigation pressing down on all in charge at the club, these were intensely difficult times. The 'new' Board, with Hart as chairman proved to be only an interim structure. Within the year the Board — or most of its members — was swept away in the wave of concern and discontent that followed the announcement of December 12, 1975 ... that Souths Juniors, the biggest and best club in the business had lost its licence.

The news carried by the Daily Telegraph *of December 4, 1975 was dramatic and bad — the club had effectively lost its licence.*

Big Leagues club loses its licence

DT 4/12/75

The Licensing Court refused yesterday to renew the South Sydney Junior Rugby Leagues Club's licence.

The club, with 51,000 members, is Australia's largest.

After the Licensing Magistrate, Mr T. Ratcliffe, SM, had announced his reserved decision, the club president, Mr L. Hart, said an appeal would be lodged.

Mr Hart said the club would continue to trade until the appeal had been heard.

The secretary-manager of the club, Mr Lawler, said:

"Naturally, I'm very disappointed in the decision."

Mr Lawler said he was particularly disappointed because the decision had been given on "technicalities."

"Not one cent is missing," he said.

Mr Ratcliffe found proved all the Metropoli-

Mr Dean

tan Licensing Inspector's grounds of objection to renewal of the club's certificate of registration.

He referred in his decision to activities of a former club president, Mr Walter James Dean, and his association with companies that had dealings with the club.

He also referred to sums of money the club had paid out without first obtaining the board's approval.

Broken

The Metropolitan Licensing Inspector's grounds of objection were:

THAT certain club rules had been habitually broken,

THAT persons derived benefits and advantages from the club not shared

MUSICALLY SPEAKING

Lionel Huntington has been musical director and bandleader at the club for more than 30 years — a Rock of Gibraltar through good times and bad. Drummer Alan Gilbert is not far behind in the longevity stakes, joining in 1968 — and being still there, driving the rhythm section as the club's 40th birthday approached. Music and entertainment has been part of the Juniors' 'way' in club life since the very beginning. Here, Lionel and Alan share some musical memories:

LH: I started in 1964 — in Terry King's band downstairs, as a casual muso. We played on Friday and Saturday nights for a dance down in the corner. The 'sharp end' of the club we called it. A guy named Mal Lowe had a band playing on the first floor, at the top of where the escalators are now. What happened was that Mal Lowe's piano player left and he asked me if I would join his band. Mal, who was bandleader and drummer didn't read music — so he came to rely very heavily on me with the 'acts'. Subsequently he had a falling out with Wintle — George reckoned he was charging too much. As a result, at the end of 1966 they auditioned bands for the job — and in February 1967 I took over as bandleader at the club. I've been there ever since. When I first started I had a ten-piece band — two trumpets and a trombone, three saxes, piano, bass and drums and guitar.

AG: In late 1966 I was in the Rocky Thomas band and we auditioned at the Juniors, one of three or four bands. It was 12 months or so later that I joined Lionel's band — around August 1968.

LH: Those were the halcyon years — from 1967 to the end of the '60s. We used to do Thursday and Friday nights — two Saturday and two Sunday shows. These

Over the years the Lionel Huntington Orchestra has featured many of the city's finest musicians. Here Lionel (in front), introduces the band — left to right: Alan Gilbert, Jack Thorncraft, Roy Ainsworth, Dick Lowe, Doug Foskett, Ray Bensted, Don Wright, Jack Iversen, Neville Blanchett (obscured), Norm Wyatt.

SOUTHS JUNIORS BAND

days we're down to a Friday and Saturday night, with an occasional extra show. All the musicians in the band now have other jobs; Alan teaches at Scots' College. Gordon White was the booking agent when I started here — following Mal Lowe — then Richard Gray, then Lionel Abrahams, the Sadler brothers Len and Hugh (Vidette Productions Pty Ltd, at the club from 1972), then Nigel Lampe of WTS Entertainment.

AG: It was during the Sadler period (in the early 1990s) that they started to charge people at the door to attend shows. Twenty dollars. It lasted about six months.

LH: It half emptied the room — and we had a real job trying to get people back. Once people get out of the habit it's not easy to win them back. The club has always had continuous entertainment on both floors — and sometimes the Oldtime Dance band working downstairs as well. That's been great for the musicians — and great for the club over the years. When

The Lionel Huntington orchestra — dressed to kill. Left to right: Lionel Huntington (on piano, holding one of their Mo awards), Alan Gilbert (drums), Jack Iversen (trumpet), George Brodbeck (trombone), Leon Gaer (bass), Paul Baker (guitar), Lee Hutchins (sax).

we have a really good show on, the place is packed. When the auditorium is not so full — times when the show is not so good … which is not often — you can go downstairs and the likelihood is that there won't be many people in the club. People beget people. They want to go where other people are — and if there is a good show on, the word spreads.

LH: The club has had a go at most things over the years. There was a Saturday night disco for a time, but it brought in a lot of riff-raff. There were brawls upstairs every Saturday — and after a while they stopped the disco. There was a piano bar at one stage too — with a girl named Paula Hibbard playing piano. That was classy, and popular.

LH: Early on, I worked with George Wintle. He always treated me fairly and with respect, although he was a guy that many people didn't like. He was a harsh man — and he will be the first one to tell you that.

AG: Hines, Hines & Dad were about the most sensational act we worked with early on. That's Gregory Hines the actor, quite a big star in Hollywood now. He came out with his younger brother and father — a song and dance act … they were extremely good tap dancers. We've worked with so many people … just about every Australian act there's ever been. And people like Howard Keel, Kathryn Grayson, Winnie Atwell, Dick Emery, Neil Sedaka — he did a live recording with us. I remember the African Ballet … the guys used to piss on their drums out the back to make the skins tighter. It is not a regular practice among drummers.

LH: In very early days one of the first acts that worked on the first floor was the Bee Gees — at a time when one of them was too young to go into clubs.

AG: They were very precocious.

LH: I wish there was a stronger word for it. Their music then was very ordinary — but they were the first ones to criticise the band. The egos were very, very big. The father was the driving force behind them. Johnny O'Keefe was another singer who used to work at the club back then.

LH: There was the Cherry Blossom Revue from Japan and a bloke called the Rubber Man who was so desperate to stay in Australia that he threw himself under a bus. It stopped in time, but he subsequently disappeared — and so did half the company. They had all decided they wanted to stay in Australia. That happened with some Russians who came out too.

LH: Norman Wisdom was a big hit. He used to have a straight man

'Oooo you are awful … but I like you!' The outrageous Dick Emery was an immensely popular visitor to the club.

Buddy Greco brought his cool style to the club in the 1990s — and wooed the fans.

with him — a tall, bald bloke who would not crack a smile all the way through the act. It was hilarious — Wisdom would do everything he could to make him laugh, and the audience would be in tears. But the guy just wouldn't crack a smile.

LH: We had the occasional drama. A guy came up the backstairs one night toting a gun and there were some fisticuffs [in interviews for the book there emerged other references to this incident, of 'cold steel' being pressed to the temple of a high profile performer one night]. And there have been one or two acts over the years who have been quite painful to work for — but I must say there are very few indeed that I didn't enjoy working with. The more professional a person is — the easier it is to work with them. The art of working with a singer is to virtually get inside their head and breathe with them … get to know their personality. Kathryn Grayson was a case in point … a big star. She didn't bring out an MD and she didn't know what to do because she wasn't used to being in the situation of not having a director with her. Once I understood that she wanted me as a musical director, as a sort of security blanket — things worked out fine. Sometimes people surprise you. Buddy Greco was here this year … still playing great piano, but for some reason very unsure of himself. He was very nervous, and inevitably the nervousness washes off to an extent on the

American group The Coasters looked sharp and proved popular when they came to the Juniors.

people around. He was uncomfortable with himself — and there was this 'thing' going on the whole time he was here. The fact is that the acoustics are different in every room … the sound is different, the set-up is different and everything takes a while to settle in. You don't make crash judgments the first time you hear something. But that's exactly what Buddy Greco did.

AG: When you have been together as long as we have, you can suss things out pretty quickly. I don't think there is another band in the business that has stayed together as long as we have.

LH: We've lost a few over the years. Johnny Costello (trombone player) died and so did one of our sax players, big Doug Foskett. Doug was quite a character — they used to call him Dining Room Doug, Debonair Doug or Dashing Doug … a classy sort of guy who died much too young, of cancer. Then there was Kevin Balenzuela, otherwise known as 'Bicycle Wheels' because no-one could spell his name. He was a great saxophonist … a karate fanatic who swam just about every day … and died of a heart attack. He just had a bad heart.

LH: The room at the club (main auditorium) is a good one. Take everything off the band — the microphones etc — and play and it is acoustically a good room. But we are at the mercy of the sound technicians. But with all the different acts the one continual problem we have is to get the sound 'right'.

LH: By the way, we have won three Mo Awards. I think that means more to people in the business than it does to us — because whether we get that sort of recognition or not, we'd still be playing with as much enthusiasm as we do. We look at the award as 'just one of those things' — but no doubt it is coveted among other bands. The big thing about this band is that we can play for June Bronhill singing stuff from the operas — then we can make an instant switch to rock 'n' roll. It's a utility band, with parameters that are quite broad. In a situation like this we've got to be able to cover everyone who comes in. We've had whip-cracking acts … gun-twirling acts … the lot.

LEFT: *Elvis lives — at Souths Juniors! In gold lamé suit Elvis impersonator Max Pellicano looked exactly the part when he came to play.*

BELOW: *Roy Hawkins — popular with his re-visiting of 1950s rock 'n' roll.*

AG: I remember we had a ladder-climbing act one time. There was a bit of a mishap and they fell backwards and ripped the curtains.

LH: For a time the club ran 'Sportsmen's Mornings' on a Sunday. There was free booze on, and strippers, and the guys would be here in droves for a good old free drink and a perve.

AG: There got to be so many blokes coming along that they opened a room upstairs too. The acts used to have to go up top and entertain, then come down.

LH: After one Sunday morning when we had finished and packed and gone home, I had a phone call from Darcy Lawler (then secretary-manager). It seems that one of the strippers had decided to 'entertain' a few of the audience privately in the band room, out the back. Darcy had caught them in the act, so to speak. 'Where were you at 11 o'clock?' he asked me. 'I was here, at home,' I responded. 'Well, do any of your blokes know anything about what was going on backstage?' he asked. 'What are you talking about?' I said to him.

I think it's fair to say that life has rarely been dull at Souths Juniors.

CHAPTER 6

WINTER OF DISCONTENT

On June 12, 1975, Darcy Lawler as secretary of South Sydney Junior Rugby League Club Limited, made application for the renewal of the Certificate of Registration held by the club for its premises at 558A Anzac Parade, Kingsford. The Metropolitan Licensing Inspector objected to the granting of the application on the following grounds:

·   that certain rules of the club were habitually broken;
·   that persons had derived a benefit or advantage from the club which was not shared equally by every member;
·   that the financial affairs of the club were not under the control of the committee elected annually by the general body of members;
·   that correct books of account showing the financial affairs of the club had not been kept in relation to:
     (1) Loans by the club to employees
     (2) Loans by the club to Walter James Dean;

Wally Dean had been made a life member of the club in a manner contrary to Article 13 (b) of the Articles of Association of the club.

So began a winter of discontent for the club and its members — with genuine uncertainty now about the future of an organisation already rocked by the findings of the Royal Commission. The club's immediate fate lay in the hands of the Metropolitan Licensing Court.

OPPOSITE: *South Sydney Juniors Board of Directors, 1974–75.*

THE DIRECTORS

DARCY LAWLER
Secretary/Manager

LEN HART
Chairman of Board of Directors, Member of Committee of South Sydney District Junior Rugby Football League, Deputy Chairman Souths Juniors Bowling Club Director of N.S.W.R.L. Country Club and Narellan properties. Patron of Men's Golf Club, Men's and Ladies' Squash Clubs, Snowy Club and Water Ski Club.

NORM CHRISTIE
Assistant Secretary Manager

DENIS JOHNSON
Patron of Cricket, Darts, Snooker.

ARCH HENDERSON
Deputy Chairman of Board of Directors, Treasurer of South Sydney District Junior Rugby Football League, Director Souths Juniors Bowling Club. Patron of Men's Indoor Bowls and Table Tennis.

FRANK KILCRAN
Member of Committee of South Sydney District Junior Rugby Football League Patron of Ladies' Indoor Bowls, Camera Club, Karate, Old Time Dance.

HARRY CRACKNELL
Director Souths/Juniors Bowling Club Patron of Fishing, Swimming, Touch Football and Tennis.

HENRY MORRIS
Director Souths Juniors Bowling Club. Patron of Bridge, Canasta, Ladies' Golf and Theatre Club.

VIV WEMYSS
Member of Committee of South Sydney District Junior Rugby Football League Patron of Art Club.

4

Club officials present a cheque for $10 000 to Prince Henry Hospital for the Coronary Care Unit. Left to right — D Johnson, H Cracknell, L Hart (chairman), Mr F Campbell (treasurer and director of Hospital Group) and Prof R Blacket (Director of Medicine).

Business went on as normally as it could under the circumstances, but with an eye always to an uncertain future. All year it dragged, with the club's appearance before the Licensing Court to show cause why it should not have its licence revoked, not listed until November. In October, at the annual general meeting, the Board was returned to office, with Len Hart back as chairman. Finally the Licensing Court hearing kicked off in the early days of November — with each sitting keenly attended by members of the media, and the story unfolding daily in the press.

The headlines told the tale: 'Police object to renewal of leagues club licence'; 'Club cash paid out before approval, court told'; 'Chairman's name linked to suppliers'; 'Court told of lending operations in Sydney club'; 'Leagues club gave money without approval, court told'. And so on.

On December 3, 1975, came the fateful verdict. Having initially reserved his decision on completion of the taking of evidence, Licensing Magistrate Mr T Ratcliffe SM, announced that he was refusing to renew the club's licence. Mr Ratcliffe found proved all the Metropolitan Licensing Inspector's grounds of objection to the renewal of the club's certificate of registration. He referred to activities of former club president Wally Dean and his association with companies which had dealings with the club.

Mr Ratcliffe SM did not mince words, writing of: 'Chairman Dean, manipulating his fellow directors either with their conscious agreement or negligent acquiescence, to run the club for his personal aggrandisement both in relation to profitable venture for his companies, and as a private, interest-free banker.' He found the directors as being generally 'recreant in their duties … they allowed Dean to do as he wished' and chided Darcy

Lawler as 'not a good minute-secretary'.

Magistrate Ratcliffe's 12-page verdict concludes: 'I have come to the conclusion in all the circumstances that the relevant matters are not such as not to warrant the refusal of the grant of this application. Accordingly, I refuse the application for renewal.'

It was a stunning blow to the club. 'Naturally, I am very disappointed,' Darcy Lawler told the media, claiming the decision had been made on 'technicalities'. 'Not one cent is missing,' he said. Chairman Len Hart declared that an appeal would be lodged, and that the club would continue to trade until the appeal was heard.

In January 1976, a petition signed by hundreds of members called for an extraordinary general meeting of the club to consider:

> 1) A vote of no confidence in the Board of Directors and Management.
> 2) That all Board positions be declared vacant immediately.
> 3) That an election of Directors be called for.

A second petition called for the resignation of Darcy Lawler in view of the loss of the liquor licence previously held by Lawler. In the event of Lawler refusing to resign the petition demanded that 'appropriate action be taken by the Board to dismiss him personally'.

By then there were already changes on the club's Board.

Denis Johnson resigned as a director on January 8, and Arch Henderson a couple of weeks later. Leslie Banton and Barry Dunn were appointed to take their places. Soon afterwards chairman Len Hart and his deputy Frank Kilcran also resigned from office.

Henry Morris walked into a minefield when he joined the Board — the double whammy of the Royal Commission and the NSW Licensing Court's refusal to renew the club's licence.

Henry Morris today has great sympathy for the 'good, honest men', the directors who gradually faded at that time from the scene in the double-whammy of the Royal Commission and the licensing dramas. 'They bore a stigma for what went on around them and that's most unfortunate,' said Morris. 'To a large extent they were sacrificed because of the situation that existed. I feel for them, still. I think what happened was really unjust to those people, I really do. And it hurt them deeply. They were decent men who worked hard for the club. I think they were unlucky victims … that the [Licensing Board] push was really to get rid of Wally and to a degree Darcy … who under the Act at that time couldn't be found responsible for the things that had gone on. But there had to be change after some of the things that had taken place — obviously — and the directors who left understood that. I can assure you they were never anything less than warmly welcomed after it. They were beautiful football blokes … and recognised everywhere as decent people. They just copped the backwash.'

For his part, Darcy Lawler survived the move to oust him — the Board voting to stick with the secretary-manager, despite some apparent reservations revealed by directors in later conversations. Under the terms of the Act in force at the time Lawler was assessed as a servant of the club — charged with the duty of carrying out the instructions given to him by the Board. Effectively he was not judged — as Dean and some others were judged. And because of it, he held on, maintaining a position of power and influence within the club for a further 18 years. Henry Morris recalls the discussion on Lawler and whether he should go or stay being 'very heavy' on the night of the big meeting. 'The Junior League clubs stuck solid, as they always do — and the Board rejected the moves to sack Lawler,' he said.

(Lawler clung on until the very end. In 1993 in a heart to heart talk chairman Morris said to him: 'Darcy, the time has come … go with a bit of glory. We don't want any blues or squabbles.' But until the issue was forced Lawler was adamant he would stay on — although taking a 'backseat'.)

The precipitating factor leading to the demise of the club's directors had come on Christmas Eve 1975 — in the issuing of summonses from the Licensing Court to Messrs Hart, Henderson, Kilcran, Cracknell and Johnson, requiring the directors to establish that they were fit and proper people to be members of the committee of the club. The club's legal representative told the Board that the allegations involving the five directors would be identical with the allegations raised in the objection to the renewal of licence. News of the summonses reached the Board on the same night as the petition, handed to Norm Christie by club member John Willis, to terminate the services of Darcy Lawler at the club. A week

… and now for the bad news: A report from The Australian of December 1975, recording the NSW Licensing Court's decision not to re-issue the Juniors' licence.

Court refuses to renew largest club's licence

AUSTRALIA's largest club, the 51,000 member South Sydney Junior Rugby League Club, yesterday was refused renewal of its licence by the NSW Licensing Court.

Renewal of the club's certificate of registration was opposed by the Metropolitan Licensing Inspector on several grounds.

After the reserved decision by the Licensing Magistrate, Mr T. A. Ritchie, SM, was announced, the president of the club, Mr L. Hart, said an appeal would be lodged immediately.

Mr Hart said the club would continue trading, pending the $1 million.

Mr Ratcliffe found proved all the grounds of objections by the licensing police to renewal.

He referred to activities of former club president, Mr Walter James Dean, and his association with companies which had dealings with the club.

"The picture is of chairman Dean manipulating his fellow directors either with their conscious agreement or negligent acquiescence to run the club for his personal arrangement, both in relation to profitable ventures for his companies and as a private-interest free banker."

after the event, far too many not approved by the board at all.

The grounds of objection by the Metropolitan Licensing Inspector were:

THAT certain club rules had been habitually broken; that people derived benefits and advantages from the club, not shared equally by every member; servants of the club voted at the annual meeting, contrary to provisions of the Liquor Act; the financial affairs of the club were not under the control of the annually-elected committee; and correct books of account were not being kept in relation to loans to employees and to Walter James Dean.

later came the petition, signed by 340 members, calling for a vote of no confidence in the Board of Directors and club management. Arch Henderson resigned from the Board that night. Chairman Len Hart and his deputy Frank Kilcran followed on January 29 — chairman Hart giving as his reasons family and health, coupled with the frustration of constant legal proceedings over a number of years.

It was on that night, a Thursday in a summer of ongoing turbulence for the club that Henry Morris was elected chairman of Souths Juniors, on a motion proposed by Barry Dunn and seconded by Les Banton. Viv Wemyss was elected deputy chairman. Taking the chair, Henry Morris thanked members for their confidence in him and declared that he trusted the Board would work as a united group in the interests of the Junior League and the licensed club.

A committed worker for the club, Len Hart, pictured in 1975. Worn down by the continuing dramas, Hart resigned as club chairman in January 1976.

Just three nights later, the entire Board of the club resigned in response to the demands of the petition aired at an extraordinary general meeting held earlier that night. The general meeting was not without its dramas — notably when Ray Vawdon declared he believed the meeting was invalid, and that he would take no further part. Within days came a summons issued by Vawdon for the entire Board (currently at only five members) plus secretary-manager Lawler to appear in court (the club won that battle). Harry Cracknell, last link with the 'old' Board, announced his resignation. With the club on a battle footing yet again, Darcy Lawler announced there were 16 candidates for the Board elections to be held in mid-March.

The election between the latest version of a 'reform group', a team representing the intra-clubs and the Morris team was fiercely fought. Henry Morris believes the intra-club 'ticket', led by the touch football

Barry Dunn polled most votes in the 'last great battle for control' of the Juniors. The new Board was entrusted with taking the club into a new era.

group, came about mainly as a signal of discontent with Darcy Lawler. Bad feeling was generated by some of the 'literature' handed out — the elected directors subsequently declaring the reform group pamphlets 'in bad taste and not in the best interests of the club'. The announcement of the ballot drew a gathering of 650 to the auditorium. The full result of the last great battle for control of Souths Juniors was as follows:

Les Banton 3282
John Begg 1151
George Bishop 75
Frank Cookson 2680
Barry Dunn 3454
Pat Fanale 2631
Pat Hennessy 1403
Barry Jurd 1254
Sol Landsman 800
Phillip Martin 157
Henry Morris 3291
Leonard Smith 1396
Bill Spyrou 2629
Ray Vawdon 918
Viv Wemyss 3842
John Willis 1263

The new Board elected to take the club into a new era and, hopefully, successful future (the appeal against the Licensing Court decision was still in progress) was: Henry Morris, Viv Wemyss, Les Banton, Frank Cookson, Barry Dunn, Pat Fanale, Bill Spyrou.

Henry Morris remembers the night of the big meeting with great clarity. 'It was an extraordinary sight all right,' he says. 'They were hanging from the rafters. We got presented with a petition signed by the members, mainly orchestrated by the touch football, to sack Darcy. The Board in turn wouldn't sack Darcy — and they tried to move a vote of no confidence in the Board at that meeting. That was my first big meeting — and I just bluffed my way through. It was lucky I had a bit of council training behind me (Morris was an alderman of Botany Council at that time). It was a testing night — but everything started to settle down after that.'

Says Henry Morris: 'It was a great challenge, at the start of a brand new era. I don't think I've ever been more excited than I was that night [of the meeting]. And we got through what lay ahead — despite the fact that we weren't given much in the way of good guidance. We had to pick up the pieces ourselves, find our own way. Maybe that was for the best.'

With a new Board in place, the club had one last hurdle to jump before it could begin the hoped for 'new era' — the licensing appeal, heard before Justice Phillip Head in late March. The Board Minutes of May 13 contain an intriguing item, a letter conveyed by the club solicitor Jack Heaney from Justice Head, reading: 'I wish to inform the legal representatives of the parties that I understand a statement has been made to the effect that the present 'Club Committee' takes its orders from the previous committee and is in office only for the purpose of this appeal. I cannot be more precise, nor am I able to elaborate upon the above.'

Henry Morris remembers Justice Head well. 'A dry, legal sort of bloke … but very fair.' And one thing stays strongly in the chairman's mind, the day of a visit by the judge to the club when all was spick and span and just right. 'Mr Morris,' said Justice Head, 'we'll give you and your new Board an opportunity. But I just hope you aren't merely window-dressing.' Says Henry Morris: 'the phrase has always stayed in my mind … window-dressing. And it wasn't that — we were sick of the drama and troubles. We just wanted a fair dinkum, well-run club. The judge advised us to always get professional advice — and to make sure we had a good team of auditors. 'You are only ordinary working class people … you are not expected to or are not trained to know all the fine details involved in running a club,' he said. 'Get professional advice.' And ever since, we have always done that.'

Kevin Humphreys, then in the early days of his appointment as 'supremo' of the NSW and Australian Rugby League, delivered a strong character reference for the club in the appeal hearing. Ultimately all the studious preparation by Jack Heaney and his legal team, supported by the Board paid off when Justice Head ruled in the club's favour in the early autumn of 1976. The licence would be renewed and life at 558A Anzac Parade could go on. Henry Morris's reflections on the period these days bring back memories of a precarious time. 'We were very, very much at risk,' he says of the nervous weeks in which the appeal to the Licensing Court was prepared, then heard. 'Perhaps we were a little slow to get going in the period that followed … we were feeling our way to an extent, but at least we worked our way through it and put stability back into the place. For a while we thought we only had to open the doors for people to flock in. We progressively realised there was a lot more to it than that — and particularly so as the competition got tougher.'

The popular Viv Wemyss, deputy chairman when the re-alignment of the club began after the 'troubles' of the early '70s.

Les Banton — elected to the Board in March 1976 after the 'last great battle' — an election that drew 650 to the club auditorium.

DARCY LAWLER: CONTROVERSY HIS COMPANION

Controversy followed Darcy Thomas Elgan Lawler throughout his public life — and even beyond. After his death in 1994, shock allegations emerged concerning Lawler's practices as a rugby league referee, focused mainly on the 1963 grand final. But there was ringing praise, too. The long-serving and widely-respected league administrator Eric Cox in 1999 called Darcy Lawler: 'The best referee I ever saw — a champion at a time the game was as hard and as demanding as it has ever been. A man of great authority on the field.' The different views pretty much summed up the way it was with Darcy Lawler; throughout his public life, opinions on him ranged right across the spectrum.

Away from football, the early years of Darcy Lawler's long administrative career at Souths Juniors were inevitably touched with controversy too, considering the findings that emerged from the Moffitt Royal Commission in 1974, and subsequent allegations elsewhere. Directors of the time were held responsible for events that had taken place at the club and Lawler, as an employee, rode through.

When he died, in February 1994, just a month after he had stepped down from his job as secretary-manager of the Juniors, a journalist rang famed Australian Test front rower Noel 'Ned' Kelly for a comment on Lawler, the referee. Kelly declined. 'There was nothing good I could say about Darcy Lawler, so I was better off saying nothing,' explained Kelly later. In his book *Hard Man*, Kelly was subsequently scathingly critical of Lawler. In 1962 at a time when rivalry between Australia and Great Britain was at its height on the football field, the manager of the touring British side, Stuart Hadfield, lashed out furiously, labelling the Test referee 'the biggest cheat that ever went onto a field'.

A former milko in the Maroubra area, Lawler swept to power at the Juniors on the 'new deal' ticket of Wally Dean at the now-famous elections of 1966. Elected a director (and vice-president to Dean), he became the club's secretary-manager within five weeks — on the decision of the recently-reinstated George Wintle to resign. It was a job he was to hold for 27 years — the club's 'nuts and bolts' man in a quarter of a century of extraordinary change and growth. In 1965–66 when he arrived at the club, accumulated funds stood at 899 801 pounds ($1 799 602). At the end of his last year as secretary-manager, 1993–94, the current cash assets were $17 947 000 and total members' equity stood at $28 387 000. Whatever individual viewpoints there may have been on Lawler and his qualities — and they differed greatly — there is no question he must be rated a player in the club's ever-upwards surge.

Views on Lawler and his contribution range across the spectrum. In an interview for this book, Joan Child, Lawler's secretary throughout the long years of his tenure, said of him: 'He was a hard, tough sort of man — but he had a good sense of humour. Darcy made his rules, then was inflexible on them.' Long-standing deputy chairman Barry Dunn was succinct in some 1999 reflections:

'I wasn't too popular with blokes like Darcy Lawler and Wally Dean — but when I got onto the Board, Darcy had to change his views a bit. I still wasn't his No. I boy by a long shot ... and for sure he wasn't mine.' Berkeley Burns, ex-mascot secretary says simply of him: 'Darcy ruled with a rod of iron.'

In rugby league folklore and history Lawler is pictured as a 'colourful' and 'controversial' referee — notwithstanding his stern manner on the field. His career was a long and fruitful one — from 1948 to 1963 — a period in which he refereed 16 Test matches and a number of grand finals. For a long period he was undeniably No. 1 in the game. Hard and unflappable, Lawler was unquestionably tough enough and shrewd enough to handle anything the game of rugby league could throw at him. But the picture of Lawler's life in refereeing has pro-

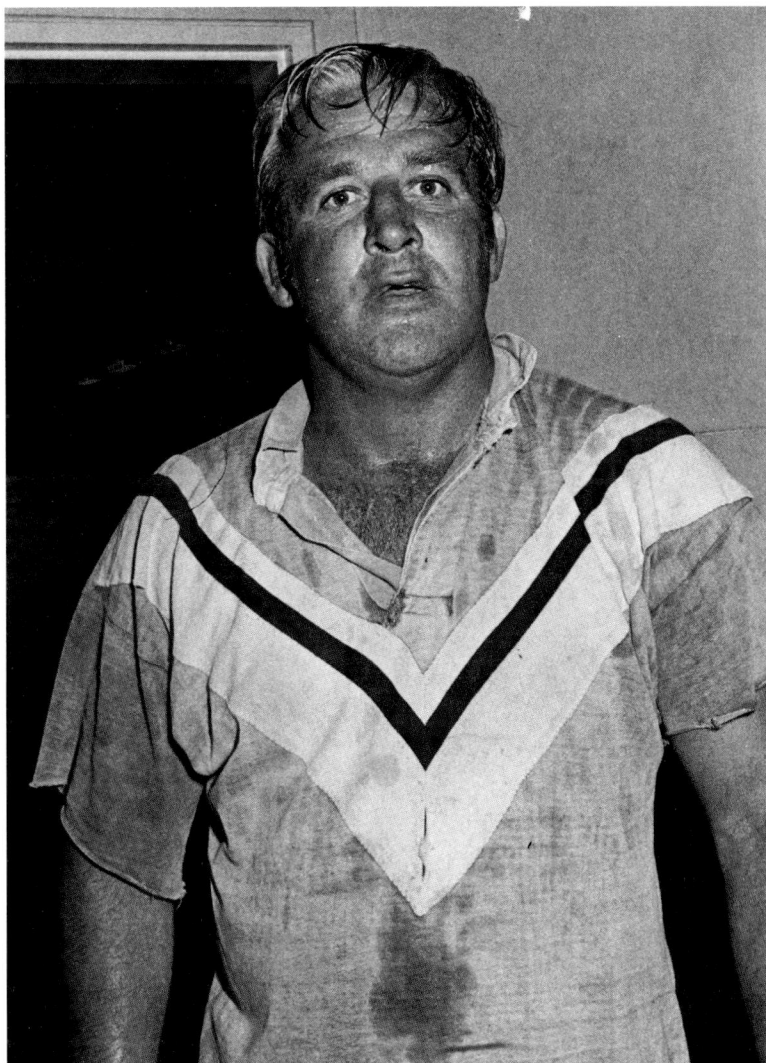

ABOVE: *Rugby league legend Noel 'Ned' Kelly — he went public in the 1990s with his opinion that Darcy Lawler 'robbed' Western Suburbs in the 1963 grand final against St George.*

gressively darkened in the years since his death — a sudden ending, from a heart attack, as he lay on the couch at home one night not long after his departure from the Juniors. Growing claims in recent years suggested that the rumours that had existed for years were soundly based — that Darcy Lawler had manipulated matches at times.

Noel Kelly, for one, appeared to hold no doubt. In his 1996 book Kelly relates — among other tales about Lawler's colourful life as a referee — the story of the St George-Western Suburbs mud battle in the grand final of 1963. He relates how Wests forward Jack Gibson, bound for later fame as a coach, came into the Magpie dressing room before the match and said to him: 'Mate, we can't win ... Darcy has backed them' (St George). Gibson has independently confirmed the story, nominating the go-between who 'put Darcy's money on'. In the slogging grand final that ensued, close calls went to St George — notably a still-discussed try by Saints winger Johnny King … with Wests players screaming that King had been 'held'. Penalties were 18–7 to St George and scrums their way on a 2–1 ratio. St George won 8–3. Wrote Kelly: 'I will never forgive Darcy Lawler for what he did that day. I have no doubt we were robbed.' St George players strongly contest the view expounded by Kelly — adamant that they won the game fair and square.

Resilient as a referee — Lawler proved himself a considerable survivor in the licensed club game, too. When the remnants of the Wally Dean era were swept away in the aftermath of the Moffitt Report, Darcy Lawler stayed. In 1976, 300 club members signed a petition to have him sacked as secretary-manager. The petitions followed the refusal of the Metropolitan Licensing Court to renew the club's licence. Again Lawler fought his way through the storm — and stayed on. When the intra-clubs mounted a ticket to oust the incumbent Board at that stage in 1976, Lawler was the main bone of contention. 'Yeah, it was mainly about a conflict with Darcy,' Henry Morris remembers. 'It was an extraordinary night … they were hanging from the rafters. The thing was that all the other Board members [from the Dean era] were gone. Blokes were crooked that Darcy was still there. That was my first big meeting as chairman and I bluffed my way through it. When the Board wouldn't sack Darcy they [the meeting] tried to move a vote of no confidence in the Board. Eventually we scuttled that, and things settled down.'

And Darcy Lawler held his place — a fixture at the club for the next 18 years … and very much a part of its story of ongoing success and growth. Henry Morris remembers him this way: 'Darcy was not an educated man, but he was cunning … oh yeah, he was cunning. He wouldn't get away now with what he did in the industry in those earlier days. The unionism wasn't too strong, and it was before anti-discrimination boards and those sort of things. Darcy would stand-over people — and get away with it. He was a tough nut, Darcy. A hard bugger … a ruthless man in many ways. And funnily enough considering his background, he didn't have a great love of the role that football took in the club. He was never a great supporter of us supporting football. You have no idea how Darcy used to hate going to the footy meetings. I genuinely think he got to hate football. He certainly didn't want any money spent on it.'

Darcy Lawler — 'the best referee I ever saw,' said the much admired league man, Eric Cox, of him. Lawler, his life linked to the ongoing story of the Juniors attracted strong opinions — for and against — throughout his life in football and clubland.

A famous moment from the grand final of 1959. St George's Harry Bath, who is looking straight at referee Darcy Lawler is about to be sent from the field, along with Manly's Rex Mossop (out of picture).

Morris believes today that Lawler held a long-standing grudge against Souths (the Rabbitohs). 'He hated Souths in those days. He certainly wasn't looking to do the club any favours because of his belief that they had done the wrong thing by George Bishop somewhere along the line.' (George Bishop, prominent referee of the 1940s and '50s, was a friend of Lawler's and something of a guiding light through Lawler's own refereeing career. Like Lawler, he was involved in a highly controversial grand final — the Souths-Wests game of 1954.)

Lawler, so shrewd and quick thinking, was a survivor through his life. At the time of the Liquor enquiry, with things hotting up at the club, there was persistent talk of Wally Dean and Murray Riley hatching a plan to get rid of him. With prominent policemen eyeing the club, Lawler proved just too quick on his feet for them — and when it came to the crunch, he was still there … and it was Dean and Riley who had departed.

When Darcy Lawler died in January 1994, former Australian captain Ian Walsh offered a closing observation: 'Whatever you thought of him you couldn't deny that he was a real character,' said Walsh.

As a final view on a man whose hard-nosed attitude polarised those around him — but who stands as a major figure in the story of Souths Juniors — Walsh's words said it about as well as it could be said.

KINGS OF THE 'CUP'
A POTTED HISTORY, BY THE LATE TOM BROCK

One of the President's Cup 'production line' — the outstanding fullback and goalkicker Kevin 'Lummy' Longbottom. Photo courtesy of Ern McQuillan.

In rugby league's foundation year, 1908, South Sydney and Balmain were the only district junior league organisations. Newtown joined them in 1909.

In 1908, Mr W Munn presented a trophy, the 'Munn Cup' to be played for by the leading clubs in each Junior League. Souths' representatives, Waterloo Oaks, won the Cup in 1908 and 1909 — and it thus became their property.

By 1910, when Mr (later Sir) James Joynton Smith became president of the NSWRL, junior competitions had commenced in the North Sydney, Western Suburbs, Eastern Suburbs and St George districts. To encourage such development, Joynton Smith donated a trophy — the 'President's Cup' — to be contested by representative teams from each Junior League — rather than by individual junior clubs. In the early years, teams met each other once and the team with the best record won. As this format tended to interfere with the regular competition in the Junior Leagues, the Cup was subsequently changed to a knockout basis.

When Souths lost 7–0 to Easts in the 1920 final, the young Rabbitohs were listed in the *Rugby League News* (published for the first time that year) as wearing red jerseys, with Easts in black. That season Souths trained at the Sydney Cricket Ground under the direction of Owen McCarthy, a former South Sydney hooker.

There were no age qualifications until 1922 when the competition was restricted to players who were under 21 at the date of its first round each season. The *Rugby League News* of May 13, 1922 commented: 'Some of the juniors think there should be no restriction, but the object of the competition is to let the senior clubs see the promising players of the district and promote them into the grade teams with their football in front of them — instead of picking players who are too old to become top-notchers.' In the June 10, 1922 issue the magazine added: 'The restriction will have the effect of the youngster being selected (for grade) before he has dropped into the 'junior groove' that is so hard to rid oneself of ...'

(Players listed *** in the following team lists played for South Sydney district club and for Australia. Those marked ** played first grade for Souths. Those marked * played lower grade football for South Sydney.)

Surprisingly, although Souths were runners-up in 1915, 1920, 1926 and 1929 they did not first win the President's Cup until 1936 when Martin Clayden* captained a team, coached by old Souths prop forwards Dave Watson and Bill Gollan, which defeated Balmain 22–2 in the final. Clayden's team-mates were Tom Vose**, Alan Schafer**, E 'Tibby' Shellack*, Tommy O'Keefe*, D McKenzie, N Byrnes, Claude Baker*, Arthur Goddard*, T Ross, Ron McFarland, R Brennan, Jack Cahill*, E Craigie*, N Johnstone, A Griffiths, Ted Baker.

The young Bobby McCarthy — dressed to kill. One of the alltime Rabbitoh greats, McCarthy came through the ranks of the juniors to stardom — a brilliant role model for the youngsters of the district.

Ron Coote, with Norman 'Latchem' Robinson behind and Bob Abbott in the background, accepts the prestigious Harry Sunderland Medal as Australia's player-of-the-series in the 1974 Ashes battle against Great Britain, the second time he had won the award.

Souths won its second Cup in 1942, coached by former international and Souths captain Alf 'Smacka' Blair and captained by 16-year-old five-eighth Les Bell**. They beat Canterbury 15–2 in the final. The other players were Keith Aitken**, Jeff 'Gunboat' Smith, Vic Wilson*, S Dean, Jack Faris*, Steve Norrish, Doug Doney, Paddy Byrne, Terry O'Brien, Eddie McQuillan, Vince Lawrence**, Keith Booth, George Dykes, Ernie Riddell*, Jack Leo**, Bill Mullane**, Alan Cummings*.

Souths won again in 1943, coached by former Wests international prop Bill Brogan and captained by Bill 'Chocca' Sherwood**. They downed St George 16–6 in the final. The rest of the squad was Frank Bonner**, Jack Lannon*, Jim Mangan**, Dave Beiber, James Clifford*, Jack 'Jumbo' Clare*, Doug Barwick**, George Kempshall**, G Keith, Ken Mudge, Harold Manning, Kevin Lampard*, Dave Lawlor, Johnny Williams, John 'Scotchy' Gersbach, J Kettlewell, Jeff Smith, Eddie McQuillan.

In 1951, Australia's 1946 Test halfback Clem Kennedy jnr coached Souths to the first of his remarkable eight President's Cup victories. The players were: Joe Arnold* (captain), Billy Bailey*, Ken Keen*, Perce Purchase*, Jim Buchan, G. 'Mick' Wolters, Bill Harris*, Trevor Ozanne*, Noel McCarthy*, Joe Renshaw**, John 'Pepsi' Cotis*, John Keating*, Jack Durrington*, Mick Horan*, Alan 'Scotty' Dennis*, Keithe Scully*, G Sherwood, Billy Dempsey. The team of '51 beat Easts 14–9 in the final — a match delayed until late July because of disqualifications and appeals.

In 1953, Clem's winning squad was John Waugh* (captain), John

Cotis*, Cec Healey*, Bill Craigie, John Dobbie, Sid Dornay*, Wally Faris*, Alan Flockton**, John Glynn*, Bob Honeysett**, Ron Hogan*, Mick Horan*, Frank Nicol, Maurie O'Brien, Tony Pearsall, Bob Sait**, Keith Tracey*, Frank Westcott*, Brian Wright**, J Wilson. Souths beat St George, 6–4 in the final.

Under Kennedy's coaching Souths were runners-up to Balmain in 1959 and their 1960 success commenced an unparalleled sequence of 26 games without loss until they were runners-up to the Tigers, six years later. In a knockout competition this was a remarkable achievement, spread over seven seasons and fielding what was virtually a new team each year.

The winning players in 1960 were Kevin 'Lummy' Longbottom** (captain), Bob Richardson**, Eric Robinson**, Ray 'Butch' Summerhayes**,

ABOVE: *Eric Simms was a President's Cup player in 1965 when called into South Sydney first grade side. It was the beginning of a superb career during which Simms established himself as one of the greatest goalkickers in the game's history. He scored 1841 points for the Rabbitohs.*

LEFT: *Gary Stevens came to grade from the juniors in 1964 and through the mix of hard work and talent built himself into one of the game's finest — and hardest-tackling — backrow forwards. He played 155 games for Souths and represented his country.*

$2.00   Volume 1

THE RABBITOH

OFFICIAL PUBLICATION OF THE SOUTH SYDNEY RUGBY LEAGUE FOOTBALL CLUB

A couple of juniors who made it in a big way, Mario Fenech (with ball) and Craig 'Tugger' Coleman, adorned the cover of the first edition of the Souths magazine, The Rabbitoh.

Bob McKenzie**, John Davis, Laurie Rubagotti*, Kevin Roberts**, Bill Stokes**, David Stokes, Ken Kay**, Dave Wood**, Graham Creer, Bill Hales, Don Wiggins, Les Woodley, Barry 'Doc' Daley, Geoff Skene. They beat Easts 11–7 in the final.

Clem Kennedy's subsequent winning squads were:

1961: Jeff Byrne* (captain), John Hynes, Bruce 'Larpa' Stewart*, Steve Lawrence*, Brian Speechley, Merv Wright*, Harold Thompson*, John Lawrence**, Alex Penklis*, Dennis Lee**, Barry Beiber*, Dave Martin*, Bob McKenzie**, Ken Brown*, Greg Christensen**, Alan Peterson, Barry Atkinson*, Ian Davidson, Bill Hales. They downed Easts 12–7 in the final.

1962: Bob McKenzie** (captain), John Hynes, Dave Perrin**, Merv Wright*, Warren Thompson**, Bryan Scanlon*, Terry Davoren*, Herb Martin*, Bob McCarthy***, Barry Atkinson*, Alex Penkilis*, Norm McLeod, Tim Stuart*, John Crowe*, Ken Murray*, Wayne Stevens**, Col Downing*. This side took the final 19–10 against Balmain.

1963: Barry Atkinson* (captain), Herb Martin*, John Newman, John Brown*, Col Downing*, Ron Paterson*, Wayne Stevens**, Billy Tong*, Ron Coote***, Chris Armstrong**, Ken Murray*, Tim Stuart*, Dave Martin*, Ron Ingram, Dave Paulson, Keith Canty, Ken Vessey, Graham Kennedy*. Souths 7, St George 5 in the final.

1964: Barry Atkinson* (captain again — and in the team for an unprecedented fourth year), Col Downing*, Paul Kain*, Ian Cook*, Ray 'Gus' Coward, Neville Creer, Brian Finnegan, Alan Heiler**, Gary Hughes*, Joe Lawler, Herb

Martin*, Chris O'Reilly*, Dave Paulson, George Piggins***, Eric Simms***, Aidan Smith, Gary Stevens***, Ken Vessey. Fielding three future internationals, Souths beat Parramatta in the final, 10–5.

1965: Jim 'Jumma' Norman* (captain), Gary Wildman, Eric Simms***, David Brown, Ken McDonnell, Russell Amatto**, Doug Ardler*, Ralph Grace**, Terry Saxby, Eric Hamilton, Damian Pryke, Bob Fleming*, Geoff Taylor, Alan Webb, Bertie Longbottom*, Gary Mashman, Paul Kain*, Neil Hayward*, Ian Cook*.

In 1968, Keith Booth maintained the district's fine record by coaching Souths to their 12th Cup triumph, 5–0 against Canterbury in the decider. His team was Les Brown* (captain), John Skelton* (who was captain in the final after Brown broke his leg in a qualifying game), Kevin Ardler, John Bowen, Paul 'Doggie' Williams, Frank Curry**, Savva 'Steve' Kosta**, Tom Larkin*, Paul Grant, John Sullivan*, Gary Fitzhenry*, John Chenhall, Mick Kirk*, Shane Day**, John Barrett, John Duncan, Robert 'Legs' Turner, Brett Stevens, John Atherton*.

Souths had their most successful year in 1969 — winning all three junior competitions (President's Cup, Jersey Flegg, SG Ball). Keith Booth's President's Cup squad was Darrell Bampton** (captain), Bob Bolin**, Steve Van*, Steve 'Joe' Annesley*, Joe Heaney, John Mussell, Billy Murphy*, John Atherton*, Ken Berrigan, Paul McCartney*, Robert Turner, Barry Maguire, Vic Swibel, Robert 'Duke' Bergan*, Jeff Withers**, John Barrett, John Lawrence, Peter Wall*, Brett Stevens. The final against St George was won 14–5.

TOP: *The President's Cup competition has been a stepping stone to bigger things for the young men of South Sydney since 1910. Here, some action from a Souths-Sydney City game in the '90s.*

ABOVE: *Souths-Easts rivalry extended from rugby league's first year in Australia, 1908 — and was as keen at President's Cup level as any other.*

STANDING:- L. Hart (Committeeman), A. Henderson (Treasurer), J. Schroder (Selector), V. Wemyss (Manager), N. Burne (Asst.Secretary), K. Booth (Coach), R. Ellison (Deputy President) J. Collis (Trainer), F. Kilcran (Selector), G. Montgomery (Selector), W. Stig (Selector).

SITTING:- J. Barratt, J. Atherton, J. Heaney, W. Murphy, K. Berrigan, D. Bampton (Captain), J. Withers (V.Captain), J. Mussell, P. Wall, S. Annesley, R. Turner.

FRONT:- J. Lawrence, B. McGuire, B. Stevens, P. McCartney, N. McIntosh (Ball Boy), V. Swibel, R. Bergan, S. Van, R. Bolin.

The picture tells the story — a champion young Souths side, skippered by a man who headed on to a notable career with the district club, on and off the field (Darrell Bampton).

Brian Murray was in charge of the 1971 Cup winners, a team comprising: Stuart Airlie* (captain), John Mussell, Malcolm Hay, Bruce Roach*, Paul Baker, Steve Clarke, Phil 'Mousey' Austin, Billy Lindwall, Paul Hills**, Steve Ellis, Maurie Stynes, Tom Moylan**, John Kolovos*, Phil Grinham, Angelo Matthews, Larry Norman, John Wilson*, Greg Longhurst**, Steve Annesley*, Rod Webb*. Souths 13, Canterbury 10 in the final.

Murray's team again triumphed in 1972 — this time in a close one, 14–13 over Canterbury. The winning team was:

John Wilson* (captain), Dave Gray*, Peter Roberts*, Terry Bentley*, Jim Kolovos, Gary Haig*, Phil Austin*, Greg Longhurst**, Bob Lees*, Graham Whalley*, Sam Votano, Bill Moore*, Leon Harvey*, Alan Abbott, Steve Layman, Colin Campbell*, Ken Barron*, Col Westaway*, Tom Moylan**.

In 1974, Col McKeough guided the Under 21s to another victory. Steve Loughnan* was his captain, with Geoff Birtles*, Peter Maher*, Danny

Johnston*, Geoff Bultitude**, Gary Haig*, Bill Russell*, Jim Harriott, George Lycakis, Mick Ecob*, Kim Harkins*, Terry Gibson**, Wayne Wright*, Gary Wright**, Jamie Griffiths*, Stafford McDonald*, Ken Barron*, Alan Abbott, Chris Moraghan*, Glen Porter**. Souths won the final 14–6 over Wests, after extra time.

McKeough was at the helm again in 1977 with Morrie Griffiths** as captain and Greg Kilham*, Brett Franklin, Bruce Richards*, Luke Farrell*, John Christopher*, Mick Bucknell*, Col Cheeseman**, Brian Sommerville*, Guy Gilliman, Steve Clare, Rod Cronon, Lee Maton, Mark Hall, Tony Cavallaro, Mark Barron**, Paul Sawdy, Chris Studden, Mark Sinclair. The final was close — an 8–7 win over Cronulla.

In 1980, Rod Gorman was coach when Tony Studden* captained the Cup winners: Gary Whitehead*, Col Mason*, John Cummings, Craig Mullins**, K McKenzie, George Longbottom**, Gary Martine, Robert Simpkins**, Jim Wells, Greg Evans**, Vic Watts, Mario Fenech**, Tony Woodcroft*, Michael Brown*, Steve Wakeley*, Wayne Eirtt, Chris Emery, Rube Kennedy*, Klaus Perkovic*, Col Porter. In their highest scoring final Souths beat Balmain 20–14.

Rod Gorman coached again in 1982 when Souths beat neighbours Easts 14–8 in the final. The team was: Tony Woodcroft* (captain), Allan Riddoch, Mark Hanlon, Dave Le Brocque*, Tony Taylor, Michael Brown*, Glen Fitzgerald*, Scott Brodie*, Rick Small, Tommy Roberts*, Klaus Perkovic*, Kerry Webster, Wayne Lonergan**, Bryan McCarthy, Jeff Charlton*, John Thomas, Vic Watts, Greg Cheung, John Sadiek*, Brent Donnelly, Rod Power.

For his third win in 1983, coach Gorman had Klaus Perkovic* as captain with Darren Dunn*, Jeff Charlton*, Mark Donohue, Paul Brandtman*, Scott Brodie*, Brent Donnelly, Michael Griffiths, Michael Andrews**, Mark Ellison**, Peter Markham, Craig Weeks**, Glen Fitzgerald*, Eick Small, Darryl Neville**, Gavin Goodman, John Thomas, Paul Thornton, Brad Webb**, Mauro Viera*, Mark Henson. Souths took the final 16–10 over Easts.

From the 336 representatives listed in these 20 winning President's Cup teams, 185 players have made South Sydney's grade ranks, including 67 who have appeared in first grade premiership games and five who have represented Australia. There have also been those who played grade league for other clubs including first graders D Doney, J Clare, W Harris, G Martine and B Stewart — and those who played first grade rugby union: J Cotis, T Davoren and M Stynes.

At least nine other Australian internationals came through Souths' President's Cup squads in non-winning seasons: Frank O'Connor (1925), Denis Donoghue (1947), Brian Hambly (1955), Ernie Hammerton (1945), Bryan Orrock (1948), Ian Roberts (1985), Paul Sait (1966), Perce Williams (1928), Graham Wilson (1958) — plus Bob Banham (1933) who represented New Zealand.

With 20 victories South Sydney dominated the competition from 1910 to 1987 while the President's Cup was the championship of the junior leagues. Easts (14 wins) were Souths' nearest rivals.

Such a magnificent record demonstrates that Souths' President's Cup team have not only been of great value to their Junior League — but also to the district's senior club … and to the wider game of rugby league itself.

CHAPTER 7

THE MODERN ERA:

CONVERSATIONS WITH HENRY MORRIS

When Henry Morris, 30, took over as chairman of the biggest, highest-profile outfit in clubland in 1976, he was extraordinarily young for such a position — but, as Morris says, his pitchforking into the top job within the Juniors was entirely the result of turmoil within the club that was nothing short of extraordinary. Sharpened by his experience as an alderman on Botany Council, Morris progressively proved he was made of the right stuff as chairman — although he is self-critical at times when he reflects on the early years that followed the 'troubles' of the 1970s.

'We fell asleep for some years … no risk,' says Morris. 'There was honestly this feeling abroad that you only had to open the doors of a licensed club and you were going to make big money. We were comfortable and happy to go along with the managerial advice of the time that we were still going okay, still making a good profit. We fell into that complacency trap, and we are entitled to some criticism for that. We were coasting — same as Ron Jones and his Board up at Easts [Eastern Suburbs Leagues Club].

'Fortunately, we woke up in time. We now have smart, professional people in the key areas — and we take their advice. You need good people — particularly in the areas of secretary (General Manager) and gaming manager. We're in good shape in that area with Geoff Knight and Paul Muir.'

OPPOSITE: *Henry Morris proved to be the leader that the club needed to find when he was pitchforked into the presidency in 1976. Henry grew up with the creed: Always barrack for Souths, and always vote Labor. His reign was marked by the steadiness of the leadership and the consolidation and growth of the club.*

Morris was a man richly steeped in the traditions of his district when he took over as chairman of the Juniors. He says: 'My old man taught me two things when I was growing up. He said to me one day, 'I'm going to tell you something — always barrack for Souths and always vote Labor.' I had those things drummed into me when I was just a kid and they stuck. I've only varied once — I had a blue with Laurie Brereton [ex-Botany Council alderman, NSW and Federal Governments minister]. I started playing football when I was about 13. I was going to Redfern Oval from when I was very young; I saw [Clive] Churchill, Bernie [Purcell] and those fellas. Souths have been part of my life … all my life.'

The disagreement with Laurie Brereton, State member for Botany, caused Morris to be barred by the Labor Party. He remembers the night of the opening of the Chinese Restaurant at the club when then NSW Premier, Neville Wran, came along to do the honours. Because he was temporarily on the outer with the Labor Party Morris wasn't permitted to sit at the official table. He recalls Wran pulling him aside afterwards with the words: 'This is only for political purposes, son. Jill [Wran] and I will come up and have dinner with you one night'. They never did. Former Chief Magistrate Murray Farquhar was also a guest at the club one night, and after a few drinks opened up in astonishing fashion about some of the things that had 'gone on' during his time on the bench.

Morris started his career in the Juniors with Botany RSL G Grade, around 1959 after playing league at Botany and Gardeners Road schools. (He remembers Gardeners Road as a 'mad rugby league school'.) 'At that time kids didn't really have the diverse range of choices that kids have today,' he recalls. 'Around our area you were seen as a bit strange if you didn't play rugby league. We used to call soccer 'wog ball'. Everyone played rugby league.' The pattern on the days of Souths home games was always the same — play your match then pack up and head across to Redfern to watch the Rabbitohs. Morris remembers Redfern on the big days as a 'sensational place' and is saddened now to see the place faded and worn, with the grandstand being eaten by concrete cancer.

After years with Botany RSL, Morris went to La Perouse (C grade) — then back to Botany to help re-form Botany United in 1966. There, still a teenager, he became secretary (as he had been in two seasons at La Perouse). He was the youngest club secretary in the League, and went on to become treasurer of the Souths Junior League, taking over from Archie Henderson. Morris explains the path he took:

'Botany RSL could only go to a certain age because of the Youth Club … 17, I think it was … so a few of us wayward blokes went over to La

Perouse. We had a couple of years there, then came back and formed Botany United in 1969 … a continuation of the Botany RSL Club. The team wore blue and gold, the same as Botany RSL.' At La Perouse he played with a Souths' and international star of the future, the great Aboriginal fullback and goalkicker Eric Simms.

They were crowded, busy days — trying to kick-start a brand new club. 'I was as keen as mustard,' Morris remembers. 'I had a little Volkswagen in those days. I was coaching at Botany RSL as well as trying to get Botany United going — and I used to pick up all the kids and throw them into the back of the VW. Then I'd be down the pub, selling raffle tickets. Football was the go then. For me, it was my whole interest.'

As a delegate with La Perouse and then Botany United, Morris walked into regular Monday night meetings that were full of fire and brimstone. They were held in the mid to late '60s in the Griffiths Hall at Kennedy Street, Kingsford. 'There were some lively nights all right …

A BAD NIGHT AT THE CLUB

A cocaine bust by officers of the Drug Squad at the club in June 1992 ended the highly-promising career within the club of Junior's assistant secretary-manager Darcy Lawler jnr. In the June 5 raid police arrested seven men who were allegedly sitting at a table which displayed white powder. Lawler jnr, 32, a man well regarded in the club was subsequently charged with possessing a prohibited drug, 1.8 grams of cocaine, and one count of self-administering a prohibited drug. Lawler, who had been assistant secretary-manager for 14 years and regarded as 'heir apparent' to the secretary-manager's job which his father held, was placed on a 12-month good behaviour bond.

Lawler's one mistake cost him dearly, extinguishing a career of promise. His letter to club directors (June 9) held in club files, reflects his pain and embarrassment. 'I deeply regret the embarrassment this situation has caused and sincerely apologise, to you, the directors, the club's secretary-manager, to club members and to all my workmates,' he wrote. 'I have been an employee for 14 years and I thank you for that opportunity and the experience I have gained. I would like to be remembered for the valuable contributions put forward by myself and my management team and not for one blemish that I am deeply ashamed of.'

In a subsequent personal reference, club chairman Henry Morris wrote generously of Darcy Lawler jnr's abilities — calling him a man of 'integrity, honesty and reliability'. Lawler was not the first to pay heavily in his life for one serious lapse — and the June '92 episode was a painful one for both him, and the club.

John 'Chook' Jones, a long-standing foot-ball and club director of renown who gave much to the club

A champion team from Coogee Randwick Wombats, with Souths' stars Julian O'Neill (left), Darrell Trindall (right) and coach Glen 'Porky' Pollock (middle).

some famous arguments,' he remembers. When he gave his support to George Wintle, who was fighting for his life in the club in 1966–67 — moves were made, driven by Darcy Lawler and Wally Dean, to have Morris expelled from the Junior League. 'It was pretty bitter … I wondered what the hell I had walked into,' he says. Morris remembers clearly his first meeting with George Wintle in 1959 after a match he had played for Botany G grade. 'My hand was all swollen up and on the Monday morning I went to see him to get a chit, so I could go to the hospital. You were supposed to get the chit at the ground if you were injured. I was overawed by the man … I had seen him at the grounds, of course. Well, he 'upped' me for not getting the chit after the match — and then he ended up giving it to me.'

Notwithstanding that beginning, Morris recalls Wintle with great respect and affection. 'I call him the founding father,' he says. 'What a worker he was … he sold programs, ice creams … did the lot. He was absolutely passionate about the Junior League and the Club. They treated him awfully … the good thing is we've welcomed him back into the fold in recent years, and that's the way it should be.' It was Henry Morris who was behind the move to restore Wintle's life membership — an honour stripped during the bitter battle of earlier days. Under his chairmanship Wintle was welcomed back to the club and made a fuss of … as he should have been.

Morris's home club, Botany United, grew from an initial one grade, to 14, eventually merging with Botany RSL to form one club in 1975 — a move that coincided with Henry Morris's progression to the Board of Souths Juniors. Morris stayed as its secretary and delegate to the Junior League through all those growing years — along the way got elected to Botany Council for a six-year term. He was there when the infamous bribery allegations emerged — touching rising political star Laurie Brereton among others.

A Botany boy, born and bred, he still lives in the district. His father Henry was in Henry jnr's words 'a mad Rabbitoh'. Not much else was discussed at the Morris dinner table. Henry Morris jnr

played his football in the front row, and made Souths Jersey Flegg side …
'my claim to fame,' he says. He played until 1974 — just two years before
he became chairman of the biggest licensed club in Australia.

'It was a fierce competition,' he says of days in Botany United
A grade. 'But the mateship was always the great thing about it. You belt
the s— out of blokes and vice versa for 80 minutes on the football field …
then you end up having a drink together and becoming lifelong mates.'

The club's ongoing commitment to the reason for its being — the
weekend football in the district — has never been in question. 'That [the
support of the Junior League] is the reason the club was formed in the
first place,' says Morris simply. The
timeless message gets through via
such means as the eye-catching
advertisement placed in the *Weekly
Southern Courier* in the 1990s:

'FREE — compulsory insur-
ance, jersey, socks and shorts, football to each team. No joining fees,
no registration fees, no ground
fees.

'The South Sydney Junior
Rugby League warmly invites
young men to play the game.'

Throughout its life — and
even through the turbulent years
— Souths Juniors has skilfully bal-
anced its dual obligation, of looking after the football, and of
attending too to the needs of
40 000–50 000 social members. The
sheer size of the club and what is
required to run it in recent years is
mind-boggling. The shopping list
for a week, for example, might
include the following: two thousand chickens, 700kg of fish,
2 000kg of red meet, 150 legs of
pork. From 10 o'clock every morning the club that George built
buzzes with activity — a mini-city

BELOW: *La Perouse (with ball) v Mascot. Weekend action on the park.*

BOTTOM: *A cluster of South Eastern Juniors close on a La Perouse ball-carrier.*

NO LENDING HAND

In 1983, with the 'troubles' now seemingly well behind, the club was dragged briefly into another Royal Commission — the one established to enquire into the activities of the Nugan Hand Group. Henry Morris's succinct letter to the Royal Commission, reprinted here explains how a seemingly innocent investment option taken by the Juniors in 1976 involved the club unwittingly with a bank which was to become the most notorious in Australia's recent history. The club survived the experience better than many others — retrieving every last cent of funds, plus the generous interest paid by Nugan Hand. They did better than counterparts St George; the Saints dropped $1 million. Following is a slightly truncated version of Henry Morris's 'history' of Souths Juniors' link with the Nugan Hand Bank:

'About June or July 1976, I met Denis Pittard [ex-Australian Test five-eighth] who was known to me through our mutual association with South Sydney Rugby League, and in the course of conversation he enquired whether the club … had any money to invest. I informed Mr Pittard that it would be a matter for the Board of Directors. Subsequently he arranged to meet me at the Souths Juniors Club and filled me in on details of the company and the investment proposition. Subsequently I believe Mr Pittard saw Mr [Cliff] Murphy — the club's internal accountant and auditor — and the letter left by Mr Pittard was later referred to the Board, with observations by Mr Murphy.

'As a result of the recommendations of Mr Murphy, and after checks by him with the then — Rural Bank, which was the club's banker, as to the authenticity of the Certificates of Deposit (which came from the National Bank of Australia), an amount of $500,000 was invested on August 19, 1976 … The Directors, when approving of the advance of $500,000 were influenced by the rate of interest available from other banks at that time. The amount was repaid to our club on August 18, 1977. In the meantime we received from Nugan Hand Bank cheques for interest.

'On August 18, 1977, being aware that the advance of $500,000 was repayable, the Directors approved of the re-investment of that amount, with a further deposit with Nugan Hand of $500,000, making a total investment of $1,000,000. These deposits matured in September 1978 and were renewed until September 1979 with the approval of the Directors. In the meantime interest had been paid regularly to the club by Nugan Hand.

'On September 14, 1979, certain of the Directors of the club proposed that the investment through Nugan Hand Bank be increased by a further $1,000,000. This was opposed by two of the directors, Viv Wemyss and Frank Cookson. The motion to invest the amount of $2,000,000 was carried. However, apart from the $1,000,000 already invested and renewed for a further 12 months, no further moneys were invested. Mr Lawler as secretary-manager, following legal advice and because of the adverse publicity that had arisen concerning

Nugan Hand, recommended to the Board that no further investments be made. The Directors accepted Mr Lawler's recommendation.

'On September 6, 1979, the $1 000 000 outstanding was repaid to and rebanked by the club with its own bank, the then — Rural Bank. At various times between August 1976 and August 1978 approaches had been made by Mr Pittard and Mr [Steve] Hill [of Nugan Hand] to have Nugan Hand conduct some of the ordinary banking business of the club, but this was at all times refused.'

Later, both Henry Morris and Darcy Lawler had to attend the enquiry that followed the bank's collapse. 'We were fortunate to get out before the whole thing blew up,' says Morris. 'Our involvement in the enquiry wasn't much — just to table some documents and to give the details of the investments that we had made.'

It was champion five-eighth Denis Pittard, pictured skipping away from a Billy Smith tackle, who linked the club up to the Nugan Hand Bank. Subsequent investments proved successful — although not without some later heartache.

catering in so many different ways to its diverse population. For 1999 as Souths Juniors celebrated its 40th anniversary as a licensed club full membership for a year cost $15 — a dollar or two more than a night at the movies — and the charge for associate membership was $10.

In conversations for this book chairman Morris reflected on the 20 years of comparative stability that followed the fiercely troubled years of the 1960s and '70s. The fine detail of the club's story is told in the year-by-year profiles on these pages. Following here, Henry Morris, a committed and respected figure at the helm for more years than probably even he can believe, takes a personal look at aspects of life at the Juniors over the years:

THE ENTERTAINERS:

'We've had wonderful people here over the years. Neil Sedaka and Howard Keel and Kathryn Grayson and the Supremes and so many more. The quality of the entertainment has always been a big part of what we do at the Juniors. We're proud of the fact that we've had some of the world's finest entertainers here, for our people. Wally [Dean] used to entertain them, take them out on boats … all that kind of stuff. We stopped all that. Nowadays we go and meet them when they arrive and I'll go backstage and say hello now and then. But we don't get much involved. These are professional people, doing a fine job for us. We've always had a resident band, and a resident ballet. Entertainment of the highest quality has always been part of the Juniors.

'Probably the best thing we ever did was to re-do the auditorium and get rid of the three bloody big horrible columns that used to be there. It was a big job … they put these huge support beams across. Darcy [Lawler] reckoned it couldn't be done, and he had advice that way. But it was done — and the auditorium is terrific now.'

ABOVE: *The cast of 'Magic of the Minstrels', 1986.*

BELOW, LEFT: *The entertainment at the Juniors comes in all sizes, shapes and styles.*

OPPOSITE PAGE, TOP: *The show was 'Tribute to the Big Bands' and members of the Souths Juniors Ballet joined headline act 'The Andrews Sisters' for a celebratory photo.*

OPPOSITE PAGE, MIDDLE: *Fast-stepping, high-kicking … the always popular Souths Juniors Ballet.*

OPPOSITE PAGE, BOTTOM: *Mark Lloyd and some of the cast from 'Enter the Night'.*

THE BOXING:

'Fight night boxing was a big event here for a long time. People in this district seemed to love the fights. Bernie Hall [ex-champion boxer who became a trainer] ran it for us for a long time. He was a tough old bloke. He'd stand over the judges half the time and it seemed that the boys from Bernie's corner won most of the time. I don't know how many letters we [the Board] sent to him making the point strongly that the judge's decision had to be absolute law — whether the fighter came from Bernie's camp or not. He was a tough character, Bernie. I saw him challenge Jeff Fenech in the auditorium one night. Fenech was up at ringside booing and heckling him and Hall just turned on him. 'Shut up you little ———,' he said. 'This is my night.' He wouldn't take a backward step, Bernie. We had the amateurs here too — with Arthur Tunstall at the helm and they'd play to a packed house. Kids from about eight upwards. The club has been a terrific supporter of the amateurs.'

ABOVE: *Fight night was always a popular attraction at the club — a chance to have a beer and watch a scrap. Over the years, the Juniors have been great supporters of amateur boxing, providing opportunity for youngsters with their sights set on the Olympics.*

RIGHT: *Most often the fights played to packed houses, providing their share of colour and controversy.*

VICTORY FOR PEOPLE POWER

The combined might of the Leagues Clubs of South Sydney — Juniors and Seniors — proved an immovable object in a bitter battle over poker machine tax in 1997. With chairmen Henry Morris (Juniors) and George Piggins (Seniors) in the vanguard the two clubs fought furiously against an iniquitous tax proposed by the NSW Labor Government. The plan was that from September 1, 1997, clubs generating between $1 million and $2.5 million in poker machine gross profits were to be hit with massive tax rise of 33 per cent. To a staunch Labor man like Henry Morris the Labor Party's proposal was a significant betrayal of its own people and principles. There was fury at the realisation that such a tax would cut clubs to the bone:

- Reducing the services on offer to members.
- Penalising charities and other social welfare agencies, recipients of millions of dollars each year from the club industry. Said Henry Morris as the tax loomed, in July 1997: 'We have just donated $750 000 to the Prince of Wales Hospital, but we have had to say this is the last time.'
- Leading to rises in membership fees, dining room prices, the imposition of entertainment charges, staff reductions and general cutbacks.

Already heavily pressured by the progressive concessions made to hotels, the clubs fought back. Plans were set in place to stand high-profile candidates against key Labor Party figures Bob Carr, Andrew Refshauge and Ernie Page in the next election. There was speculation that George Piggins himself would take on Premier Carr for the seat of Maroubra.

People power, commonsense and the muscle generated by the Juniors and others finally won the day. Realising the hornets' nest they had stirred up — and the potentially damaging quality of the opposition — the Labor Party took several steps back from their original proposal.

Smithy's Gaming Room with its spectacular centrepiece — a scale replica of the 'Southern Cross'.

THE WRESTLING:

'The wrestling was popular too. Mike Cleary [ex-rugby league international, later NSW Minister for Sport] used to do the calling when it first started. We'd have Ronnie Miller and Larry O'Day and all that mob. In the end we had to stop the wrestling because some of the members got too excited, too involved. They thought it was fair dinkum. Can you believe that? They'd rush down to ringside … that sort of thing and it was looking like it was going to get out of control.'

HARD YARDS:

'Over the years we have spent a fortune, upgrading a 1959 building into something that would be suitable for the '90s and beyond. We had some problems all right. Getting rid of the asbestos that was used in building of that time, for a start. Sometimes I wonder whether we should have pulled the whole thing down and started again. We didn't — and it has cost us a fortune over the years.'

ABOVE: *Flowers on the table, good food and wines at the ready … the Sky Lounge set up and looking at its best for a private function.*

LEFT: *In the range of food offered the focus has always been on variety, and excellence.*

TOP: *Karate classes for the young ones, with expert advice on tap.*

CENTRE: *It's a close call and the gathering for a precise measuring decision is worthy of the United Nations. Indoor bowls remains ever-popular.*

BOTTOM: *Half an hour of water-aerobics at the Juniors — and you're GUARANTEED to feel better.*

LOYALTY:

'The loyalty of many people is behind the success of this club. I think of people like Claire James and Joan Child. And honestly the way they were treated in earlier times was bloody terrible. But they stuck solid because they loved the place. The club was built on the contributions of people like them. The club was very, very lucky to have them, and I'm not sure if we'll ever be able to thank them properly. Joan Child was an absolute rock for Darcy — she'd do all the correspondence, do everything for him. And Claire is a person full of heart and compassion. She loved the Junior League and she virtually ran it; she had to — Darcy certainly wouldn't have. He wouldn't have known what colours half the sides wore. Claire and Joan ... they were equally brilliant.'

THE JUNIOR LEAGUE TODAY:

'Claire James used to virtually run it on her own. Nowadays we have a staff of five full-timers. We employ two development officers, a chief executive officer and two secretaries ... plus a trainee. The commitment to rugby league is as strong now as it's ever been. I have no doubt it will always be that way. Our commitment to junior football in the district is enshrined in the articles of Souths Juniors [four members of the Management Committee of the Junior League on the seven-man Board]. It's something that has been tested in court — where the articles were proved valid — and I'm sure it's there for evermore. My personal wish is that the Junior League will always be strong within the licensed club.'

TOP: *Happy prizewinners at the end of a club rock 'n' roll contest.*

ABOVE: *That good ol' rock 'n' roll.*

RIGHT: *The Orbit Room.* Photo courtesy of Ern McQuillan.

BELOW: *The club's popular Racing Game.*

THE MEMBERSHIP:

'We've progressively become a league of nations over the years — pretty much reflecting the changes in Australian society. I honestly wouldn't have a clue as to the range of countries represented within the club now — but it would be huge. We're over 50,000 members now (53,000). There were 246 when George [Wintle] kicked it off back in 1959. We give people automatic life membership when they have been members for 35 years.'

THE MONDAY NIGHT MEETINGS:

'The meetings were pretty much my introduction to the [licensed] club. They used to give each delegate two tickets. We'd come back to the club ... and you'd get two beers and a little meal at the snack bar. The Monday night meeting routine has been going for as long as anyone can remember, starting these days at the end of February, and ending in September. They're pretty tame these days, compared with what they used to be. They were fiery all right ... especially at the time of the big split. Friend turned against friend, club against club. And there were people wounded along the way who were good rugby league people.'

FRINGE BENEFITS:

'We're proud of the extra things the club can offer that can make life just that little better for members … the hotel-motel on the Hawkesbury (Una Voce) … the blocks of units up the coast … the [Souths Juniors] Bowling Club, a bold initiative from years ago … all the intra-clubs catering to hobbies and interests … the two luxury coaches we have for members … the boats … the determination to look after our staff — we have a staff bus that drops home anyone who works late. At the holiday places we have always subsidised the costs [Una Voce has been a steady loser over the years] because we believe that while we're travelling okay we should be subsidising things to make life a little easier, a little more comfortable for our members.'

ABOVE: *The tennis courts at Una Voce in full swing on a busy weekend.*

BELOW: *Walkers head back to Una Voce — a bright blue sky above and beautiful bushland all around.*

THE FUTURE:

'Well, we're in good shape — but we need to be constantly vigilant, constantly on the pace. The competition out there is stronger and sharper than it's ever been — what with pubs getting poker machines and updating their operations. We've got to stay awake, got to keep working at it. We're committed now to major extensions that will take us into the next century, over the car park. We're going to do that whole bottom floor out for 24-hour trading. There'll be major changes all round … we're shifting the swimming pool … expanding the gymnasium. The competition is tough; the pubs have got their poker machines, and 24-hour licences, some of 'em. The pressure has never been heavier for clubs — to be smart, innovative and professional. I believe that after all these years of relative stability, we're pretty close to a changing of the guard here. Much as I love the place I believe I have just about run my course. It's a double-whammy every week — doing the football, then looking after the licensed club. It would be terrific if we only concentrated on the licensed club. But the Articles of Association say that four-sevenths of the Board must come from the management committee of the footy. That's been tested — and survived — as a basic foundation stone of this club. Four from the Junior League — and three from the floor … although we put out a four and three ticket. Y'know … they're just bloody mad about their footy here. Every Monday night during season we have about 180 delegates at the club

BELOW RIGHT: *In 1995–96 the Juniors showed the depth of the club's commitment to the local community with a $750 000 five-year sponsorship deal with the Sydney Children's Hospital, Randwick.*

BOTTOM RIGHT: *Stephen Fisher was appointed Director of the Juniors in April 1997. He is also a Director of South Sydney Junior League Bowling Club Ltd and patron of four intraclubs.*

OPPOSITE PAGE, TOP: *The beginning of a great partnership as the club put its weight behind the Sydney Children's Hospital at Randwick. Left to right, Professor Les White (Sydney Children's Hospital), Margaret Child (Secretary to the Board), Ron Harder (Operations Manager), Les Banton (Director), Brad Stanford (Promotions Officer), Henry Morris (Chairman), with young patient Adam Howland helping out.*

OPPOSITE PAGE, BOTTOM: *In 1978, then-Rabbitohs coach Jack Gibson acclaimed the contribution of the great clubman and hooker George Piggins with a special presentation. Then, there was no inkling of the battles that lay ahead for Piggins in the 1990s as he fought to save the district club in the face of the vast changes wrought by the Super League war and eventual News Ltd control.*

38TH ANNUAL REPORT
1995-1996

Souths Juniors kicks in for kids

South Sydney Junior Rugby League Club Limited
ACN 000 213 575

for the meeting — and they're here because they love their football … although I'm sure they enjoy the few beers and the bit of tucker that we put on afterwards. So that's how it is. When you're in it, you're in it. But the time comes when you have to pass the baton. Sometimes I think to myself … there's gotta be another life out there. I've been here a long time, and the footy has worn me down a bit. In all the time I have been here I have missed only two meetings. Once was when I had to go to the Judiciary and the other time I was crook. That's two meetings missed in 20-odd years.

'The South Sydney squabble that blew up [Morris's confrontation with Rabbitohs president George Piggins in 1998; see separate story] kept us all together, kept us here a little longer than some of us intended. But I feel I'm near the end of my term at the club. We're on the verge of a new regime. My determination though is that the Junior League [the football side] will always be strong in this club. I just want to leave it all in top shape … and with a great future.'

LEFT: *Professor Les White and Dr Andrew Refshauge cut the ribbon to celebrate the club's five-year sponsorship deal with the Sydney Children's Hospital.*

BELOW: *Souths legend Bernie Purcell, with Harry Malo at the big support night for Harry hosted by the club in 1999.*

OPPOSITE PAGE, TOP: *When the SES boys and girls came to help save the smashed houses of Kensington in the wake of Sydney's extraordinary hailstorm of 1999, South Sydney Juniors was there to say 'thanks' — opening its doors and dining areas to all workers and volunteers. Here, president Henry Morris makes a presentation outside the club, flanked by (left to right) Brian Troy, Gaye Cameron and Peter Micallef.*

OPPOSITE PAGE, BOTTOM: *Kids from the Sydney Children's Hospital said 'thanks' in the nicest possible way following the 1996 announcement of the club's sponsorship support of the 'Souths Juniors Wing'.*

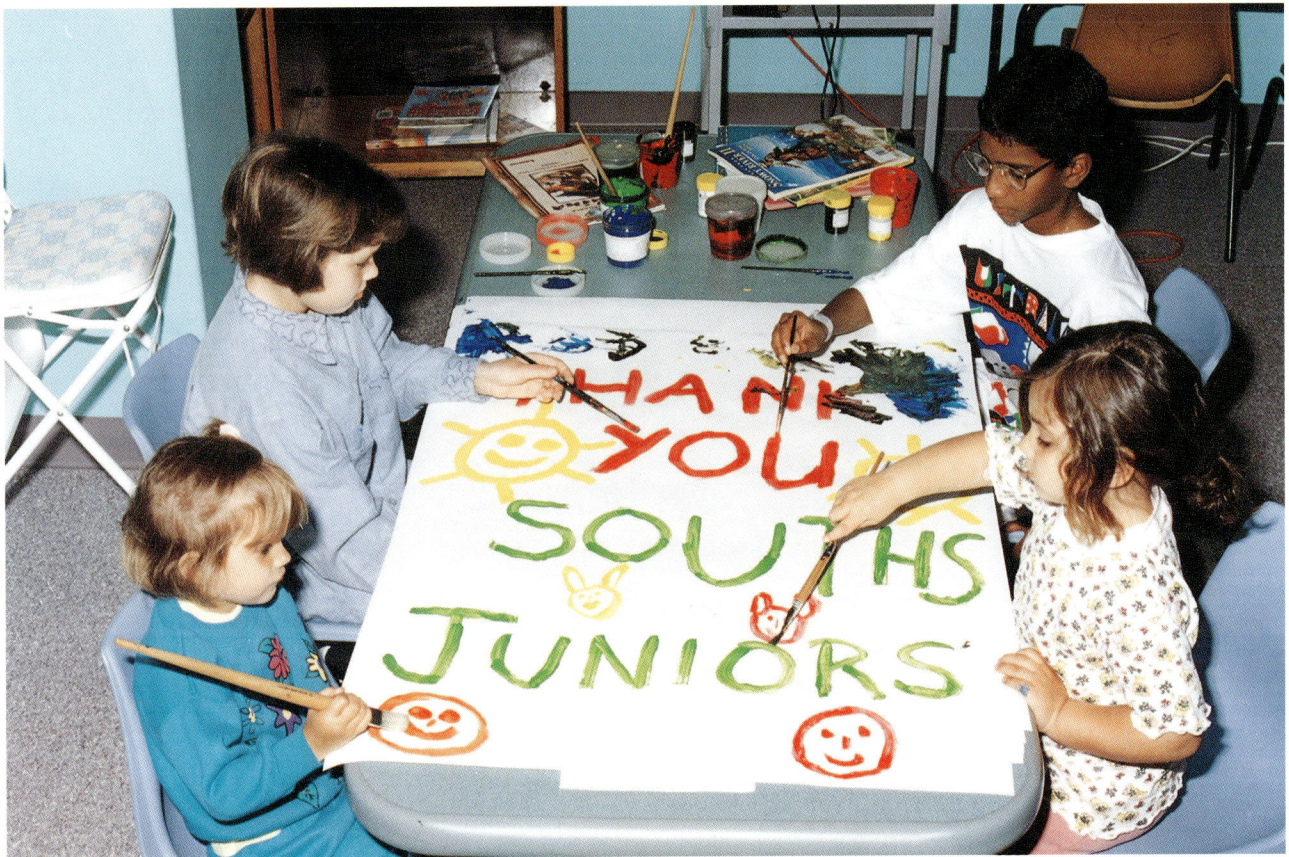

FRANK COOKSON REMEMBERS ...
A PASSION FOR MASCOT

George Treweek. The much-admired rugby league writer Tom Goodman rated him the finest second rower he ever saw. In Frank Cookson's story-bank — handed down over the years — is the tale of the day that Treweek 'belted the bloke with the one arm'.

'I started going to the regular Monday night meetings of the Junior League in the mid '60s, representing Mascot. They were pretty lively times — at the end of the [George] Wintle era, and just when Wally Dean had taken over. We used to meet down at Snape Park tennis courts — the Juniors held the lease on the courts and the club house. It was different then to the way it is now at the weekly meetings. We sat pretty close together and you just had to rise off your seat to talk. You didn't need a microphone. The meetings [in the club] now are not as spontaneous — people have to get up and go to a mike and there isn't the same cut and thrust of debate.

'My links with the Junior League go a long way back. We've always been at Mascot Oval — and we trained at L'Estrange Park for many, many years. My father and uncles played back in the 1920s — and they used to train down at L'Estrange Park. There's a lot of tradition within Mascot Club. We've got fourth generation kids playing down there these days. The Evans family, for one. Old Charlie Evans was the top fighter of his day. They tell the story of the one day he was playing for Mascot in a match in which one of the second rowers on the other side only had one arm ... just a stump on the other side. Well, the bloke with one arm belted Charlie — and Charlie bashed him back, and got sent off. 'What did you do that for?' said George Treweek [bound for later fame with Souths and Australia]. Next thing, with Charlie heading for the showers the bloke with the stump whacked George too ... and then George was getting stuck into him.

'Mascot Club went through some hard times. In the mid '60s the club was almost extinct. But a combination of hard work and a number of good people brought it back — and Mascot has been pretty much the premier club ever since. I think they have won every club championship, bar about four, between 1969 and 1998. We had a breakaway in the 1960s — a club called Mascot Jets was formed in 1962. There was some discontent around and a bloke named Harold Fogarty who was a terrific worker for Mascot gathered up some players and started the new club. Quite a few of our blokes went and played with them, but they lasted only one season — then everyone came back.

'I still go to Mascot Oval every Sunday in the season. I have a passion for the joint. I suppose it is what a 'club' ideally should be about — every-

With hair brylcreamed, boots shined and in blazers and scarves, the winning Mascot A grade side were a proud lot when photographed in 1952.

one knows you … and you know everyone … plus their kids and their grand-kids. The guys I coached when I first started now have got grandkids playing for the club! There have been some great players come out of the club — Ian Roberts, Eric Lewis, Percy Williams for a time, Brian Hambly, George Treweek, Alf and Frank O'Connor, Mario Fenech, George Piggins, 'Chicka' Moore.

'Things have changed in junior football. The raffle ticket is pretty much gone. Back in the '60s most clubs used to rely on two bob raffles to get them through. In fact we still run raffles at Mascot and they help pay for some of the funding — but there is a lot of sponsorship in Junior League now. Everyone gets a good go from Souths Juniors — the gear and the allowances and subsidies and prize money. The players really don't have to put their hands in their pockets.

'My personal opinion is that the standard |of play| has dropped in the last 8-10 years. I look around the district today — and there are only four or five Under 19s sides. Ten or 12 years ago there were 16 sides playing. It just seems there is a dramatic drop-off in numbers all-round in football. And the fact is that without quantity, you can't be guaranteed of getting quality. Kids have got that many things to do these days. I don't believe the League is doing the game's future any favours with the current structure. Once we had stepping stones all the way to third grade and beyond … Ball, Matthews, Jersey Flegg and President's Cup … all of them as Junior League competitions. Now they have dropped the Thirds, made the President's Cup an open age competition … and left a huge gap down to the Under 19s. Now where do the kids in that gap go? Probably out of football. Effectively, the current administrators have dropped two grades — citing costs as the reason. That's a load of garbage. Because of the inflated pay structure these days it costs more to pay one middle-of-the-road player than it would to run a whole competition for kids. In the interests of keeping young blokes in the game

Some proud award winners pose with one of the great-achieving Rabbitohs of modern times, front-rower Ian Roberts.

they should be creating competitions … not destroying them.

'The other thing that has changed in Junior League is the behaviour of spectators. Some of the parents on the sidelines are a bloody disgrace. I suppose we have all given a referee a bagging somewhere along the line. But it's got out of hand. There seems to be a new generation of people in the game who have no respect for anything.

'The Juniors' relationship with the senior club (Souths Rabbitohs) has been much discussed. I'd say it has always been good at the times we have been giving them something. When all the drama was on this year I had a million people ringing me and asking me why the Juniors wouldn't pour a pile of money in each year to fund the senior club. I told them all the same thing: 'It is not the function of Souths Juniors to keep Souths Seniors going.' And that's the truth of it. Our brief at the Juniors is to look after junior league … junior sport in the area … not to pay professional footballers. Honestly, it is ridiculous to suggest that it is the Juniors' responsibility to underwrite the Seniors. And people talk about the Juniors' grant as 'peanuts'. I wouldn't mind getting peanuts like that — $1.5 million a year! I believe the Juniors have been very generous in their support of Souths. And, of course, everyone at the Juniors hope there is some way the club can survive. In normal times, they'd be all right. But once this mob [Super League] came along it was a different ball game with different agendas. The other side of the coin, of course, is that of the 50,000 members at Souths Juniors, a large percentage don't have an interest in football. Their interest lies in going to the club and enjoying themselves.'

Frank Cookson — 'I still go to Mascot Oval every Sunday in the season. I have a passion for the joint.'

GEORGE PIGGINS, HENRY MORRIS —
AND THE FIGHT FOR FOOTBALL'S FUTURE

One of the saddest events of the 1998 rugby league year was the high-level squabble between two great Souths men and soul-brothers in football — Henry Morris (Juniors) and George Piggins (Rabbitohs). At issue was the standing and responsibility (if any) of the South Sydney Junior Leagues Club to the district club's threatened future under premiership football's new regime of the NRL/News Limited. Could the Rabbitohs continue to 'stand alone' in league's new future? That was the question. Via a succession of strong and emotional statements by George Piggins in the media, the Juniors, with $19 million in club reserves, were progressively painted as the 'bad guys' — for a perceived lack of (total) support to the cash-strapped Rabbitohs. The cry went up for the two South Sydney clubs to merge — to 'Save the Rabbitohs' and preserve their heritage in the district. The falling out between the two strong men of South Sydney football was an unfortunate residue of a particularly thorny issue. The pair of them — Piggins and Morris — had stood shoulder-to-shoulder to mount pressure on Premier Bob Carr and head off the suggested and iniquitous increased poker machine tax in 1997. Now they were at each other's throats.

Through local and metropolitan media Souths' chairman Piggins in his fight for the club he loves, hit hard and repeatedly on the issue of Juniors' support for the senior club:

In the *Daily Telegraph*: 'The Juniors have the capacity to help the Seniors. They turned over around $80million last year and have a reserve of $15 million [sic]. Together with the senior licensed club and the right business plan we could easily manage what it takes for the Rabbitohs' survival … and I guarantee it would not drain the Juniors' resources one iota.'

In *The Messenger*: 'Souths Juniors not assisting us is the only way they [News Limited/NRL] can get rid of us. Come on Henry [Morris] you have an obligation to the people of this district. The future of the South Sydney club is in your hands.'

In the Sydney *Bulletin*: 'There's only one merger we want and that's for the one between the Seniors and the Juniors. Together we're unbeatable. The Junior League players of the district deserve to have a senior team to which they can aspire.'

In the *Sun-Herald*: 'The Juniors' support is essential. I feel like a beggar but I'm happy to go cap in hand.'

Eventually, tired of the steady stream of letters calling him 'traitor' and the ones accusing him of selling out the Rabbitohs — Henry Morris hit back publicly. 'You can't keep on getting belted around the lughole without retaliating,' he said. Relationships between the two clubs fell to an alltime low — and especially so after Monday July 6, 1998 when the Board of South Sydney Juniors voted that the $1.5 million per season funding grant to the Rabbitohs that had been in place since 1997 would continue for 1998 and '99 only — and would cease from 2000. As Morris declared then — and was later proved — that position was definitely not, however, 'a closed door'.

In the wake of the announcement, George Piggins made an emotional declaration that his club now had no option but to seek a merger. 'The club is definitely endangered,' he told *The Australian*. Said Morris: 'George forced the issue. I said to him … 'don't do it … don't force it, the timing's not right'. But he went ahead. George was standing over us — which was probably quite fair for him from a tactical point of view — stating that with the turnover we have here we're not spending enough on senior football. But that's not our charter … just not our charter. The fact is that we have extensions of $10–$12 million planned at the club and we are being careful because of the possible impact of the GST. We said to them: 'If you want a commitment now for 2000 and beyond, we can't provide it.' But we never closed the door on them. It was always a wait and see situation.'

Morris told the *Sun-Herald* at the time: 'I'm cranky. We're sick and tired of too much pressure. We love Souths … we're passionate about the club, but we can't be railroaded. It can't go on. They just can't stand over us. We're not a bottomless pit.'

Later, to *Rugby League Week*: 'At our club I'd say that only a quarter of the members (50 000) have an interest in rugby league. There's such a mix of people … very many of them wouldn't care if it was a ping-pong club. It's been said that everyone who goes through the door of our clubs loves the Rabbitohs. I can assure you they don't. Yet our commitment to rugby league since 1959 has been beyond question. Right now we have an office staff of five, and spend $1.45 million per year on running the Junior League. That's our brief — that's what we're here for … Juniors first, and then Souths.' Morris quoted the club's 1959 memorandum of association which reads in part: 'To assist generally in the promotion, conduct and propagation of junior rugby league football in the rugby league football district of South Sydney.'

The ongoing war of words strained relationships to breaking point between the two men … and the two clubs. After one emotional meeting between the two Presidents, Morris said of his business partner and longtime friend:

'Look, I admire him in a lot of ways. His strength and the belief in his principles are never in doubt. He wants his football club to survive, and that's terrific. But, Jeez, you've got to look at the big picture.' Included in that 'bigger picture' said Henry Morris was the reality that in rugby league's changed world there was no longer much sympathy among ordinary people for the idea of throwing vast amounts of money at football clubs. 'Many ordinary working class people are filthy on them,' said Morris. 'When they read about ordinary players getting $300,000 or more a year … gee, there's not much sympathy for that.' Morris chided Piggins: 'Instead of looking at the performance of our club, you should be looking at your own [Leagues Club]. Their own licensed club can't give them any money yet they want to come and get three or four million out of us every year. I know what would happen if we did it. Our members would rebel.'

Morris described suggestions that the Juniors were not generating adequate money considering the annual turnover of the club as 'scurrilous'. 'I asked them — if you think we can improve our profitability here, how do you suggest we do it? Up the prices on everything at the club? It's a steal what we provide for members in the gymnasium and in so many other ways. We lose over $1 million on providing entertainment — but we're prepared to do that, because that is the way the club is. It is in giving away things to members that the success story of this club lies.'

Along the way, 83-year-old George Wintle entered the battle, firing off his own bullets at the seniors, and Piggins. In a widely read letter in the *Daily Telegraph* he wrote: 'I ask this very pertinent question — where was the senior club in 1957 when the Juniors were slogging through the courts for two years to gain a licence? Certainly not by the Juniors' side.' George Piggins returned serve with an equally strong letter.

The history of the sometimes uneasy relationship between the two clubs was tilled, over and over. Said Morris:

'George [Piggins] has said it and so have some of the others that Souths Juniors owe the Souths Seniors because in 1959 when we got our licence, they didn't oppose us. The theory on that continues that having a club here [at Kingsford] has been to their detriment. Well, I can't see that. They're poles apart. I don't believe it's a valid argument.'

In late August '98 after weeks of controversy, commonsense and a shared interest (to keep Souths alive and healthy) finally brought a settlement. At a media conference, chairmen Morris and Piggins announced jointly that Juniors' support of the Rabbitohs — at $1.5 million per year — was safely in place for the next three seasons. Part of the $4.5 million package involved a restructuring of the [Souths] football club. Temperatures cooled — and the two clubs were back on track ... both of them cheering for the same thing: a long and productive future for the famed 'Rabbitohs'.

'The position is this,' said Henry Morris. 'Our unanimous stance is that we will, of course,

The old 'splinter of a building' on Anzac Parade grew by the years into a mighty club.

help Souths where we can — but we will maintain our own independence. That's the way it will be."

By August 1998, the two great South Sydney clubs and the men at the helm, were totally united in the common cause. The task now was no less than to save the Rabbitohs as the NRL pressed relentlessly on, seemingly determined to cut the competition to 14 clubs for 2000 and beyond at whatever cost. Souths were ranked among the clubs in danger. The Juniors Board met, and pledged ongoing support of $1.5 million for the next three years — as the fight for life by the game's most famous club continued.

On Friday, Oct 15, the NRL delivered its bombshell — Souths were out of the 2000 Premiership. The battle entered a new phase.

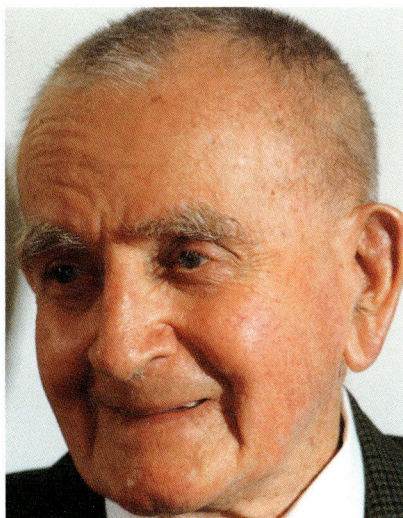

ABOVE: *As the Juniors and the District Club worked in 1998-99 to find unanimous common ground in their support of a great cause — the fight to save the Rabbitohs — Henry Morris steered the ship through stormy waters, often under pressure but battling resolutely on.*

LEFT: *At 83, George Wintle joined the fray in the ongoing Juniors-Rabbitohs negotiations — firing off a stiff letter to the* Daily Telegraph.

GOING TO THE DOGS

The day the Juniors hosted the 'champion' greyhound from the UK at a glittering function ranks as one of the most colourful in the club's long history. In 1975 chairman Wally Dean joined with *Daily Mirror* sports journalists Bill 'Break Even' Mordey and Jeff Collerson and another partner to bring Irish dog Super Approval to Australia for stud duties. Super Approval was listed as track record holder over 518.5 yards at London's prestigious White City track. It was not until the deal had been done, however, that the new owners learned the news that only one race had ever been run over that distance at the track. There was a further problem with Super Approval, too — of which more later.

News that the 'record-breaking' run was maybe not quite as good as it seemed was not even a small hurdle to a much ballyhooed luncheon function at the club, attended by the glitteratti of the Sydney media. Being somewhat colourful characters themselves Mordey and Dean organised a spectacular media launch, replete with Irish pipers and dancers, gallons of Guinness and mountains of food. Invitations had gone out on a card bearing the dog's paw mark; the welcoming party held up top, in the club's Star Room. There was a slight problem getting Super Approval into the place, owing to the fact that patrons at Souths Juniors since 1959 have traditionally been two-legged.

Finally the pooch was decked out in a gold lamé rug and brought up more or less incognito in the service lift. At the opening of the doors, his arrival was greeted by the Irish pipers, lines of dancing girls, the raising of the glasses of frothing Guinness and much cheering. Not surprisingly, Super Approval was a little taken aback. 'In fact,' said Mordey candidly in telling the story, 'he s— himself and wouldn't come out of the lift. He was cowered in the very back corner.'

Eventually the star of the show was lured out of the lift and the party began. At a certain point a TV cameraman working the lunch asked Mordey if there was any chance the dog could be posed with a piece of food. 'No problem at all,' said Bill — and heaped a smallish hill of ham, lobster and chicken onto a large plate. The image on the TV news that night was a beauty … but the aftermath somewhat troublesome. After the sight of the dog wolfing down the food had appeared on TV that evening, a club member rang Souths with a not unreasonable question: was that particular plate destroyed after the dog had had his lunch (the plate being out of the club's crockery)? Well … no, as it turned out, it hadn't been. There followed a general panic, checks with the Health Department etc. As a result, every piece of crockery used at the lunch had to be destroyed.

Super Approval duly went to stud where he also proved to be something of a problem, owing to his significant lack of interest in the opposite sex. Fortunately for the owners the record-breaking plate-licker finally found the spark – and went on to a moderately successful stud career.

Mordey recalls being at a low-grade midweek Queensland provincial meeting a couple of years later, when a Super Approval dog won a race. The crowd was a couple of hundred, the prizemoney about the same. It was a long way, said 'Break Even' Bill, from the glitz and glamour of the historic Day of the Canine at the Juniors.

The 'plate-licker' (literally) which came to Souths Juniors one day in 1975 and caused a stir. Super Approval was a moderate greyhound, as racer and sire — but given a Hollywood-style welcome to Australia, thanks to 'Break Even' Bill Mordey and a glittering function in the Star Room.

CHAPTER 8

CLUB LIFE
YEAR BY YEAR

The club's year-by-year annual reports give the clearest picture of all of the evolution of the South Sydney Junior Leagues Club Ltd. The reports present a fascinating profile of a changing, growing club. Sadly, an extensive search mounted by the club and researchers for this book failed to uncover a full set of reports from the foundation year of 1959. The first report held by the club in its archives and its details noted in this book is that for 1961. The next, for 1961–62, is designated as 'Fourth Annual Report and Financial Statement'. Of the critical reports of 1959 and 1960, no trace was found. But the ongoing Junior League reports from earlier years provide a valuable picture of the steady movement towards the opening of the club in November 1959.

South Sydney District Junior Rugby Football League, 50th Annual Report and Financial Statement, presented at School of Arts, Coward Street, Mascot, Friday, Feb 21, 1958:

PROJECTS AND PROSPECTS

'We are right in the throes of organising a licensed sporting club called the SSJ League Club Ltd. Premises have been secured on the corner of Wallace Street and Anzac Parade, Kingsford and application has been made to the Licensing Court for a provisional license. It is hoped by the time this report is presented we will have started our reorganisation of the interior.

OPPOSITE PAGE, TOP: *The heartbeat of a community — South Sydney Junior Leagues Club, Kensington. Pictured in 1999.*

OPPOSITE PAGE, BOTTOM: *The gentlemen of the Board, 1997. Back row (standing, left to right): Ron Floyd, Stephen Fisher, Frank Cookson, Ken Williams. In front, seated: Barry Dunn (deputy chairman), Henry Morris (chairman), Ron Ellison.*

'Your committee have taken this major step because it was thought we were big enough to own our own home and centralise the already expanding activities of the SSJRF League. A company was formed under the guidance of Mr Clif Murphy, our accountant. A substantial deposit was paid on the building which costs 32 500 pounds and we have secured very liberal repayment terms. Articles of Association have been formulated and already we have a membership application of 300. Our prospects could not be better and we feel that this club will be the biggest in the area within a short space of time. All profits will be ploughed back into sport and charitable organisations.'

The Junior League's office bearers at this critical time in the history of South Sydney junior football were:

Patron: W Fletcher, President: D Thompson, Treasurer: O Nilson, Hon. Secretary: G Wintle, Management Committee: D Thompson, O Nilson, G Wintle, T Craigie, E Coupland, J Kelly, W Fletcher (District Club Rep.).

South Sydney District Junior Rugby Football League, 51st Annual Report and Financial Statement, presented at Kensington Club, Cnr Anzac Parade and Wallace Street, Kingsford, at 7.45 pm on Friday, February 27, 1959.

AUDITOR'S REPORT

'The Junior League has entered into a conditional agreement for the purchase of freehold property to ensure that premises will be available for the club to lease. The agreement with the owner of the property must be completed or rescinded by October 1959. If the Junior League elects to rescind the agreement to purchase it will be liable for the payment of two years rent, amounting to 2080 pounds for its occupance of the premises. The League also proposes to spend 2500 pounds on building improvements which amount is not recoverable from the owner of the property in the event of non-purchase.

'Should the club obtain a provisional licence before October 1959, the Junior League intends to exercise its option to purchase the property.'

1959

'Several problems confront us; one is the handling of the liquor bar at Redfern Oval and this is receiving the earnest consideration of your committee. Another is the financing of our building in Kingsford. The League Club has met setbacks in its application for a liquor licence but this matter is gradually being resolved. We have had 12 months effort in this regard so patience must be the order of the day.'

The licence was granted in the nick of time and on December 19, 1959, South Sydney Junior Leagues Club Ltd opened its doors …

1961

Annual Report and Financial Statement 1961

South Sydney Junior Rugby League Club Ltd.

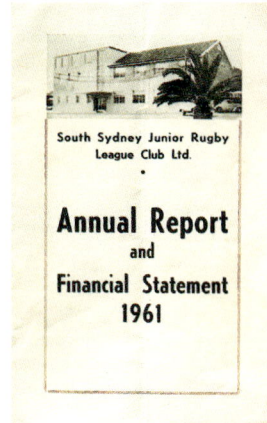

Directors: Darcy Thompson (president), Steve Ryan (deputy president), Jack Kelly, Alfred 'Tim' Wallace, Tom Craigie, Ernie Coupland, Keith Holmes.

'The financial report reflects a position of financial solidarity that couldn't have been envisaged in our wildest dreams,' wrote George Wintle in his report for the year — recording the club's net surplus for the year of 68 788 pounds. Acclaiming the achievement of obtaining a gross profit on bar trading of 17 234 pounds ('due entirely to the honesty and effort of our bar staff') Wintle's generous wider acknowledgement of the contribution of the club staff to a successful year is a feature of the report.

Turning his attention to the poker machines, he wrote: 'We have heard that they are 'filthy' articles, weapons of the devil, breakers of homes, starvers of children etc etc. But let's state this: without these 'naughty' things the great state of NSW would be without many things. We are proud to say that we have nearly 100 per cent playing membership although of course we have the odd 'bod' who isn't putting the odd 'bob' through. We will keep plugging along to bring these people into the fold.'

In 1961, the club supported the 'Windgap' Home for sub-normal children and became strongly involved in the Randwick Meals on Wheels project. Five days each week volunteers gathered at the club to take three-course meals out to people unable to fend for themselves.

The report contains an important 'formalising' of the commitment to South Sydney Junior football. George Wintle recorded: 'We have taken over as a project the South Sydney District Junior Rugby Football League because that organisation has through the alteration of Rugby League policy and through the efforts to assist your club in the initial stages, become entirely dependent on our financial resources.' The club assisted 116 teams in nine grades — 2500 players in all — and sponsored a 10-day New Zealand tour for the Under 17s, and a three-day trip to Toowoomba for the President's Cup team.

The intra-clubs were by now firmly established. Indoor bowling was popular, with 100 male and 70 female members (out of the total of 220 Associate Members who 'graced the club with a dignity that places it above the ordinary'. Marrickville was the main base for the golf club (membership closed at 100) — with the club 'not making much progress' in its attempts to secure block bookings on other courses. Plans were revealed for 'tennis club, fishing, sailing etc'.

Third stage extensions were underway. 'The cottage resumed is being demolished — the [new] building will be of aluminium-cased plate glass front, and most modern.' Estimated cost was 50 000 pounds.

Wintle concluded this way his overview in the modest 11-page annual report: 'We are justly proud of our effort, and can quote that since opening in December 1959 and being heavily in debt, we now own a building worth 72 000 pounds and could possibly be able to finance the 50 000 pounds extension without recourse to bank overdraft. We will always be aware of the need to build an edifice where nice people can go in comfort and immunity — and cognisant of our responsibility to the community.'

Costs
Entertainment — 12 248 pounds
Donations and grants — 7355 pounds
Salaries — 5134 pounds
Dining room — lost 997 pounds

Returns
Entrance fees & subscriptions — 5267 pounds
Net bar profit & poker machine revenue — 99 326 pounds

SURPLUS for year — 68 788 pounds
Accumulated funds — 115 200 pounds

1961–62

Jackpot 1, purchased for 7000 pounds ($14,000).

Directors: D Thompson (chairman), S Ryan (deputy chairman), E Coupland, T Craigie, J Kelly, A Knight, A 'Tim' Wallace.

Club membership at June 30, 1962 numbered 2706, and the annual report tells of a highly successful year, returning a net surplus of 93612 pounds. The club had acquired the adjacent block of land, stretching from Anzac Parade to Wallace Street and measuring 38ft 11ins in width — and plans had been drawn to extend the existing premises over the whole of this area on the ground floor, part of the mezzanine floor and two-thirds of the second floor. Estimated cost of the work was 60000 pounds. The extraordinary energy of the club in those early years was shown in the long list of plans afoot. They included:

· Provision of another car park.
· Renovations to six tennis courts at Snape Park, plus new clubhouse (cost 10000 pounds).
· Erection of a major sports and amenities centre at Kingsford Junction.
· Improvements to Coral Sea Park, Maroubra.
· Securing of land on the central or north coast for a holiday resort.
· An application to the Lands Department for the lease of 27 acres near Prince Henry Hospital for a nine-hole golf course.
· A lease granted by Botany Council of 22 acres at Astrolabe Park — with plans to build a two-decker clubhouse, four bowling greens, a large oval (to accommodate 20000 fans), an Olympic swimming pool, 6 tennis courts, 6 basketball courts, gymnasium and squash courts. Estimated cost: one million pounds.
· Partnership with nine other rugby league clubs to purchase 212 acres at Narellan for the building of the Rugby League Country (Golf) Club.

The extent of the club's determination to expand so widely, so early in the Juniors' life was little short of breathtaking.

Poker machine numbers were up to 65, five of them two-shilling machines. Payouts averaged 600 pounds per day. The club by then owned land, buildings, furniture and fittings with a book value of 185487 pounds. The report declared: 'You, the members, own the lot. Some of you would have a bigger moral claim than others, but in the words of Shakespeare — 'That's the way the cookie crumbles." The club's philosophy on the dining room at that time was made abundantly clear. 'Meals aren't our business. In this club they are an amenity, nothing more or less.' The Meals on Wheels project continued in full swing — 70 hot meals (soup, a good dinner and sweets), five days per week. The Children's Christmas Party attracted 1000 children and 1000 parents. In inter-club notes there was strong focus on the boat *Jackpot 1* purchased for 7000 pounds by the licensed club for the Fishing Club.

The club estimated forward commitment costs (including the ambitious Astrolabe Park project) at 1435000 pounds. 'We are building up assets, not cash,' commented the annual report.

Costs

Entertainment — 19582 pounds
Donations and grants — 14000 pounds
Salaries — 8859 pounds
Dining room (loss) — 6167 pounds

Returns

Entrance fees and subscriptions — 7701 pounds
Net bar profit & poker machine revenue — 158891 pounds

SURPLUS for year — 93612 pounds
Accumulated funds — 177744 pounds

George Wintle's 'Weekly Newsletter' was always a lively read.

1962–63

Directors: D Thompson (chairman), S Ryan (deputy chairman) J Kelly, E Coupland, T Craigie, A 'Tim' Wallace, A Knight.

Never short of enthusiasm or praise for events unfolding at the club, secretary-manager George Wintle opened his report for the year on the front foot: 'At a risk of repeating oneself, I can say again that the growth of your club has been nothing less than fantastic,' he wrote. 'We have increased our membership since December 1959 from 246 to the present figure of 7 120.' Secretary Wintle announced that the building additions announced the previous year had been set back two months by inclement weather but were now 'almost completed'.

The 1962-63 annual report was modest in size (16 pages) — but robust in content, reflecting a year of further remarkable growth. With the purchase of two further cottages adjacent to the club, plans were announced for a second ambitious building program. Via the plan drawn up by architect John Scobie the club was to undertake:

- Construction of the ground floor swimming pool (25 metres long, 34 feet wide).
- Building of new stairs at Anzac Parade, leading up to the mezzanine gallery.
- Extension (by 72 ft x 45 ft) of the main club lounge on the first floor, with additional improvements.
- The building of four squash courts on the second floor.

Total cost of the building work was estimated at 120 000 pounds, with work to be completed inside 12 months.

The club had also purchased that year Una Voce, the 60 acre property with accommodation for 100 guests — at Lower Portland on the Hawkesbury River. Purchase price was 25 000 pounds. The club had also secured for 4500 pounds a second property — 'The Dolphins' — on the other side of the river, providing parking and private launch access to Una Voce for members. In an active, expansionary year the club had bought two blocks of flats at Torrens Road, The Entrance — for 24 000 pounds. For the use of holidaying members the flats provided accommodation for 50 people, at 'very reasonable rates'.

Concluding his report, George Wintle wrote: 'We are proud of our accomplishments ... we are a legitimate organisation that can hold its head high. Don't ever think we will reach a stage where we have too much money — it's being spent all the time, and will continue to be spent on members' amenities and encouragement of youth.'

The club's directors came in for glowing praise: 'All have been most meticulous in their attendance to club duties ... [they] have saved the club thousands of pounds. These men are all workers and have made the club their life. They have never forgotten our humble beginning and that makes them big men.'

Costs

Entertainment — 26 708 pounds
Donations & promotional expenses — 19 989 pounds
Salaries — 11 760 pounds
Dining room & snack bar (loss) — 11 919 pounds

Returns

Entrance fees & subscriptions — 13 335 pounds
Net bar profit and poker machine revenue — 251 640 pounds

SURPLUS for year — 150 794 pounds
Accumulated funds — 328 538 pounds

1963–64

Pride of the Juniors in the early '60s — the new pool.

Directors: D Thompson (chairman), S Ryan (deputy chairman), J Kelly, E Coupland, T Craigie, A 'Tim' Wallace, A Knight.

The graph continued steeply upwards — the surplus for the year a record 238 775 pounds. Accumulated funds now stood at 364 530 pounds. Commented George Wintle: 'The surplus for the year will be termed 'profit'. It may not be fully understood that such surplus is the result of our members fully using the club and its facilities because of the pleasure, comfort and comradeship it affords them.' Club membership had increased from 1959's 246 to more than 12 000. 'The list of persons waiting to join grows daily,' recorded the Report.

Work was proceeding full steam on a number of projects:
- Gymnasium improvements (providing the most up to date facilities in Sydney).
- Completion of the heated swimming pool with its five racing lanes, viewing gallery etc.
- The squash courts, featuring a special air intake arrangement 'unique in Australia'.

Una Voce at Hawkesbury was by now fully operational, with plans for ongoing improvements at the holiday centre. Flats at The Entrance and Shelley Beach gave members a wide range of holiday accommodation choice. Rates varied from 5 pounds 5 shillings per week (off season) to 9 pounds 9 shillings per week. It was reported that more than 1000 people had attended the club's Annual Ball — held at the (NSW) University Hall. Ticket cost was a modest one pound five shillings per person.

A further, major developmental step had been taken during the year with the deposit paid on three and a quarter acres of land on Botany Bay — for construction of a two-storey club house and the five greens that would comprise the South Sydney Junior Rugby League Club Outdoor Bowls Club. The all-in cost was estimated at 250 000 pounds.

The entertainment program at the Juniors for 1963 was this:
- Thursday night — old time dance.
- Friday night — dancing to Malcolm Lowe and his five-piece orchestra.
- Saturday and Sunday nights — bands on both ground and first floors.
- Every second Tuesday — jazz concert. Every alternate Tuesday — films in the lounge. Every third Sunday — Cinemascope, in the gymnasium. Wed-Saturday — Eric Smith at the Hammond organ.

George Wintle looked back on the year and commented: 'It has been an honour to serve as secretary-manager.' As was now traditional the Wintle report was glowing in its praise of the staff (now over 180) and the directors — reflecting his belief that the growing success of the club was very much a 'team' effort.

Costs

Entertainment — 38 299 pounds
Donations & promotional expenses — 18 245 pounds
Salaries — 15 148 pounds
Dining room & snack bar (loss) — 27 573 pounds
Una Voce (loss) — 5 416 pounds

Returns

Entrance fees & subscriptions — 23 770 pounds
Net bar profit & poker machine revenue — 374 081 pounds

SURPLUS — 238 775 pounds
Accumulated funds — 567 313 pounds

1964–65

Directors: D Thompson (chairman), S Ryan (deputy chairman), J Kelly, E Coupland, T Craigie, A 'Tim' Wallace, A Knight.

For the first time the modest annual report document (16 pages, 22 x 14 cms) carried a photograph inside — of Una Voce, nestling on the banks of the Hawkesbury. The resort had been improved by the addition of modern bathrooms, a new children's dormitory and new furnishings. The club had added properties at Forster and Lake Tabourie to its growing collection of holiday venues for members. It was reported that Souths Juniors at this stage had contributed 17 000 pounds to the Rugby League Country Club at Narellan — then comprising three championship nine-hole courses.

Continuing its determination to serve the local community the club in 1965 opened a Senior Citizens' Centre at Kingsford. The Centre was voluntarily staffed but backed by the club. Free morning and afternoon tea was provided plus a midday meal — for two shillings. The club's luxury cruiser *Stella* which cost 25 000 pounds, departed from Rose Bay Wharf three days a week on Sydney Harbour cruises. Longer trips included to Una Voce, Botany Bay, Terrigal and Newport. Primarily for members the boat also hosted parties of sick, handicapped or underprivileged people — plus school groups.

The club was only six years old — but offered a remarkable range of activities through the facilities offered for squash, tennis, swimming, the steam room, gym, billiard room, library to the intra-club activities: art classes, euchre, snooker, indoor bowls, beginners French, old time dancing, rummy, movie nights … and many more.

GW Wintle's 'state of the nation' assessment in the annual report was brief: 'I cast my mind nostalgically back to our opening date, 19th of December 1959, when we had 246 members who possibly viewed the future with trepidation. Time is a wonderful factor — it makes or breaks and in our club we have been fortunate to rise to a position of opulence without being ostentatious — bigness, while still being humble.' Wintle wrote of the '17 000 very good people who grace our club with dignity'. 'We can look forward to the future with full confidence and your directors already have plans which envisage the spending of one million pounds on improvements and additions which will bring amenities and comforts to members unheard of in the past.' It was to be George Wintle's last report as secretary-manager.

Costs

Entertainment — 56 148 pounds
Donations & promotional expenses — 23 092 pounds
Salaries — 16 997 pounds
Dining room & snack bar (loss) — 35 338 pounds
Una Voce (loss) — 9 866 pounds

Returns

Entrance fees and subscriptions — 38 794 pounds
Net bar profit & poker machine revenue — 559 880 pounds

SURPLUS — 332 488 pounds
Accumulated Funds — 899 801 pounds

1965–66

The way we were, mid '60s.

Directors: Darcy Thompson (chairman), Stephen Ryan (deputy chairman), Thomas Craigie, Ernest Coupland, John Kelly, Alfred 'Tim' Wallace, Athol Knight.

The annual report of 1965–66 makes no mention of the club's major event of the year — the exit of George Wintle, founder of South Sydney Junior League. Brief in its presentation the report is signed off by Robert (Bob) Laforest, the man appointed as the club's new secretary-manager. Wintle, at loggerheads with the club's directors was dismissed from his job as secretary-manager — while he was on annual leave. The sacking set up a chain of events which began the club's 'Troubles' — years of bickering, innuendo and drama. The 1965–66 annual report gives no hint of it. It is a relatively sketchy document compared with the reports of later years, thin in content and reporting a reduced profit of $475 139 — down almost $200 000 on the previous year's figure (Australia had made the switch to decimal currency on February 14, 1966 — and the report for 1965–66 thus was an historic one, the club's results listed in dollars and cents rather than pounds and shillings).

Club membership in 1965 had risen to 19 459, divided into the following classes:

- Ordinary members 12 442
- Associate members 7005
- Life members 12

The report displayed the club's willingness to take a loss on facilities that it believed were beneficial or necessary for members. Among them the dining room, snack bar, running

of Una Voce, the tennis courts and the holiday units lost $141 940.

Auditor Clifford F Murphy chided the club's activities on three technical grounds:

- Disposing of a freehold property owned by the club without the sanction of a General Meeting of the company.
- The payment of 'large sums of money' to South Sydney Junior League without the authority of the Board of Directors.
- An authorised payment of $500 to an associate member.

'We look forward to a bigger and better 1967,' wrote chairman Darcy Thompson.

Costs

Entertainment — $142 534
Donations & promotional expenses — $63 287
Salaries — $43 738
Dining room & snack bar (loss) — $129 211
Una Voce (loss) — $22 268

Returns

Entrance fees & subscriptions — $77 523
Net bar profit & poker machine revenue — $1 050 803

SURPLUS — $475 139
Accumulated funds — $2 274 741

1966–67

Col Joye (left) and Barry Crocker (right).

Directors: W Dean (chairman), R Ellison (deputy chairman), F Kilcran, N Christie, L Hart, M Hart, A Caldon. (Two members of the Board resigned during the year — Darcy Lawler, who became secretary-manager, and George Bell.)

Larger in format, printed on glossy heavy-stock paper, the 1966–67 annual report took on a new look — in line with the fact that the club was in new hands after the bitter battle for power. The new directors were pictured on page 2, chairman Wally Dean on page 3 and new secretary-manager Darcy Lawler on page 5. The report of '66–67 is strongly pictorial in content, carrying photos of almost every facet of the club's operations. For the first time an 'outsider' reading the report would get a real sense of the club and its facilities — inside and away from 558A Anzac Parade.

Chairman Dean lashed out in his report: 'The months since January have not been without their difficulties, most of which have been caused by influences and activities unrelated to the business and trading methods under which we have operated. Your present Board inherited many unhappy legacies. Building plans were incomplete and impracticable in many details. The Bowling Club was in a bad way, without a working constitution and many other matters needed urgent and effective action.' Dean pinpointed the assistance given by the club to young sportspeople and observed: 'This is our primary objective at all times. The first and most important aim of our club is to foster football and bring on the young men in our district.' Souths Junior League was now the biggest in the country, with 3000 players.

Secretary-manager Darcy Lawler identified a significant 'upswing' in profit in the second half of the financial year. The profit for the six months to December 31, 1966 was $86 502 and for the six months to June 30, 1967 — $245 210. Lawler called the season past, the 'best ever'.

The Directors' report to members reflected the troubles of the months past. There was reference to 'contingent liabilities' of $520 000 in the balance sheet relating to the settlement of four actions against the club claiming damages for defamation. The report noted: 'Two of the actions were commenced by the Club's auditor and his former partner following remarks of a derogatory nature contained in a circular to members issued at the instigation of the previous Board of Directors. The present Board is of the opinion that the remarks were unfair and unjustified and apologise to Messrs Sears and Murphy.'

South Sydney Juniors now had 21 'intra-clubs' — plus the regular daily gym classes. Familiar faces appeared among the photos of entertainment 'stars' of the year — including those of Col Joye and Barry Crocker. Among changes listed under the new regime were: 'the innovation of Resch's beer, more lavish entertainment, allowing the children the use of the pool and the Dining Room … 'bringing the family closer together'.'

Costs

Entertainment — $242 939
Donations & promotional expenses — $78 850
Salaries — $59 056
Dining room & snack bar (loss) — $174 510
Una Voce (loss) — $21 770

Returns

Entrance fees & subscriptions — $107 902
Net bar profit & poker machine revenue — $1 084 119

SURPLUS — $331 712
Accumulated funds — $2 606 453

1967–68

Maroubra Diggers 'M' Grade, semi-finalists, 1968.

Directors: W Dean (chairman), R Ellison (deputy chairman), A Caldon, L Hart, M Hart, A Henderson, F Kilcran.

'The opening of the Club extensions in May this year has stamped your club as probably the biggest of its kind in the world today,' wrote chairman Wally Dean in his 'President's message'. 'There has been a continual flow of executives from other clubs throughout the nation coming to our club to peruse it, collect ideas and gather information. It would appear that our club has been accepted as the 'trail blazer' in big club developments in Australia.' Among visitors to the club in 1968 were members of the British World Cup (rugby league) squad — who were hosted on a day out on Sydney Harbour, aboard the *Southern Belle*.

(The extensions were widely and admiringly featured in the popular press. '$2.5m Facelift For Leagues Club' read one newspaper headline.) The report spoke glowingly of Souths Juniors 'rags to riches story' and made much of such features as:

- Three escalators — a first in an Australian club.
- A poker machine gambling 'Casino' — also unique in Australia.
- A huge tiered auditorium, setting another club 'first'.

Chairman Dean reported membership up from 26 248 the previous year to 30 649 when the balance sheet went to press. By the end of the year membership had risen to 38 000. The surplus was the second highest on record — $519 662. Secretary-manager Darcy Lawler reported that the cost of the new building, completed in May, was $1 774 878 — with a further $403 495 spent on furnishing, carpets and new poker machines. Deputy chairman Ron Ellison reported the junior league 'population' supported by the club at more than 3500. 'It is indicative that our efforts have been highly rewarding when one considers that in our densely populated area we have the lowest delinquency rate in the state.'

The total of 3500 junior players was almost 1000 up on the 2519 of the previous year. The report acclaimed the district's champion footballers — and singled out the deeds of Eric Simms (50 points) and Ron Coote (try in each match) in the World Cup. 'Our club has been referred to as the 'Cradle of Champions' — a title we accept with pride. No rugby league area in the world has been able to produce champions as prolifically as South Sydney Junior League.' The report picked a team of South Sydney Junior League products who 'would have reached the first grade semi finals this year': Kevin Longbottom, Alan Heiler, Arthur Branighan, Brian Moore, Wayne Stevens, Leo Toohey, Eric Simms, Ron Coote, Bob McCarthy, Paul Sait, Dennis Lee, John Hynes, Graham Wilson. Reserves: Gary Stevens, Ray Branighan. There was reference to the winning of seven President's Cup competitions in the previous nine years.

Costs

Entertainment — $300 403
Donations & promotional expenses — $93 046
Salaries — $60 521
Dining room & snack bar (loss) — $201 541
Una Voce (loss) — $25 126

Returns

Entrance fees & subscriptions — $169 815
Net bar profit & poker machine revenue — $1 390 235

SURPLUS — $551 399
Accumulated funds — $3 126 115

1968–69

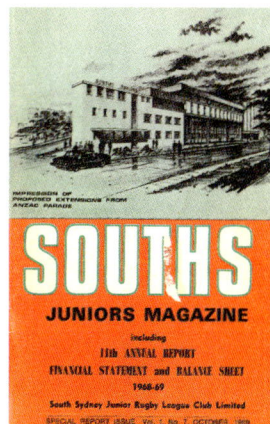

Directors: W Dean (chairman), R Ellison (deputy chairman), L Hart, M Hart, F Kilcran, A Caldon, A Henderson.

For the first time the club's annual report (the 11th) was contained within the pages of Souths Juniors Magazine. The report told a story of continuing growth. The rising scale of membership in the years 1967–68–69 was 26 248 30 649 45 734 and the surplus $331 712, $519 662, $621 999. For the first time net profit from bar takings and poker machine revenue topped $2 million ($2 063 683). The number of intra-clubs was now up to 32. The club had added qualified nursing staff to the ranks of employees — to be in attendance throughout the opening hours each day.

In his report, deputy chairman Ron Ellison set out a philosophy of the management: 'It has been the policy of the directors to adhere strictly to one rule: 'Never lose sight of what the normal member desires from his club.' To this end we have such things as: the Sportsmen's Mornings, the new Bistro, escalated entertainment, further extensions to the present club, the success of the Ball, the staging of night boxing, the picture theatre each week.'

The list of charity, welfare and sporting bodies benefiting from donations from the club stretched over more than a page and comprised more than 80 different organisations.

The report carried a pictorial tribute to the South Sydney Juniors representative sides — and to their achievement of June 15, 1969. On that day teams in the red and green won the SG Ball, Jersey Flegg and President's Cup finals — the first time a club had achieved the 'clean sweep'.

Costs

Entertainment — $701 983

Donations & promotional expenses — $87 355

Salaries — $77 171

Dining room & snack bar (loss) — $262 275

Una Voce (loss) — $21 396

Returns

Entrance fees & subscriptions — $377 468

Net bar profit & poker machine revenue — $2 063 683

SURPLUS — $656 097

Accumulated funds — $3 748 114

1969–70

The racy 18–footer — 'Souths Juniors'.

Directors: W Dean (chairman), L Hart (deputy chairman), F Kilcran, A Henderson, B Shannon, D Johnson, H Cracknell.

A shake-up on the Board saw three new directors help guide the club through the year — with Harry Cracknell, Brian Shannon and Denis Johnson replacing Ron Ellison, Morton Hart and Jack Caldon. Len Hart took over as deputy chairman. The club reported a net surplus of $557 823 — up $11 000 on the previous year. Assistant secretary-manager Norm Christie wrote of 'huge rises' in operating costs, with amounts expended on entertainment and other members' amenities rising by more than $168 000. Christie called the $557 000 profit result 'magnificent'.

Christie offered an insight into the operations of the dining room and snack bars — areas which had always lost money in the club's annual running. In 1969–70 the losses were up, with Christie revealing that the club in fact made a profit on the actual food — but that the determination to keep price levels low for members, carried a substantial loss on the wages bill.

A run-down on dress regulations showed that standards set during the George Wintle era were still, largely, in place. Suit, collar and tie was still a requirement for male members much of the time (at all times in the dining room). Ladies could wear 'sportswear' up to 7pm each evening — after which frocks or suits were the standard. Head scarves and jeans were not permitted at any time.

Chairman Wally Dean revealed two major projects under consideration:

- A convalescent hospital, with payment of 'nominal' charges.
- Formation of a co-operative society for the financing of home units.

The chairman estimated that costs incurred for entertainment during 1969–70 averaged $60 per member. 'When compared with the annual subscriptions charged, this repr sents something like 1000 per cent return on investment,' wrote Dean.

Richard Gray, Entertainment Manager, reported that the line-up of acts in a highly successful year included: D'Aldo Romano, Neil Sedaka, Kathryn Grayson, Howard Keel and Nelson Sardelli. Waxing enthusiastic, Gray described the club as 'the Mecca of entertainment in the southern hemisphere'. In 1969–70, the club had a new addition to its 'fleet' — the 18-footer *Souths Juniors*, seen in regular competition on Sydney Harbour. Junior rugby league numbers during the season were: 187 teams from A to N grade, and 4 106 players.

Costs
Entertainment — $871 205
Donations & promotional expenses — $105 542
Salaries — $81 826
Dining room & snack bar (loss) — $304 206
Una Voce (loss) — $22 561

Returns
Entrance fees & subscriptions — $361 914
Net bar profit & poker machine revenue — $2 268 101

SURPLUS — $557 823
Accumulated funds — $4 305 937

1970–71

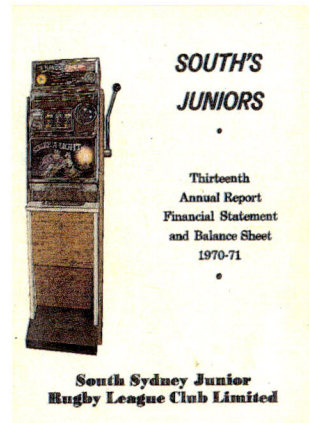

Directors: W Dean (chairman), L Hart (deputy chairman), F Kilcran, A Henderson, B Shannon, D Johnson, H Cracknell.

Two poker machines were pictured on page 2 of the annual report. Around them were the stark details of annual costs now being borne by the club: Taxation — $1.2 million; Suppliers — $2 million; Wages — $1.5 million; Entertainment — $1 million. Announcing a significantly reduced surplus of $208287 (down more than $300000 on the previous year), chairman Wally Dean wrote: 'It will be obvious to you when analysing the financial report that the profit decrease has occurred because of the compounding inflationary trend that has become part of our everyday lives. We have been forced to raise Club membership fees and for this no apology is offered. The increase can be tied directly to the present State Government, whose taxation of poker machine profits could have plunged us to a catastrophic financial fall. Our club is paying the penalty of being a well-organised and controlled business with assets in excess of five million dollars. Economically, restraint could have been placed on expenditure for intra-clubs (now 34 in number), entertainment and other subsidised amenities but such is not our intention — now or ever.'

Norm Christie's report threw more light on the financial position. The club's turnover had reached a record figure of almost $13 million during the year, the assistant secretary-manager reported. 'But added costs from State taxation and wage increases reduced overall profit (to $208287) from what should have been the staggering sum of $972714. Poker machine taxes jumped by $197722 and with a 17.2 per cent salary increase the wages bill rose by $240898. Entertainment was $325807 above that of 1970 for artists and musicians.'

Club membership at June 30, 1971, numbered 50301. In supporting a junior league competition of more than 4000 players, the club spent $105000. A further $70000 was provided for the organisation and running of a Senior Citizens Welfare Centre.

The report of 1970–71 gave a revealing insight into security measures undertaken by the club at that time: 'Senior government officials have described the security for counting and weighing of money at Souths Juniors as being the best of any licensed club in NSW. Four armed independent guards take responsibility every evening and maximum security is maintained 24 hours daily. The guards supervise as the House Manager and senior staff weigh the money which is then placed in a safe until morning when new staff re-weigh and count it. At no stage does your secretary-manager or members of the Board of Directors have anything to do with the counting. Under the double check system of night and morning weighing the money count never varies more than $14.'

For the first time the annual report carried advertising — a fullpage ad for Mick Simmons sports store, and another for the Coronet Carpet Co Ltd.

Costs

Entertainment — $1 118 224
Donations & promotional expenses — $107 852
Salaries — $116 337
Dining room & snack bar (loss) — $317 429
Una Voce (loss) — $23 598

Returns

Entrance fees & subscriptions — $473 459
Net bar profit & poker machine revenue — $2 199 798

SURPLUS — $208 287
Accumulated funds — $4 514 224

1971–72

Cover photo from the 14th annual report.

Directors: W Dean (chairman), L Hart (deputy chairman), F Kilcran, A Henderson, H Cracknell, D Johnson, B Shannon.

Tightening poker machine security and with a substantial cut to the entertainment budget, the club returned to the days of booming profits in 1971–72 — returning a surplus of $537329. Chairman Wally Dean explained: 'Following a profit drop last year because of the compounding inflationary trend in everyday living, your Board took steps to arrest and improve the situation. The emphasis has been on security of poker machines because of an increasingly well-organised group of illegal manipulators. The Board also felt that more money than necessary was being spent on entertainment — and the talent provided do not justify the huge expense. This year the club's entertainment costs have been cut by more than $150000.'

The club in 1971 switched to Top Artists Promotions Pty Ltd — with strict advice that the agents were to stick firmly to budgets. Despite the $150000 reduction in budget the club hosted two Australian 'firsts' in entertainment during the year — The African Ballet and English singer Max Bygraves. Special permission had to be obtained from the Guinean Government before the African Ballet made their appearance. The Ballet had never appeared anywhere but in traditional theatres, and never before an audience drinking alcohol during the show. After observing audiences in the auditorium at other shows administrators of the African Ballet gave their okay for the show to go ahead. For hard-to-get Max Bygraves, who had never appeared in Australia, chairman Wally Dean flew to London to help with the signing. The other big show of the year was the Tokyo Revue, for which the lavish costumes had to be insured for $100000 before the cast left Japan.

Other highlights of an eventful year included:
- The club becoming the first in Australia to operate its own luxury coach. Purchased at a cost of $33000 and featuring stereo speakers, tinted windows etc, the coach was for the use of junior rugby league teams.
- Membership of the 34 intra-clubs topping the 10000 mark.
- The South Sydney Rabbitohs winning the premiership for the fourth time in five years.
- The President's Cup and Jersey Flegg sides winning their respective competitions.
- The demolition of the old Una Voce guesthouse with plans approved for the building of a 33-room motel-type replacement — to cost $500000.
- In the club premises, the Opal Bar was completed and opened.

Costs
Entertainment — $1065700
Donations & promotional expenses — $142311
Salaries — $123008
Dining room & snack bar (loss) — $263099
Una Voce (loss) — $28168

Returns
Entrance fees & subscriptions — $477134
Net bar profit & poker machine revenue — $2396133

SURPLUS — $537329
Accumulated funds — $5051553

1972–73

Showtime stars — The Bachelors.

Directors: W Dean (chairman), L Hart (deputy chairman), F Kilcran, A Henderson, H Cracknell, D Johnson, B Shannon.

A profit of more than $600 000 and the near-completion of the Una Voce re-development project were highlights of an eventful year. It was a difficult year of spiralling costs and turbulence in the associated industries — beer and power — but the club came through strongly. Adding to the pressures was the battle being waged by 'brother' club South Sydney Leagues, which was forced to close its doors for three months before being revived by a 'Save Souths' campaign. Wrote Wally Dean in his President's report: 'It has been a controversial year with suggestions that our club be involved in a takeover of South Sydney District Club. This was given long and serious consideration and several meetings were held with senior officials and officers of South Sydney. Finally, it was decided that although we have close ties with the District Club our main interest lies with our own members.'

In his report secretary-manager Darcy Lawler reported total wages to staff as $1 657 000 and that poker machine and licence tax commitments had increased by $73 000 to a record $1 293 340. The report paid strong attention to the 'Souths Juniors Tourist Hotel' being erected on the site of the old Una Voce. Within the club itself there was an obvious sense of pride in the new gymnasium. The decor of the club was upgraded during the year with new carpeting, furniture, and the provision of new bars.

The problems of a challenging year spread as far as the Junior League. South Sydney JRLFC president Wally Dean outlined the situation: 'The season has been most difficult with the decision of the NSWRL to place an age limit on players. We were very disturbed at the original attitude of the head body, which limited the playing of this great game to 12-year-olds. Recently this was altered to cater for the Under-10 group. No doubt public opinion forced this change; our administration was flooded with protests over the restrictions.' The licensed club injected more than $100 000 into the Junior League in 1972–73.

Costs

Entertainment — $1 102 741
Donations & promotional expenses — $116 575
Salaries — $134 609
Dining room & snack bar (loss) — $239 970
Una Voce (loss) — $5667

Returns

Entrance fees & subscriptions — $452 050
Net bar profit & poker machine revenue — $2 475 750

SURPLUS — $608 000
Accumulated funds — $5 659 553

1973–74

With the Junior rep sides, it's always been a 'team' effort.

Directors: W Dean (chairman), L Hart (deputy chairman), F Kilcran, D Johnson, B Shannon, A Henderson, A Cracknell.

A record surplus of $690 000 and hints of even better days ahead highlighted the annual report of 1973–74. On new plans for the club, chairman Wally Dean didn't give too much away, writing, 'The Board insisted management maintain strict security with poker machines and I feel we are now reaping the full benefit. Although at this stage I am unable to elaborate there are plans under study which could prove even more beneficial.' Dean reported the new tourist hotel at Una Voce as 'a tremendous success'. For the first time the club's total wages bill had topped $2 million ($2 023 371) and poker machine and licence tax commitments were nearing $1.5 million. Wrote Darcy Lawler: 'These spiralling increases that have occurred within 12 months are most perturbing and members, like myself, may well wonder where it will all end.' Club membership was at record levels and for the time, membership was closed.

Secretary-manager Lawler acclaimed the feats of Souths' junior representative sides — with President's Cup, SG Ball, Under 14s and the M grade coaching class all winning their respective competitions. One hundred and forty-seven teams played rugby league in the competition run by the Juniors. The new initiative of the M grade coaching class was ranked a big success. 'I feel this step [of forming the class] will ensure these youngsters are kept in rugby league until they attain the age to enter fully fledged competition,' wrote Wally Dean. 'Perhaps if they had been ignored they would have been lost to other sports.'

Costs

Entertainment — $1 159 154
Donations & promotional expenses — $178 105
Salaries — $156 168
Dining room & snack bar (loss) — $322 272
Una Voce (loss) (listed as 'Tourist Hotel loss') — $53 945

Returns

Entrance fees & subscriptions — $476 608
Net bar profit & poker machine revenue — $2 850 745

SURPLUS — $698 216
Accumulated funds — $6 357 769

1974–75

Cruising … aboard the club's Southern Belle.

Directors: L Hart (chairman), A Henderson (deputy chairman), D Johnson, F Kilcran, H Cracknell, H Morris, V Wemyss.

The Wally Dean era had ended at Souths Juniors and Len Hart, a director since 1967–68 presented his one report as chairman of the Board. Henry Morris and Viv Wemyss were new faces on the Board, replacing Dean and Brian Shannon. No mention was made in the annual report of the troubles being confronted by the club — although chairman Hart in his report wrote of 'enormous difficulties and pressures due to increased taxation and spiralling wage bills'. Hart added: 'Because of spiralling costs and the high inflationary trend we have been forced to restrict some amenities that had been provided in the past.' Net surplus in the face of a difficult and confronting year was down to $210 474, the lowest for many years.

Darcy Lawler pinpointed the rising costs: Wages, $2 690 960 (up $667 589) and poker machine and licensing taxes, $1 186 695 (up $417 960). Lawler rated the profit return for the year 'extremely good' considering the rising costs. Lawler noted a Board decision which was to prove unpopular with members — the charging of an entrance fee to shows when 'topline artists from overseas' were appearing.

The new Una Voce features strongly in the report of 1974–75, via a three-page spread profiling the hotel which had been built on the site of the old guesthouse. 'The Directors have attempted to bring within the reach of all the opportunity of having a holiday in the most convivial surroundings at the cheapest possible rate,' noted the report. 'One thought is foremost in our minds — that you make your leisure hours pleasure hours amidst the picturesque settings.'

Wally Dean, as president of Souths Junior League, presented the good news of 3 126 registered players in 1974–75 — from A to N grade. 'Years ago it was the belief of dedicated men that the game of rugby league was one way in which to educate our youth not only to play football but to meet good friends and comrades and above all learn sportsmanship,' wrote Dean. 'Thus, through the dreams of these men, the South Sydney District Junior Rugby League was formed.'

Intra-club numbers now stood at 30, and the number of charities and local organisations receiving financial support from the club was 41.

Costs
Entertainment — $1 200 487
Donations & promotional expenses — $184 010
Salaries — $213 118
Dining room & snack bar (loss) — $350 733
Una Voce (Tourist Hotel) (loss) — $104 345

Returns
Entrance fees & subscriptions — $462 799
Net bar profit & poker machine revenue — $2 451 288

SURPLUS — $210 474
Accumulated funds — $6 568 243.

1975–76

South Eastern M grade — Tommy Bishop Shield winners, 1975.

Directors: H Morris (chairman), V Wemyss (deputy chairman), L Benton, P Fanale, F Cookson, W Spyrou, B Dunn.

Henry Morris's first report as chairman of the Board — the beginning of a long reign — brought positive news in an improved operating profit, and new initiatives within the club. Reported Morris: 'The increase in net profit was anticipated by the Board which has in a short period implemented many cost saving techniques without depleting club amenities. Price rises, the fuel of inflation, have been minimal. To illustrate this the total administrative and overhead expenditure rose by less than 2.5% in the same year that the national inflation rate passed 12%.' The new chairman reported that the net worth of the club had increased to a record $6.9 million with working capital near $2 million. The Board was vastly changed with 1974–75's newcomers Morris and Viv Wemyss the only directors to hold their places. Chairman Morris reported that the club had been awarded costs of $22 382 by the Supreme Court of NSW in the matter of Denis Leslie Ryan (plaintiff) and the club and others (defendants). On the 'new look' Board as the club headed into its next era were five new directors: Les Banton, Pat Fanale, Frank Cookson, Bill Spyrou, Barry Dunn.

Poker machine and licensing taxes topped $2 million for the first time — with the club's wages bill now up to $2 700 000. Notwithstanding, the profit of $293 000 was an improvement on the previous year and a sign of better days ahead. Within the club the Bistro was dismantled — to make way for a Chinese restaurant, causing some disruption. The addition of a beer garden, BBQ and movie projector added to the facilities at Una Voce on the Hawkesbury, where manager Ted Lawler reported a successful year. The club had a new addition to its staff — 'bunny girls' in suitably short skirts who rounded up jackpots for poker machine players and generally helped in the poker machine area. One of many cheques presented by the club to schools, services and charities in 1975–76 went to the Blind Dog Appeal.

On the football field, 3113 players in 162 teams battled it out in Souths junior league. Souths' SG Ball side, under the coaching of Graeme Hill, again won the prestigious junior competition. The 'Tommy Bishop Shield' for M graders stayed in the district for the third successive year — won by the 'Mighty Midgets' from Maroubra.

Costs

Entertainment — $1 163 020
Donations and promotional expenses — $179 071
Salaries — $240 593
Dining room & snack bar (loss) — $278 820
Una Voce (loss) — $91 234

Returns

Entrance fees & subscriptions — $415 485
Net bar profit & poker machine revenue — $2 648 453

SURPLUS — $293 692
Accumulated funds — $6 861 935

1976–77

The cast of 'Showboat' — a big hit in 1977.

Directors: H Morris (chairman), V Wemyss (deputy chairman), L Banton, P Fanale, F Cookson, W Spyrou, B Dunn.

Operating profit was making steady progress after the slip (to $210 000) in 1974–75 — with 1976–77's return at $384 375 after tax. Chairman Henry Morris described the year as 'very rewarding', accrediting the improved profit figure — in part — to 'the practice of holding regular Board meetings which allow for early solution to new problems and a constant review of costs and income'. The chairman's report gave a snapshot of how Henry Morris viewed the club industry, and obligations at the 'Juniors': 'I feel great advancement has been made in the club movement as a whole and since the licensing of clubs the progress attained by Leagues and Sporting clubs has upgraded the social life, entertainment and other amenities for the average family man and woman. Although our club boasts the biggest membership in the state we have endeavoured to maintain an intimate atmosphere.'

The annual report had gone 'up market' in style — with a four-colour cover format and colour photos of 'Showboat' playing to a full house in the auditorium. Entertainment during the year was at an especially high level — with the line-up of overseas stars appearing at the Juniors including Warren Mitchell, Al Martino, Cilla Black, Dick Emery and Matt Monro. 'We have been particularly proud of the presentation of the musicals 'Annie Get Your Gun' and 'Showboat', reported Len and Hugh Sadler of Vidette Productions.

Senior staff at the club were: Darcy Lawler (secretary-manager), Norm Christie (assistant secretary-manager), George Radolf, Peter Strachan (house managers), Ron Harder, Bob Moore (bar managers), Ted Lawler (manager Souths Juniors Tourist Hotel), Dick Pigneguy (skipper of

Southern Belle). Daily tariff at Una Voce (all inclusive) was $11 — with reduced charges for children. A new addition was a nine-hole putting green.

Secretary-manager Darcy Lawler profiled the new Chinese restaurant which had proved a considerable success. He wrote: 'The luxury Chinese Restaurant is decorated in a most congenial Chinese atmosphere. Ming blue walls and ceilings are contrasted by two sets of beautiful red silk lanterns. The colonnades setting complete with green roof tiles, the magnificent carving of the dragon — these and many other features have made this the most beautiful dining room in Australia. To top it all, we even have a FAIR DINKUM rickshaw on display.' The restaurant was officially opened on December 3, 1976 by NSW Premier, Neville Wran QC.

For the President's Cup side it was yet another successful season — with the 8–7 win over Cronulla-Sutherland in a strongly-contested final capping a fine year. One hundred and fifty teams, comprising 3184 players from A to N grades made up the 1976–77 season.

Costs

Entertainment — $1 464 385
Donations & promotional expenses — $188 732
Salaries — $333 912
Dining room & snack bar (loss) — $304 266
Una Voce (loss) — $107 992

Returns

Entrance fees & subscriptions — $448 173
Net bar profit & poker machine revenue — $3 031 563

SURPLUS — $384 375
Accumulated funds — $7 246 310

1977–78

The Souths Juniors coach — a much-used amenity.

Directors: H Morris (chairman), V Wemyss (deputy chairman), P Fanale, B Dunn, L Banton, W Spyrou, F Cookson.

After years of consolidation, club profits took the quantum leap in 1977–78. A trading year described as 'outstanding' by secretary-manager Darcy Lawler produced an after-tax profit of $644 000, up $260 000 on the previous year. 'The net result came as no surprise,' reported chairman Morris. 'It had been carefully planned by the directors and management.'

It was a year of expansion — featuring the purchase of a luxury coach for use of both the Junior League and the intra-clubs, plus 'Sundown units', an attractive block of holiday flats at Forster. The 24-page annual report reflected the aura of success that was a reality of the year. For the first time the report was in full colour, featuring fullpage (colour) photos of the Souths Juniors Ballet and of the resident band, led by Lionel Huntington. Ninety per cent of the many photos used came from the Juniors' own Camera Club. Darcy Lawler assured members that despite 'huge increases' in beer and spirits prices, the club would do its utmost to keep price levels below charges 'outside'.

Junior League numbers held fairly firm — 136 teams from A to N grades, and a total of 2968 players. Members were reminded of the proud record of the Junior League: 12 wins in the previous 18 years by the President's Cup side; eight Jersey Flegg trophies since 1961 (Canterbury next best on three wins); five wins by the SG Ball side since 1965. 'But we are not restricted solely to rugby league,' wrote Darcy Lawler. 'There is a carry over to the summer sports of cricket, tennis, swimming and athletics and in addition there is a host of social activities provided which often would not be available to the youth of the area.'

Ted Lawler's report recorded a dramatic year at Una Voce. 'The year past would have to be called the Year of the Big Floods,' he wrote. 'The biggest since 1867 according to the records. However the rain did not stop members and their families from arriving. They came over hills, around mountains, over rivers in boats and all kind of vessels … and everyone had a ball.' Tariffs were now at $90 per week (adults) or $12 per day (adults) and from $2–$6 per day (children — depending on age).

Costs

Entertainment — $1 507 374
Donations & promotional expenses — $193 955
Salaries — $369 647
Dining room & snack bar (loss) — $252 058
Una Voce (loss) — $122 921

Returns

Entrance fees & subscriptions — $458 195
Net bar profit & poker machine revenue — $3 281 282

SURPLUS — $644 124
Accumulated funds — $7 890 434

1978–79

The 'Sundown' units — at beautiful Forster.

Directors: H Morris (chairman), V Wemyss (deputy chairman), L Banton, P Fanale, F Cookson, W Spyrou, B Dunn.

The graph continued on its upward path — a buoyant year producing a record profit of $870 627. In its 20th year the modest club kicked off by George Wintle and his fellow believers had grown into something approaching an empire. Costs now were enormous with both total wages ($3 277 376) and poker machine and licence tax ($2 035 347) at their highest ever levels. The continually spiralling costs provided an ongoing challenge to the Board and senior management. Commented Darcy Lawler: 'These continual and never ending rising costs are most disturbing and members, like myself, may well wonder what will transpire in the future.' Lawler described the struggle of the year past as 'very hard'.

Colour photos in the annual report recorded the club fashions of the time. Office staff wore brown tunics with white blouses, Joy in the cloakroom sported a bright green outfit and snack bar staff were in orange. Male bar staff wore dress shirts and bow ties. The introduction of colour to the report gave new life to the photos of the club's units and flats — at Forster (two blocks), Shelley Beach and The Entrance. New, all-weather tennis courts at Snape Park — in fitting red and green colours — were close to completion.

President's Cup, Jersey Flegg and SG Ball sides all made the semi-finals — and the youngsters in the Ball side went on to win the competition, building on their growing tradition.

Recording a busy year, licensee manager Ted Lawler recounted the history of Una Voce, by now a very different building from what it had been. 'The history of this great club amenity goes back to earlier in the century when it was owned and jointly operated by Mr Bruce King and Mr Fred McKinley, who bought the property from Mr G. Gospers around 1920–22,' he wrote. 'Disagreements arose, so King purchased McKinley's share — and aptly named the guesthouse 'Una Voce', meaning 'One Voice'. King's 28-foot boat the *Signet*, equipped with a steam engine, was sailed out from England — and used for ferrying guests across the Hawkesbury.'

Entertainment for the year was headed by the likes of John Inman ('Are you being served?'), Dick Emery, Cilla Black, Jim Nabors, Pat Boone, Kamahl, Julie Anthony, Marcia Hines — and featured world class presentations of the musicals 'South Pacific' and 'Guys & Dolls'.

Costs

Entertainment — $1 728 688
Donations & promotional expenses — $210 230
Salaries — $405 939
Dining room & snack bar (loss) — $236 150
Una Voce (loss) — $106 148

Returns

Entrance fees & subscriptions — $450 914
Net bar profit & poker machine revenue — $3 862 093

SURPLUS — $870 627
Accumulated funds — $8 761 061

1979–80

Zetland JRLFC, N Grade, 1980.

Directors: H Morris (president), B Dunn (deputy president), L Banton, F Cookson, J Jones, W Spyrou, K Williams.

The death of Pat Fanale and the retirement of deputy chairman Viv Wemyss gave the club Board a different look at the end of the decade. John Jones and Ken Williams were the new directors appointed, and Barry Dunn took over as deputy president. Henry Morris superintended a year which he described as being 'a difficult one for the club industry in general'. In his report, Morris explained: 'We witnessed a concerted campaign by the Federated Liquor Trade Union for an $8 per week interim wage increase — an increase above the CPI and outside the guidelines set down by the Wran Labor Government. With clubs disagreeing, industrial action resulted. Your directors sought and obtained an assurance from the Union that this increase was not to be considered as above the award and was to be absorbed in the final decision.'

Henry Morris wrote of a challenging year in which 'commodities and all costs' rose (entertainment costs by 26 per cent) — but in which there had been no decrease in members' facilities. New plans for the club which included a senior citizens centre, new rooms for the intra-clubs, an auditorium cum convention room and additional parking were discarded for the time being. Morris observed: 'The conditions requested by council were not realistic or fair.' Secretary-manager Darcy Lawler went further, declaring that the council's insistence on the remodelling of the old building could only happen at an 'astronomical, impractical and impossible cost'.

Notwithstanding the problems, the club returned an operating profit of almost $400 000. Darcy Lawler reported a wages bill of $3 764 253 (up $283 691) and poker machine and licence taxes of $2 166 169 (up $121 803). Entertainment was a problem, as Lawler explained: 'The cost of entertainment rose dramatically, due, in the main to no expense being spared to import overseas 'super stars', in conjunction with our own local talent. Obviously efforts in this area have been in vain as patronage and response by members to the show have been extremely poor and certainly did not warrant the expenditure.'

Best news for the year came from the football field — where the President's Cup and SG Ball junior representative sides won their respective competitions. The SG Ball victory represented an historic occasion — being the 100th premiership win recorded (all levels) by the South Sydney district. 'We are proud of the officials and players who are responsible for establishing our Junior League as one of the best sporting organisations in Australia.'

At Una Voce, there was continuing progress via air-conditioning for all rooms, the erection of a volleyball court, construction of a wharf with walkway — and plans for squash courts by 1981. Manager Ted Lawler expressed his disappointment at the 'continued efforts of the badge lenders' — with non-members benefiting by obtaining the cheaper tariff of $115 per week as against the non-members' rate of $175 per week.

Costs

Entertainment — $2 061 938

Donations & promotional expenses — $240 934

Salaries — $439 181

Dining room & snack bar (loss) — $317 952

Una Voce (loss) — $101 364

Returns

Entrance fees and subscriptions — $437 278

Net bar profit & poker machine revenue — $3 911 902

SURPLUS — $395 582

Accumulated funds — $9 156 643

1980–81

Directors: H Morris (president), B Dunn (deputy president), K Williams, L Banton, F Cookson, W Spyrou, J Jones.

For the first time since 1970 the club announced it would be raising membership renewal fees — up $5 for both men and women. Recording a net profit of $500 221 (up from $395 582), Henry Morris commented: 'To stay ahead of inflation, spiralling wages and general costs and to ensure the continuance of amenities it has been considered essential that membership renewals be increased.' On the other side of the coin, the club announced that the unpopular booking fee on the auditorium shows had been lifted. Wrote Morris: 'The year has been a successful one in many ways for Souths Juniors in a period of economic instability which has seen many clubs cut down or cease amenities for its members. This has not occurred at your club.'

During the year the club had undergone a 'facelift'. Reported the president: 'Members have expressed their satisfaction in the artistically designed foyer, switch and cloak room areas with the tasteful new carpet, drapes and furnishings adding a touch of warmth to Souths Juniors. The whole interior of the club has been re-painted.'

In the annual report the directors issued what amounted to an ultimatum to the Souths Juniors Bowling Club at Botany. The year ended May 31, 1981 resulted in trading loss of $11 271 for the club. Advance loans of $63 921 and unrecoverable gifts in cash of $14 869 had been granted over a period of time by the parent club. The annual report continued: 'Your Board has decided that no more grants will be forthcoming. They will still receive our support, nonetheless. The Bowling Club from hereon must be self-sufficient.'

Plans were before council for permission to build a car park on the vacant property adjacent to the club — and a new 28-seater bus had been purchased for members' outings. Darcy Lawler pinpointed increases in wages and poker machine and licensing taxes (up $210 000) and a heavy subsidy to the Tourist Hotel ($136 000) as having 'greatly reduced' the net profit for the year. Popular dishes in the Rickshaw Room restaurant, now in its fifth year in the club, included: Mongolian lamb, sizzling king prawns, pork spareribs and Cantonese whole lobster. Entertainment topliners for the year included: Patti Page, Acker Bilk, the Duke Ellington Orchestra, Jack Trent and Tony Hatch, Al Martino, Guy Mitchell, Marcia Hines and Don Lane.

Costs

Entertainment — $1 834 057
Donations & promotional expenses — $242 922
Salaries — $465 041
Dining room & snack bar (loss) — $233 588
Una Voce (loss) — $136 821

Returns

Entrance fees & subscriptions — $451 054
Net bar profit & poker machine revenue — $4 004 405

SURPLUS — $500 221
Accumulated funds — $9 656 864

A big band backing for a top international act — Buddy Greco (piano), Leslie Anders (vocalist).

1981–82

Directors: H Morris (president), B Dunn (deputy president), K Williams, L Banton, F Cookson, W Spyrou, J Jones.

Directors during a successful year wrestled with the dilemma of how to provide assistance to South Sydney (District) Leagues Club which was again finding the going tough as it tried to support the 'Rabbitohs' in an increasingly inflationary environment in rugby league. Chairman of the Board Henry Morris reported that the club (Juniors) had received requests for assistance from the district leagues club — setting out four propositions to enable their club to continue to operate. 'The proposals ranged from the Juniors taking over Souths Leagues Club Ltd and its liabilities — to various others,' reported Morris. 'After many discussions, and your Board receiving advice from the club's solicitors and auditors, all proposals were rejected. However the trading difficulties of the South Sydney Leagues Club Limited could have threatened the solvency of the 'Mighty Rabbitohs'. The provision of financial aid to promote football and other sports in our district is one of the objects for which our Junior Leagues Club was established. For this reason a new company known as Souths Juniors Sporting Association Limited was formed and a loan of $2.5 million has been made to the Sporting Association. The interest earned on this amount by the Sporting Association will go towards rendering assistance to the District Football Club and our own Junior Rugby League. The loan funds themselves will not be drawn upon and may be withdrawn at any time.'

Notwithstanding the shadow of the continuing fight to keep alive Australia's most famous rugby league club, the Juniors returned a resoundingly successful year — with a net profit of $651 000. For the first time in the club's history accumulated funds stood at more than $10 million. An undoubted highlight was the booking by the club of the Dalian Variety and Acrobatic Troupe which travelled outside

the Republic of China for the first time and which staged additional shows at the club to fulfil the strong demand. A highlight too was the innovation of the new Atlantis Forum and Seafood Restaurant (featuring a live lobster tank) on the ground floor. 'Certainly no establishment in Las Vegas could match it,' wrote Henry Morris of the Forum.

The club reported with some pleasure that the associated Souths Juniors Bowling Club was back on track — returning a trading profit of $21 152 after the loss of the previous year. Confronting a wages bill and poker machine and licensing taxes that rose by a total of more than $500 000 in a single year, secretary-manager Darcy Lawler called the ever-upwards trend 'most perturbing' and wondered where it would all end. At Una Voce, fees were at $20 per day ($25 at weekends) and $150 per week for members, claimed as the 'lowest tariffs in NSW'.

Playing numbers in the Juniors were at 2700 — healthy, if down on the record figures of a few seasons before. Congratulations were offered widely to the President's Cup team who won their competition again — for a record 19th time.

Costs

Entertainment — $1 869 260
Donations & promotional expenses — $237 424
Salaries — $531 363
Dining room & snack bar (loss) — $241 759
Una Voce (loss) — $102 156

Returns

Entrance fees & subscriptions — $653 890
Net bar profit & poker machine revenue — $4 235 450

SURPLUS — $651 124
Accumulated funds — $10 307 988

1982–83

The Rickshaw Room.

Directors: H Morris (president), B Dunn (deputy president), L Banton, K Williams, F Cookson, W Spyrou, J Jones.

Clubland faced unprecedented challenge and change in the year 1982–83 — with the introduction of random breath testing causing many people to alter long-established social patterns. In his President's report Henry Morris called the year 'a difficult one', and added: 'It has been a period in which we have witnessed in NSW massive unemployment and retrenchments with many industries tightening their belts and social habits changing. When random breath testing was first introduced in December 1982, followed by the advent of instant lotteries, we were faced with serious problems to overcome. Without panic, or the prophecy of doom, your directors and management have steered the club through this harrowing period — but still realising with the unstable economy we have a long way to go.'

The balance sheet showed the effects of tough economic times, allied with the changes in society. Net profit for the year was down to $260 646 (from $651 000 the previous year). Henry Morris observed: 'When the balance sheet is studied you will note the increased cost of so many essential items. But in attaining this net profit I am pleased to say that no amenities in the club have ceased.'

Secretary-manager Darcy Lawler pinpointed the difficulties faced: 'It has been a year of financial turmoil, incurred by recession, the introduction of random breath testing, high taxation and licensing charges, excessive rates and the ever-increasing costs of running a club of this magnitude. For example artists and musicians [costs] increased by $87 000, insurance by $57 000, rates and land taxes by $20 000, depreciation by $137 000, poker machine tax by $93 000 and electricity and fuel by $63 000.'

Lawler offered his view that random breath testing had had a 'disastrous effect' on club and hotel life. 'It has greatly affected employment, it has affected patronage, and it has affected revenue. No-one should sit behind a wheel and attempt to drive while under the influence and we should certainly discourage any person to do so. However, I hold firm to my belief that .05 is ridiculously low, particularly for a capable and efficient driver.'

Building work at the club added to the financial burden of a tough year — with the construction of the external staircase on the Anzac Parade side, along with other improvements, estimated to cost $1 million. Stringent application of fire safety requirements added to the cost.

In and around the club it was life as usual, despite the hard times. The annual report noted that the tennis courts, holiday flats, tourist hotel, fishing boat (the *Jackpot*) and the club's coach and bus were all enthusiastically utilised by club members. The club's tennis complex was selected as the training venue for the prestigious Custom Credit Squad, headed by Tony Roche and John Newcombe. The football season continued to bring great pleasure to many — and there was celebration at the achievement of Souths' President's Cup team in winning their competition — for the 20th time.

Costs

Entertainment — $2 009 000
Donations & promotional expenses — $348 000
Salaries — $583 000
Dining room & snack bar (loss) — $71 000
Una Voce (loss) — $123 000

Returns

Entrance fees & subscriptions — $682 000
Net bar profit & poker machine revenue — $4 245 000

SURPLUS — $261 000
Accumulated funds — $10 569 000

The chase is on.

1983–84

Directors: H Morris (chairman), B Dunn (deputy chairman), K Williams, L Banton, F Cookson, W Spyrou, J Jones.

'The year under review may well be considered the one that could break the back of the Club industry.' So began chairman Henry Morris's review of a most difficult 12 months. Morris explained: 'so many clubs, particularly in NSW, are struggling. The downturn in the economy, random breath testing, indexation of excise duty on liquor, alternative entertainment such as home videos, and instant lotteries are some of the problems with which our industry has had to cope. Now the Government has passed legislation for video poker machines in hotels.'

In such a climate — via shrewd planning and tight management the club returned its second-largest profit in a decade. Profit for the year was $648 613, as against the previous year's $260 646 — the club's operating cash surplus up from $1.2 million to $1.7 million. Morris wrote of the club's need to be 'continually progressive' to survive. In line with that policy was the 'artistically designed' Orbit Room — replacing the Sahara and Oasis Rooms. 'Your club is envied within the industry — for no other club can match the Juniors for the amenities provided,' wrote Morris. 'We believe that giving value for membership is the formula of success.' Darcy Lawler added the observation: 'To compete successfully we have to be better than other clubs — that is our objective and we know that 50 000 brains (the club membership) will be of great assistance in this endeavour.'

The number of intra-clubs contained within the Juniors now stood at 33 — providing a remarkable diversity of opportunity for members' recreational interests. The report of 1983–84 carried a spectacular colour photo of the new 'Orbit Room' with its kaleidoscope of coloured columns. Junior League numbers held steady, with 135 teams battling it out from A to N grades. The Atlantis Seafood Restaurant and the Rickshaw Room, both complementing each other and in (friendly) opposition, continued to give members a choice of top class dining. The Rickshaw Room announced the introduction of a special $5, four-course menu, available seven days a week. In the auditorium the star turns included 'The Ice Show', 'Tropicana is the Show', 'Artists and Models' (described as 'sexy and funny') and the 'Cherry Blossom Revue' ('full of glamour, mystery and beautiful oriental boys and girls'). Four nights and five days break at Una Voce on the Hawkesbury was still a remarkably cheap holiday in uneasy times — at $100 per person.

Costs

Entertainment — $1 833 000
Donations & promotional expenses — $336 000
Salaries — $595 000
Dining room & snack bar (loss) — $25 000
Una Voce (loss) — $96 000

Returns

Entrance fees & subscriptions — $644 000
Net bar profit & poker machine revenue — $4 419 000

SURPLUS — $648 000
Accumulated funds — $11 217 000

1984–85

The year Ron Floyd became a director, replacing Bill Spyrou.

Directors: H Morris (president), B Dunn (deputy president), K Williams, L Banton, F Cookson, J Jones, R Floyd.

The front cover photo of 1984–85's annual report said it all. Secretary-manager Darcy Lawler was pictured with Ita Buttrose, holding an impressive *Daily Telegraph* plaque. It read: 'CLUB OF THE YEAR 1984 — South Sydney Junior Rugby League Club Limited.' Henry Morris began his chairman's report with the words: 'We have experienced a truly magnificent year which has enabled our club to continue achieving rightful recognition right through the industry in NSW and to still expand on the illustrious achievements of the past.' Morris pinpointed three areas of significant achievement in a memorable year:

- A record net profit of $921 000. Operating revenue of $19 930 000 was 8.2 per cent up on the previous year, despite the difficult economic climate.
- The naming of the Juniors as 'Club of the Year' in the *Daily Telegraph* awards. Noted the chairman: 'There are over 1500 registered clubs in our state and to be judged No 1 is the ultimate.' Judging of the award covered various categories, including: amenities, support to sporting and charitable organisations, entertainment and food. Judging involved an inspection by a distinguished judging panel.
- The achievement of the district's junior rugby league sides in winning the NSWRL's Club Championship award.

Total expenditure on junior league during the year amounted to $310 000. A further $122 000 went to Souths district club in a continuing show of support and to 'upgrade their players and strengthen their club'. Over a three-year period

grants to the Rabbitohs had totalled $367 000.

The club pledged its continuing intention of providing top class entertainment for members. Wrote Morris: 'Other clubs say 'we're mad' — but we have no intention of charging an admission fee for entertainment … we consider our members are entitled to the best.' In line with that ideal, a program of renovation and refurbishing of the auditorium was announced. During the year the entertainment line-up included: Al Martino, Davey Kaye (starring in the 'London Soho Sex Show'), the Balkan Folk and Acrobatic Theatre from Bulgaria, The 'Sexy French Reveal Show' and 'Red, Hot & Sexy'.

Henry Morris and the Board recorded 'with regret' the resignation of assistant secretary-manager Norm Christie after 17 years of dedicated service to the club. Christie, who had not enjoyed the best of health in the previous 12 months was acclaimed for his 'efforts and loyalty' to the club over a long period of employment. The Board had a new member — Ron Floyd, replacing Bill Spyrou.

Costs

Entertainment — $1 904 000
Donations & promotional expenses — $404 000
Salaries — $624 000
Dining room (loss) — $16 000
Una Voce (loss) — $54 000

Returns

Entrance fees & subscriptions — $613 000
Net bar profit & poker machine revenue — $4 875 000

SURPLUS — $921 000
Accumulated funds — $12 138 000

1985–86

The SG Ball team of 1986 — undefeated premiers.

Directors: H Morris (president), B Dunn (deputy president), K Williams, F Cookson, R Floyd, J Jones, L Banton.

An extraordinary leap in profit took the club into territory never before experienced. Chairman of the Board Henry Morris presented the annual report and balance sheet with 'special pleasure' — and not surprisingly, considering that the after-tax surplus had zoomed to $1 813 000. It was the first time the club had ever recorded a profit figure of more than $1 million. The huge profit leap came in spite of a tax increase of $550 000 and wage increases totalling $505 000. 'The club's decision not to curtail members' amenities in the difficult period before was a significant factor as was the continued provision of free, world class entertainment (at a cost to the club of $1.1 million),' wrote Morris. 'Members responded accordingly — by increased patronage.' Operating revenue of $22 309 000 was up 11.9 per cent on the previous year. New work in a vibrant period for the club included the redecorating of the Chinese restaurant (The Rickshaw Room), a complete refurbishment of the auditorium and car park extensions, providing additional parking for 39 cars and 12 motor cycles. Additionally there was resealing of the existing car parks (the property of Randwick Council) — and a renovation program at the Mariner holiday flats, Forster.

Chairman Morris farewelled three long-term employees — Ron Harder, Peter Strachan and Mrs Frances Brodie — and wished them well for the future. The appointment was announced of Darcy Lawler jnr, a graduate of Ryde College with his Club Managers Higher Certificate, as assistant secretary-manager.

Success on the football field added to the lustre of the year. The SG Ball side (Under 17s) won their competition and both President's Cup and Matthews Shield sides made the semi-finals. 'I am very proud of the fact that the Junior League administration totally administers our club for we must never lose sight of the fact — regardless of how big we may grow — that this club was formed for the propagation of junior rugby league in the South Sydney district,' wrote Henry Morris. Numbers held firm in the Juniors, with 2754 players making up 134 teams. More than $300 000 went to the Juniors, and $133 000 to the district club.

Entertainment topliners during the year included Al Martino, Souths Juniors Variety Circus, Simone & Monique, Wickety Wak, Julie Anthony, Don Lane and the Astor Magic & Variety Show.

Costs

Entertainment — $1 900 000
Donations & promotional expenses — $439 000
Salaries — $754 000
Dining room (loss) — $27 000
Una Voce (loss) — $81 000

Returns

Entrance fees & subscriptions — $639 000
Net bar profit & poker machine revenue — $5 792 000

SURPLUS — $1 813 000
Accumulated funds — $13 951 000

1986–87

Directors: H Morris (president), B Dunn (deputy president), K Williams, L Banton, R Floyd, J Jones, F Cookson.

As Bicentennial year approached the Australian flag and coat of arms emblazoned the front cover of Souths Juniors annual report. 'We as a club have our part to play when all Australians come together as one,' wrote Henry Morris. It had been another year of significant achievement — producing a near-record profit of $1762953. The club's accumulated funds now stood at $15715000. The financial result was an outstanding one considering wages and taxes increases of more than $500000 in the previous 12 months and a rise in the entertainment budget of $251000. Chairman of the Board Henry Morris called the year 'a stabilisation period', with no major projects undertaken, although thoughtful planning for the future was well underway. The computer age had arrived, and the club management submitted a detailed report recommending that the Fortune Computer System be implemented throughout the club.

The club's poker machine policy continued — of purchasing 28 new machines every three months to enable members the opportunity of playing 'the latest' at all times. Treasury Department officers assessed the Juniors' poker machine systems and security — and concluded that in both areas the club was second to none.

To assist in community awareness the club donated $10000 to the Micro Search Foundation of Australia, in addition to the ongoing support of regular charities, schools, hospitals and other community projects. In the Junior League, playing numbers were up — at 2975 players, in 137 teams. Through the grades seven play-off games were needed to settle the various semi-finalists — an indication of the keenness and closeness of the competition.

Top of the bill in the auditorium during the year were Max Bygraves and Danny La Rue. Other acts which drew big crowds were Nelson Sardelli, the Fabulous Krankies, Peter Gordeno and The Gypsy Show. At Una Voce, decisions were taken in an endeavour to boost bookings at the tourist hotel during quieter periods. It was decided that reciprocal rights would be offered to other clubs Monday to Friday from the period May–September and that dates would be allocated for seminars and conventions in 1988.

Costs

Entertainment — $2120000
Donations & promotional expenses — $521000
Salaries — $699000
Dining room (loss) — nil
Una Voce (loss) — $105000

Returns

Entrance fees & subscriptions — $622000
Net bar profit & poker machine revenue — $5852000

SURPLUS — $1764000
Accumulated funds — $15 715000

1987–88

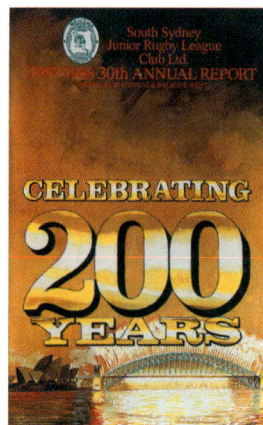

Directors: H Morris (president), B Dunn (deputy president), J Jones, L Banton, F Cookson, K Williams, R Floyd.

'Celebrating 200 Years', read the line on the front page of the annual report, atop an artist's impression of fireworks blazing over the Harbour Bridge. And for the club, it was a local celebration too. 'Proudly I report our South Sydney District Junior Rugby Football League, the birthplace of our club, is celebrating 80 years of outstanding achievements in the community,' wrote Henry Morris. Long since a thoroughly efficient business machine in its running, the club returned another booming profit — of $1 657 000. 'The profit is more remarkable when one considers the economic climate, which was responsible for the reduction in our investment income — and also increasing costs over which the club has little control — wage awards, superannuation, insurance and government licences and taxes,' the chairman noted in his report. Some of the figures were, indeed, staggering. Total staff wages now stood at $4 766 000 and poker machine & licence tax had leapt to $3 190 000. A cut in interest rates had seen return on investments diminish by $301 000.

Henry Morris offered the view that the club industry was heading into a 'new and exciting era' in poker machines. The latest in video poker machines had been installed in the club and via the continuous updating program, none of the club's 454 machines were more than three years old. Morris reported: 'The most recent innovation in pokies is the 'In-house Link Progressive Machines', which are linked by a central controller board — with the jackpot prizes shown on large display cases above the machine. At the time of compiling this report, two jackpots of $31 000 and $13 000 had been won, in addition to many smaller ones.'

Sky Channel was beamed into the club now, and appli-cation had been made to the TAB to secure an operating licence for the premises. In September 1987 the Omeros Seafood Restaurant opened in the club — the 'Omeros' name synonymous with quality in seafood cuisine. The new restaurant's slogan was catchy: 'Our only competition is mum!'

The Juniors had joined the 'World Vision' program and was now sponsoring three children from Third World countries. Adding to the club's activities aerobic and water-aerobic classes had begun for those in pursuit of fitness. Upgrading of the tennis courts took place — with high-quality lighting installed which provided greater illumination than any other tennis court complex in the metropolitan area. Entertainment for the year covered a broad spectrum — including Simon Gallaher, Danny La Rue, 'Les Sexy French Revue', Col Joy & the Joy Boys, Frances Yip, Don Lane and The Ice Show — plus a special: 'Souths Juniors Tribute to the Bicentenary'. Two floods in three months along the Hawkesbury provided problems for Una Voce — with parts of the golf course and grounds having to be reconstructed.

Costs

Entertainment — $2 155 000
Donations & promotional expenses — $532 000
Salaries — $726 000
Dining room (loss) — $37 000
Una Voce (loss) — $63 000

Returns

Entrance fees & subscriptions — $604 000
Net bar profit & poker machine revenue — $6 381 000

SURPLUS — $1 657 000
Accumulated funds — $17 372 000

1988–89

The swinging '50s — a fun night at the club.

Directors: H Morris (president), B Dunn (deputy president), K Williams, F Cookson, R Floyd, J Jones, L Banton.

The president reflected nostalgically on old days in 'Bell's Ballroom' pre-1959 in announcing a spectacular profit return of more than $2 200 000 in 1988–89 — despite an income tax bite of $416 000. Henry Morris profiled the club in its 30th year: 'The administration of such a large club with 50 000 members, 90 permanent and 305 casual staff with 456 poker machines under excellent security is an enormous job. Mr Darcy Lawler deserves our recognition, thanks and commendation for his application to this task.'

The annual report outlined the rapid change in poker machine technology: 'On link machines since their inception in August 1988 — the two systems, Grand Rapid and Super Rapid — a staggering $1 272 000 has been won on the 24 machines alone, with the biggest jackpot $100 000. Cashcade — our new bonus jackpot system — is proving very popular. Jackpot amounts of between $100–$300 are randomly triggered on non-paying combinations. $1 and $2 machines — the latest additions to our very modern installation, provide the members with machines which give a return of up to 95 per cent to the player.'

Close by for the club industry was Keno — under consideration by the Government and likely to be available sometime in 1990. Wrote Henry Morris: 'Personally, I feel caution should prevail in this regard; let us not kill the goose that laid the golden egg.'

The Board had the club under close attention and noted: 'The structure of the club is ageing. Contracts for a complete new roof, covering the whole of the club, and a new drop-ceiling in the snack bar and first floor area is nearing completion at the time of this report. More than $1 million has been spent on upgrading these areas, while a new stage, lighting and sound systems have been installed in the auditorium.' Additionally the club spent $250 000 on a complete renovation of the 13 holiday flats at Shelley Beach and The Entrance.

A TAB agency came to the Juniors in 1988–89 — and was reported to be 'operating smoothly'. In Omeros Seafood Restaurant, a whole lobster cost just $20. The Rickshaw Room responded with a banquet at only $18 per person. Entertainment in the auditorium mixed Australian and overseas acts, among them: Kamahl, the Ink Spots, Rolf Harris, 'Les Sexy French Revue', Julie Anthony, Max Bygraves, the regular boxing nights and the spectacular 'South American Fiesta'.

Returning an operating loss of $7 772 (after a loss of $17 024 the previous year) Souths Juniors Bowling Club was being closely monitored. An in-house highlight of the club during its fruitful year was the hosting by directors of an 'appreciation dinner' given to executive members of the intra-clubs — so much a part of the club's operations since 1959. One of them, the Souths Juniors Snowy Club, noted that it been running for more than 21 years — hosting six weekend trips per season to the snowfields for club members. Never far removed from its links with rugby league and junior football the club took pride in the regular presence of up to 10 junior 'products' in the Rabbitohs' first grade side during the year, with the Rabbitohs taking the minor premiership, five points clear of their nearest rivals.

Capturing the buoyant spirit within the club, Darcy Lawler observed that after 22 years he could never remember taking more pleasure from the presentation of a balance sheet — one recording the most financially successful year in the history of the Juniors.

Costs

Entertainment — $1 999 000

Donations & promotional expenses — $516 000

Salaries — $803 000

Dining room (loss) — $40 000

Una Voce (loss) — $63 000

Returns

Entrance fees & subscriptions — $605 000

Net bar profit & poker machine revenue — $9 457 000

SURPLUS — $2 223 000

Current assets (cash) — $14 733 000

Total members' equity — $19 595 000

Members of the Juniors' 'Snowy Club' ham it up for the camera.

1989–90

We are the champions!

Directors: H Morris (president), B Dunn (deputy president), K Williams, F Cookson, R Floyd, J Jones, L Banton.

An after-tax profit of more than $2 million, a 12 months turnover of an all-time high $31.6 million — these were boom times for Souths Juniors. 'It has been said that the economy is heading for a recession but our trading figures certainly do not give support to that viewpoint,' Henry Morris observed. The operating profit of $2 820 000 in fact exceeded the previous year's record figure by $181 000 — but increased taxation took a larger chunk, and the final figure was down by just $13 000 on the record — at $2 210 000. Accumulated funds (excess of assets over liabilities) now stood at more than $20 million ($21 805 000).

The year was one of almost exclusively good news. Generous support from the club's thriving year benefited many local sports and charities. The subsidiary company — Souths Juniors Sporting Association Ltd — donated a total of $705 632 to the Junior League and other sporting associations. A further grant of $100 000 went to the South Sydney District Club. A donation of $10 000 went to the Nyngan Flood Disaster Appeal and continued strong support was given to the Prince of Wales Children's Hospital and Randwick Meals on Wheels.

Nothing was more personal in the club's wide range of grants than in the backing of three children from Third World countries via World Vision. The children — from Indonesia, Haiti and Ecuador — sent regular reports to the club of their progress.

The club on Anzac Parade was now in its 31st year of life — and to show appreciation the Board recognised the sterling service rendered by 27 long-serving employees by hosting a lunch at which inscribed gold watches were presented. Said Henry Morris: 'I believe it is most important that we do not forget or lose the desire to honour our long-time employees, or the gentlemen who founded this magnificent club.'

The new TAB amenity was proving popular with members — and turnover in the first year exceeded $200 000. Souths Juniors Bowling Club managed a significant turnaround — from a $7 772 loss in 1989 to a $29 713 profit in 1990. The holiday flats at The Entrance and Shelley Beach received a facelift, as did the club roof and snack bar area — at a total cost of $850 000. In the Junior League the number of individual teams — 159 — was close to the highest ever. The entertainment line-up was, as ever, diverse and appealing: 'The Cotton Club', 'Caribbean Carnivale', Simon Gallaher, The Drifters, Greg Anderson and his horse, 'Europe by Night', The Barron Knights, the Jolson Revue.

Costs

Entertainment — $2 250 000
Donations & promotional expenses — $734 000
Salaries — $860 000
Dining room (profit) — $35 000
Una Voce (loss) — $41 000

Returns

Entrance fees & subscriptions — $610 000
Net bar profit & poker machine revenue — $10 133 000

SURPLUS — $2 210 000
Current assets (cash) — $16 438 000
Total members' equity — $21 805 000

1990–91

Saturday night Showtime — fun and frolics guaranteed.

Directors: H Morris (president), B Dunn (deputy president), L Banton, F Cookson, R Floyd, J Jones, K Williams.

Chairman of the Board Henry Morris dealt with weighty matters in the longest President's Report in his time in office.

1) A request from the (South Sydney) District Club for a 'one-off' grant to help the club with its ongoing solvency problem. Wrote Morris: 'From the outset it was felt a 'one-off' grant was inappropriate, as we could only look at the matter from a commercial point of view'. This was a difficult ongoing problem — an inbuilt wish to support the district club, such an integral part of the rugby league competition since 1908 — counterbalanced against the need for responsibility in the Juniors' use of its hard-earned funds. In the end — a reasonable compromise: based on an independent valuation of the NSWRL's Country Club at Narellan, of $15 million, Souths Juniors purchased, for $1.25 million the district club's $\frac{1}{12}$th share in Narellan.

2) Major works carried out in the club, relating to fire safety. Major capital expenditure included fire sprinklers ($151 000), fire protection furnishings ($218 000) with a further $727 000 written off club profits in respect of associated club renovations.

3) A planned ATO change in the formula used by clubs to pay their tax. The Board estimated that the change could double or even quadruple the club's taxation obligations.

Henry Morris posed the question: 'When will the taxation department stop milking clubs and let us continue to look after serving the community, our members, charities and the sporting fraternity — as we do so well?'

So, a challenging year — but a highly successful one all the same. Net profit came in at a healthy $2 062 000 after the payment of $758 000 tax. Net bar profit and poker machine revenue was up by more than $800 000. Accumulated funds were now up to $23 867 000. Membership of the club was 44 500 — with associates comprising 40 per cent of the total number.

Secretary-manager Darcy Lawler proudly listed the benefits offered to members as the 1990s began: 'Free entertainment every weekend, 33 intra-clubs, holiday flats, gymnasium, aerobics and water aerobics, four squash courts, sauna and steam rooms, library, tennis courts, holiday flats, holiday resort on the Hawkesbury.' Junior League numbers were steady, at 2796. A week at Una Voce was $300 for members, $350 for non-members.

The big nights of entertainment included: 'The Minstrel Show', 'Spice on Ice', Oriental Cavalcade, Jackie Love, Soir de Paris, Simon Gallaher and the Leningrad Music Hall.

Costs

Entertainment — $2 458 000

Donations & promotional expenses — $336 000

Salaries — $905 000

Dining Room (loss) — $9 000

Una Voce (loss) — nil

Returns

Entrance fees & subscriptions — $600 000

Net bar profit & poker machine revenue — $10 974 000

SURPLUS — $2 062 000

Current assets (cash) — $16 109 000

Total members' equity — $23 867 000

1991–92

Club Keno was introduced in February 1992.

Directors: H Morris (president), B Dunn (deputy president), L Banton, J Jones, K Williams, F Cookson, R Floyd.

Necessary alterations throughout the club took almost $1 million out of the Juniors' earnings in 1991–92. The 'abnormal item' listed as a cost on the balance sheet — of $918000 — related to the removal of a substance within the ceilings throughout areas of the club. The work, and its high cost, cut deeply into an operating profit of $1814000. Eventually the after-tax profit settled at $611000 — rated 'satisfactory' by president Henry Morris in the circumstances of a testing year. Morris described the work done at the club as an 'absolute necessity'. Capital expenditure during the year included the following: poker machines ($620000), coin counting equipment ($84000), new carpeting throughout the club ($236000) Keno equipment ($32000), new PABX system ($46000). A new computer hardware and software system was implemented at a cost of $185000, while the final cost of fire control systems throughout the club was $750000. A reduction of $694000 in interest received on investments, reflecting reduced interest rates on Australian bank bills, added further to the demands of the year.

Poker machine payouts for the year reached a staggering $11201000. Meanwhile Club Keno arrived (in February) — and a substantial upgrading was undertaken of the TAB area, with the latest in TV monitors and comfortable seating. Ahead in the continual improvements program felt necessary for a club more than 30 years old lay a total renovation of the swimming pool and surrounds. Senior staff changes punctuated the year — with Geoff Knight (assistant manager), Jim Thorne (poker machine manager) and Peter Heaney (human resources officer) — all being substantially upgraded in their employment.

Membership numbers remained steady at 44900, with members entitled to (and encouraged to) join one of the 33 intra-clubs ('from aerobics to water ski').

Similarly the playing numbers remained fairly constant in the Souths Junior League — 142 teams and 2694 players. All coaches within the Juniors were now required to be holders of Level 1 Coaching Certificates, guaranteeing quality and expert coaching for the young players.

Tony Barber, the Leningrad Music Hall, Circus of the Stars, Max Bygraves and the 'sexational and popular' Braziliano were among the shows to fill the auditorium. Charities supported in the club's long and ongoing program of community help included: Royal Blind Society, Victor Chang Appeal, Diabetics Australia, Guide Dog Association, Prince Henry Hospital, MS Society, House With No Steps, Salvation Army, Meals on Wheels, Austcare, Prince of Wales Children's Hospital, Red Cross, World Vision, Epilepsy Association, Combined Pensioners' Society.

Costs

Entertainment — $2476000
Donations & promotional expenses — $600000
Salaries — $1031000
Dining room (loss) — $52000
Una Voce (loss) — $43000

Returns

Entrance fees & subscriptions — $602000
Net bar profit & poker machine revenue — $10593000

SURPLUS — $593000
Current assets (cash) — $16547000
Total members' equity — $24406000

1992–93

Showtime glamour — with a capital 'G'.

Directors: H Morris (president), B Dunn (deputy president), J Jones, L Banton, F Cookson, R Floyd, K Williams.

With cash reserves of $18 million the club was in good shape as it moved into its fourth decade. Accumulated funds exceeded $25 million and the Current Ratio (current assets to current liabilities) was a particularly healthy 10.3 to 1. The theme was 'conservative planning,' chairman Morris reported. Nonetheless the initiative had been taken to proceed with appropriate works — and an artist's impression on the front cover of the annual report gave members an idea of how their club would look as it headed towards the new century. Plans included:

· The exterior refit, including a full-length awning.

· A new foyer — to incorporate the Membership Office, giving easier access at renewal time.

· The upgrading of toilet facilities throughout the club.

Already $330 000 had been spent on swimming pool renovations. Henry Morris promised that 'all care' would be the motto on all refurbishment work being considered by the club.

The year had been a good one — a bounce back to a net profit (after tax) of $1 344 000, despite a reduction in interest income of $297 000 because of lower interest rates. Wrote Morris: 'The success story of the club is the poker machines which we continually update to meet the demand of members. To give something back to our pokie players we conducted a special promotion this year — with a car as first prize.' Membership had topped the 45 000 mark. During the year the club rejected an approach from South Sydney District Club for further financial assistance.

The Junior League year was one of progress, and change. Rod Gorman, CEO of the Junior League, reported that five Eastern Suburbs sides had accepted an invitation to compete in the 1993 season, along with Camperdown Dragons. Wrote Gorman: 'With registration of players at an all-time high and a development program available to all players, I am pleased to report that the development of quality players from the earliest possible age is now a reality. Gone are the day of thugs in league; now players can develop their mental strategies in line with their physical attributes.' A further step ahead saw the formation of the South Sydney Junior Bunnies — Under 12s, 13s and 14s who played exhibition games against Illawarra, the Central Coast and Western Suburbs. The acquiring of a lease over Erskineville Oval led to the club developing a new gymnasium for the future development of players.

Members enjoyed a number of shows exclusive to the club, including: Harem Nights, Nelson Sardelli, Frances Yip, The Parade of New Australian Talent, Best of Broadway and Cafe Continentale. Tariff for a week at Una Voce now stood at $325 for seven nights (members) and $375 (non-members) — all meals included!

Costs

Entertainment — $2 551 000

Donations & promotional expenses — $724 000

Salaries — $1 060 000

Dining room (loss) — $111 000

Una Voce (loss) — $102 000

Returns

Entrance fees & subscriptions — $573 000

Net bar profit & poker machine revenue — $11 353 000

SURPLUS — $1 344 000

Current assets (cash) — $18 209 000

Total members' equity — $25 750 000

1993–94

'Japan by Night' — a hit in 1994.

Directors: H Morris (president), B Dunn (deputy president), F Cookson, K Williams, J Jones, R Floyd, L Banton, K Williams.

The retirement and subsequent passing of Darcy Lawler after 27 years of faithful service to the club headed the news of a year of some sadness, change and financial strength — and marked the beginning of a new era at Souths Juniors. In the midst of a bountiful year the club mourned the death of three men who had made significant contributions to what the club at Kingsford had become — Darcy Lawler, Norm Christie and Frank Kilcran. There was further change in Joan Child's decision to retire, after 28 years of diligent and selfless service as secretary to the Board, and secretary to the General Manager. Geoff Knight, having worked his way through the ranks after his beginning at Souths as a poker machine supervisor, was appointed the new General Manager, and Margaret Child, daughter-in-law of Joan, took over the key secretarial duties. During the year the Board restructured the management of the club, with Jim Thorne appointed Gaming and Computer Manager, and Ron Harder Operations Manager. 'I feel this structure will lead our club into the new century, and beyond,' commented president Henry Morris.

After-tax profit for the year came in at an all-time record — $2 637 000, a spectacular return. Operating profit before abnormals was $4 008 000 — an increase of $2 530 000 or 170 per cent on the previous years results. The turnover was a record at $45 million and operating profit of $2 876 000 almost doubled the previous year's figure. From this position of financial strength, the club opened the purse strings, spending well over $1 million in improvements. By annual report time the hoardings were already in place at the front of the club, masking the work that would produce a new facade and two new entrances. 'The end result will delight,' wrote Henry Morris. A new gymnasium, complete with sprung floor (for aerobics) and ultra-modern equipment, had opened. Renovations to the ladies' change-rooms had been part of this re-make. Toilets throughout the club had been modernised and refurbished. And in a move designed to further increase the viewing and listening pleasure of the countless thousands who attended the auditorium for concerts and shows through the year, work was underway to remove the three view-blocking columns. Structural engineers convinced the Board that such an improvement was indeed possible — and safe.

A further substantial commitment during the year was the granting of $500 000 to a community project unprecedented in the district — the building of a Sporting Academy on land owned by Souths' District Club.

Junior League numbers totalled 2700 — with some girls playing in the mini-league. The Under 17 SG Ball side proved the star outfit of the year, winning their title in the face of strong competition.

Top-rating shows in the auditorium included: 'The Mediterranean Festiva', Black Tie, Al Martino, The Ice Show, Caribbean Carnivale, Best of Broadway Musicals, Japan by Night and Doug Parkinson and the Buddy Holly Sensation. Lionel Huntington and his versatile and consistently excellent band won a 'Mo' award. Nineteen charities and organisations benefited from the club's generosity and ongoing policy of providing a 'helping hand'.

Detailing methods of the financial results of the club in 1993–94, changed. Some key indicators were:

Operating profit (before abnormal items & income tax) — $4 008 000

Operating profit after income tax — $2 637 000

Turnover from trading activities — $44 060 000

Current assets (cash) — $17 947 000

Total members' equity — $28 387 000

1994–95

Pleasant surroundings, pleasant company — a night out at the Juniors.

Directors: H Morris (president), B Dunn (deputy president), F Cookson, K Williams, J Jones, R Floyd, L Banton, K Williams.

Switching to a horizontal 'landscape' format the annual report for 1994–95 took on a glamorous new look. Pictured on the wide front cover was the club's spectacular new exterior and entrances on Anzac Parade. In many ways the club had taken the quantum leap necessary to keep its place among the front runners in the Sydney entertainment business. Never had it looked better — and financial returns for the year left no doubt that members were flocking to the glamorous new-look premises. Operating profit before abnormal expenditure was up 50 per cent on the previous year's record figures — to $6 024 000. The 'abnormal items' listed, amounting to almost $4 million, related to the extensive building program, still incomplete, but well advanced:

- Removal of the pillars in the auditorium, plus new sound system, air-conditioning, lighting system, special effects and new seating arrangements. A 'loop' system to assist hearing-impaired members was to be included.
- Purchase of the premises adjoining the club in Wallace Street — to be vacant possession by January.
- Air-conditioning — up-graded through the club.
- Dacom 5000E Player Marketing System — for attachment to each poker machine, enabling players to accumulate bonus points.
- New escalators — final approval awaited from Randwick Council.
- Members' lift.
- New first floor bar — with the proposed demolition of the existing Opal Bar.
- A 'theme room' to be built on the ground floor — to be called the Kingsford-Smith Room.

In line with the club's conception — for reasons to do first and foremost with the propagation of junior rugby league in the South Sydney district the club now employed a fulltime staff of five — a chief executive officer (Rod Gorman) and two development officers (Tom Larkin and Keith McCraw) plus a secretary and a secretarial assistant.

Addressing the ongoing 'Super League' storm in rugby league's world, Chairman of the Board Henry Morris wrote: 'Over the past 12 months there has been much upheaval that has given great concern for the future. Nonetheless, one important factor is paramount in our endeavours — and that is to safeguard and preserve South Sydney Junior Football League.' In the course of the battle between ARL forces and the Rupert Murdoch-backed Super League, Souths District Club (the Rabbitohs) had asked the Juniors for financial assistance of $1 million a year for the next five years to help them stay solvent. The Juniors Board had rejected the initial request, but resolved the following: 'That the South Sydney Junior Rugby League Club Ltd is prepared to provide up to $1 million per year to contract promising

junior players on scholarships, this to include country players — on the condition they not be called up to grade until their first year of Jersey Flegg.' The club proposed that a joint working party be set up between the two organisations to put the resolution in place.

There were further accolades for the resident Lionel Huntington orchestra — with the winning of a second 'Mo' award. Hugh Sadler from Vidette Productions continued to provide excellent fare in the entertainment line-up.

Rod Gorman's Junior League report carried thanks to the 'silent achievers' — the behind-the-scenes workers and all the voluntary helpers who made the League what it was.

The Junior League organisation would miss a great deal Claire James (Junior League treasurer of 20 years), who had decided to retire after long years of working for the 'cause' of junior rugby league.

Finances — key indicators
Operating profit (before abnormal items & income tax) — $6 024 000
Operating profit after income tax — $1 854 000
Turnover from trading activities — $54 258
Current assets (cash) — $17 208 000
Total members' equity — $30 241 000

A perfect Sydney day-out aboard the Juniors coach.

1995–96

Early morning in the gym — ready for customers.

Directors: H Morris (president), B Dunn (deputy president), F Cookson, K Williams, J Jones, R Floyd, L Banton, K Williams.

A photo of one of the beautiful kids from the Sydney Children's Hospital, Randwick, held pride of place on the 1995–96 annual report cover. The photo, and others from the hospital, recognised a five-year sponsorship deal struck between the club and the hospital under which the Juniors would contribute $750 000 to the 'Souths Juniors wing' at Randwick. The wing would house cardiology, urology and renal units, the adolescent and orthopaedic wards, plus the physiotherapy and occupational health departments. President Henry Morris was pictured handing over to Professor Les White a cheque for the first instalment of $150 000.

It was a year of much 'giving' — at the end of an excellent 12 months trading in which after-tax profit reached $2 236 000. As the agonising 'Super League War' unfolded with much focus on the viability of older, struggling clubs such as the Rabbitohs, the Juniors became the centre of much media attention. Reporting that the Board had rejected Souths Seniors request for a Juniors' takeover of the club and football operations, Henry Morris outlined the situation: 'Souths Seniors were fearful for their survival and we were well aware of the fact that if Souths no longer existed the boundaries and the identity of the Junior League in South Sydney would be in great jeopardy, with a possibility of being lost for ever. As a result, and after much discussion, your Board decided on an annual commitment, in principle of $1 500 000, to Souths Seniors … I also report to members that a special Development & Recruitment Fund has been formed for the South Sydney Junior League with $500 000 allocated for the purpose of enabling our Junior League to keep its elite players and also to invite promising players from the country to become part of the South Sydney spirit.'

Morris outlined to members that the Juniors' commitment to rugby league in the district — catering for 3500 players and 23 local clubs — had cost $1 050 000 to run in the season past. 'We boast the best structured junior league in the world and we trust that members support the Board of Directors on this most important issue,' he wrote.

In a further financial commitment — and gesture of community support — the club agreed to pay $140 000 to complete the grandstand at Kensington Oval. The grandstand would be named after Kevin 'Lummy' Longbottom, outstanding ex-Souths player and the Community Room named after Claire James, recently retired treasurer of the Junior League.

Morris wrote proudly of the near-finished building program at the club: 'It gives our club a whole new look — a look that will enable the Juniors to remain 'The Best for the Best'. During the year assets to the value of $6 300 000 were purchased — including new escalators, lift, poker machines, a new touring coach and assorted plant and furniture. Despite the investments — all of them aimed at improving the club environment for members — the club remained cash-healthy, with Total Current Assets amounting to $17 610 000.

The club industry however was facing challenging times. General Manager Geoffrey Knight reported the industry as being 'under attack' from the Australian Hotels Association (AHA) and urged members to closely read a special assessment of the situation in the annual report. The assessment warned of current proposals before State Government which could lead to the granting of club-type poker machine licences to pubs. It was estimated that the re-investment by clubs — into club facilities, charities and community organisations — of surplus revenue generated from gaming, totalled more than $700 million each year. Such ongoing investment would be at risk if the AHA lobbying was successful.

The club had a new Gaming Manager, John Willis — a man versed in casino operations around the world. During the year the club paid out $27 526 480 in jackpots and cancel credits. Steve Longbottom won promotion to House Manager — and three directors (Barry Dunn, Les Banton and Frank Cookson) reached the milestone of 20 years continuous service on the Board.

There were laurels on the football field. Souths Juniors won the GIO Encouragement of Sport Award at the annual Club of the Year awards. A representative Souths Juniors team ran out winners in the inaugural Jack Gibson Challenge Cup, organised by Cronulla.

Finances — key indicators
Operating profit (before abnormal items & income tax) — $4 319 000
Operating profit after income tax — $2 236 000
Turnover from trading activities — $59 204 000
Current assets (cash) — $17 036 000
Total members' equity — $32 477 000

Professor Les White of the Sydney Children's Hospital, chairman Henry Morris — and a cheque for $150,000, downpayment from the Juniors on a $750,000 commitment.

1996–97

The Golden Easter promotion, complete with giant chocolate rabbits.

Directors: H Morris (president), B Dunn (deputy president), F Cookson, K Williams, J Jones, R Floyd, K Williams, S Fisher (director for three months; appointed April 10 1997).

Henry Morris's understanding of the challenges faced by the Juniors in an increasingly tough market shone out of 1996–97's impressive annual report. The President's Report opened with these words: 'Never, in all the years I have presented this report, have I been so concerned about the future and survival of the club industry in NSW. Make no mistake, we are currently faced with the greatest crisis since the inception of our industry when we were allowed to use poker machines.' Chairman Morris accused the NSW State Government of showing 'no appreciation or understanding' of the club industry, or of the financial support given to sporting, welfare and community groups by clubs. In the past year, Souths Juniors had allocated $2.8 million in these areas.

The president speculated whether hotels and casinos, privately owned for profit 'would put anything at all back into the community'. The main bone of contention lay in legislation that had passed through State Parliament and which effectively increased poker machine tax from 22.5% (on gross earnings less payouts) to 30%. It was estimated the change would cost the Juniors $2.1 million in profit over a 12-month trading period. Additionally there was news that the State Government was considering that clubs pay the TAB a poker machine monitoring fee of $50 per machine, per month. For Souths Juniors this would impose an additional cost of $300 000 per annum. All of this came in the face of the imminent opening of the Sydney Casino (November). 'It is apparent the State Government will decimate the club industry unless strong action is taken,' wrote Henry Morris. The Juniors were at the forefront of the fight against the suggested changes, with members urged to support where possible the newly-formed Registered Clubs Party in the NSW Upper House.

The balance sheet for the year showed an operating loss (after tax) of $180 000. The before-tax profit was $2 627 000 — but after deducting donations of $2.8 million and allowing for tax adjustments the 'after-tax' figure was in the red for the first time. Notwithstanding, the balance sheet was a healthy one, listing Retained Profits of $32 million. Caution would be the key word for the year ahead, reported the president.

The 1996–97 report was tinged with sadness, bearing news of the death of long-serving director, Les Banton the previous October. In April (1997) Stephen Fisher was appointed to the Board. Happier news lay in the opening of the Souths Juniors Wing of the Sydney Children's Hospital at Randwick, a festive affair replete with clowns, fairy floss, pass-the-ball games and a visit from the Paddlepop Lion. Within the Juniors the new 'Jockey Club' was open for business, featuring a state-of-the-art racing machine of which there were only three in NSW. Gaming machine payouts for the year reached their highest ever level — at $37 770 326.

On Keno two South Juniors punters picked up a $2.75 million payout from a $10 bet, and seven cars were won by lucky members during the year.

On the retirement of Hugh and Alice Sadler from their long association with the Juniors, in providing entertainment, WTS Entertainment took over as booking agency for the auditorium shows. There were sell-out shows: The Four Kinsmen, Frances Yip and John Rowles.

The football year was a busy one — with an 'A Reserve' grade added and various tours undertaken, including the Under 16s development team to the Snowy Mountains, and the Junior Bunnies 13s, 14s and 15s to Nambucca Heads.

Finances — key indicators
Operating profit (before donations, abnormal items and income tax) — $2 627 000 Operating profit after income tax — ($180 000)
Turnover from trading activities — $74 159 000
Current assets (cash) — $15 397 000
Total members' equity — $32 297 000

The club by night — a welcoming place.

No shortage of entries! Anticipation builds on the night of a Maroubra Mitsubishi promotion.

1997–98

A glittering new attraction in the 1990s — 'The Emerald Forest'.

Directors: H Morris (president), B Dunn (deputy president), F Cookson, K Williams, J Jones, R Floyd, K Williams, S Fisher.

In the 40th annual report there were reflections on earlier days, of humble beginnings in 1959 when the club began its operations in Bell's Ballroom and of the struggle to get established. Chairman Henry Morris presented an annual report which showed just how far the club had progressed. Net profit for the year was $3.3 million (before tax and donations), reducing to $1.4 million. Reported chairman Morris: 'The results are very pleasing and were achieved despite unprecedented opposition from the Hotel Industry with new poker machines and 24-hour trading — and the completed Star City Casino. When will the government of this state realise that there are just too many gaming machines available to casinos and hotels that do not have the same community spirit as the club industry?'

Henry Morris addressed the principal controversy of the year — extensive publicity, creating considerable pressure and linking the club to the future (or otherwise) of South Sydney District Club. He wrote: 'I feel most of these articles were very hurtful to this club and completely unjustified. This club has, wherever possible, helped Souths Seniors financially over many years. Your Board has never lost sight of the fact that when we were granted a liquor licence back in 1959, our principal objective was the propagation of Junior Rugby League and local junior sport — as well as providing proper amenities for members, and support in general to the community. We have not failed — we will never fail in this commitment.'

There was positive news on the club's ongoing battle to get a 'fair go' from the NSW Government, particularly on the planned 33 per cent increase in poker machine tax. The chairman wrote: 'Proudly I report that your club and many

other clubs within our district resisted strenuously; we fought, we lobbied the Premier, the Treasurer and various bureaucrats, eventually obtaining an assurance that our current rate of taxation … will remain for a period of three years.' Stiff challenges remained for the club industry — with hotels lobbying for extra poker machines, and Club

Keno being introduced into hotels. 'We must protect our interest — we must have a choice in government, we must fight,' wrote Henry Morris.

On the horizon loomed another major hurdle — the Federal Government's planned introduction of a GST, expected to have a huge effect on the profitability of the Juniors, and of the entire club industry.

Notwithstanding, confidence in the future was at high enough levels for the director to agree in principle to lodge the relevant applications for extensions and renovations to the club — estimated to cost $12–$15 million.

As had been its tradition over 40 years, the club was a changing place. On the first floor now stood the Emerald Forest Gaming Lounge — a fantasyland complete with thunder, lightning, trees and a life-like elephant. There were three Cashcade Jackpot systems on the floor — Mountains of Money ($9000–$10 000), Leopards' Lair ($500–$1000) and The Emerald Forest ($9000–$10 000). New Gaming Manager Paul Muir was congratulated on the innovations.

Numbers remained solid in Junior League ranks, despite the troubled state of rugby league in its wider world since the Super League disaster. More than 3500 players — of both sexes — were registered within the 24 clubs that comprised Souths Junior League. Victory in the SG Ball competition and a place in the Jersey Flegg Final made it a year of considerable success.

In its 40th year the club had a staff of 500, headed by General Manager Geoff Knight, Operations Manager Ron Harder, Gaming Manager Paul Muir and Financial Controller Bruce Johnson. Member benefits included the giving away of 12 cars a year in major promotions — and $2 a ticket booking fee to see the likes of Helen Reddy, Julie Anthony, John Rowles and the Four Kinsmen.

Finances — key indicators
Operating profit (before donations and income tax) — $3 330 000
Operating profit after income tax — $1 358 000
Turnover from trading activities — $39 909 000
Current assets (cash) — $16 395 000
Total members' equity — $33 655 000

A spacious welcoming foyer for members and visitors.

A WEEK IN THE LIFE OF THE CLUB, 1999

- Members: 24,891 men, 22,466 women. Total: 48,727

- Intra-clubs: 32

- Club is open 24 hours per day in Smithy's Gaming Lounge

- Bar trade — per week: 80–100 kegs ordered per week, plus 400 dozen packaged beer (bottles and cans). Nine dozen bottles of spirits. 10 dozen bottles of wine (red and white) plus 215 litres of bulk wine. 15–20 cartons of orange juice (15 litres per carton). 40 dozen bottles of water. Four dozen Oasis. 204 dozen soft drinks of various types (including sports drinks). 270 litres of Post Mix

- Gaming machines: 475 — with the jewel in the crown being 'The Jockey Club' one 24-terminal simulated racing game

- Staff numbers: 106 permanent; 294 casual

- Auditorium: approximately 2500 people per week attend the shows

- Tax paid weekly: $175,000

- Weekly wages bill: $207,000

- Poker machine duty: Last year (1998) averaged out at $165,000 per week paid to the NSW Government

- Yearly Donations (charities, hospitals etc): $2.8 million.

SOME FUN AT THE CLUB

Monday	Bingo
Tuesday	Market Place
	Punters' Choice
Wednesday	Spin 'n' Win
	Kaffy's Kashboard
Thursday	You're Laughing
	Members' Badge Draw
Friday	Bingo
	Stack the Deck
Saturday	You're Laughing
Sunday	Line Dancing
	Spin a Dinner
	Go Racing

INDEX